CHOCTAWS AND MISSIONARIES IN MISSISSIPPI, 1818–1918

Choctaws and Missionaries
in Mississippi, 1818–1918

By Clara Sue Kidwell

UNIVERSITY OF OKLAHOMA PRESS : NORMAN AND LONDON

Book design by Bill Cason.

Library of Congress Cataloging-in-Publication Data

Kidwell, Clara Sue.
   Choctaws and missionaries in Mississippi, 1818–1918 / by Clara
Sue Kidwell.
       p. cm.
   Includes bibliographical references and index.
   ISBN 0–8061–2691–4
   1. Choctaw Indians—History—19th century. 2. Choctaw Indians—Missions. 3. Choctaw Indians—Government relations. 4. Missionaries—Mississippi—History—19th century. 5. Mississippi—History—19th century. I. Title.
E99.C8K53 1995
976.2'004973—dc20   94–30374
                                                              CIP

The paper in this book meets the guidelines for permanence and dura-
bility of the Committee on Production Guidelines for Book Longevity
of the Council on Library Resources, Inc. ∞

1 2 3 4 5 6 7 8 9 10

Contents

Illustrations

Preface

IN 1931, JOHN SWANTON DECLARED: "THE ABORIGINAL CHOCTAW seem to have enjoyed the enviable position of being 'just folks,' uncontaminated with the idea that they existed for the sake of a political, religious, or military organization. . . . Absence of pronounced native institutions made it easy for them to take up with foreign customs and usages." Thus they became "with great rapidity poor subjects for ethnological study but successful members of the American nation."[1] In 1934, Angie Debo published *The Rise and Fall of the Choctaw Republic*, a history of the tribe during their removal from what is now the state of Mississippi, the subsequent reestablishment of the Choctaw Nation in Indian Territory, and its political destruction as Indian Territory became the state of Oklahoma.

Swanton's pronouncement and Debo's history seem to have put an effective end to major scholarship on the tribe. The last words had been spoken. Lost almost entirely to scholarly interest were the Choctaws who remained in Mississippi after removal. Without a land base or federal recognition, they participated in none of the major issues that have defined Indian history in the later nineteenth and early twentieth centuries, including allotment and reorganization. Outside the mainstream of historical developments on the western frontier, the tribe remained in the backwaters of southern history. After 1830, many were driven off lands that had always been theirs, and they were relegated to the status of squatters or tenant farmers. The institutions of white society were not open to them, and hence there was little pressure on them to change.

In recent years, however, the Mississippi Band of Choctaw Indians has gained national attention for its economic development, and in the past few years they themselves have led the resurgence in interest in their history. The tribe has established a

Choctaw Heritage Commission and a museum and has sponsored the publication of two books on the pre- and postremoval history of the tribe.

The history of the Choctaws in Mississippi is fascinating precisely because these people exist in contemporary America with a distinct sense of their own identity. There are seven communities in which Choctaw is still a working language for community life. Their racial and historical identity persists to a remarkable degree. Choctaw Fair, in July, celebrates their identity and their connections with past traditions of the Green Corn Ceremony.

The survival and the political resurgence of the Mississippi Band of Choctaw Indians in the twentieth century are remarkable evidence of the vitality of Indian cultures in the face of government policies aimed at acculturation and social pressures based in racism.

My interest in the Choctaws has grown out of my own Choctaw heritage on my father's side and my contacts with students from the Mississippi Choctaw reservation whom I have met during my teaching career at Haskell Indian Junior College and the University of Minnesota. For the persistence to finish the task, I owe a debt primarily to my Choctaw grandmother, Susie Thompson Kidwell, who raised me, and to the continued queries of my parents, "When is the book going to be done?"

I am indebted also to many librarians and archivists who helped guide my search for materials. Among them are John Aubrey, librarian of the Ayer Collection at the Newberry Library in Chicago, Robert Kvasnicka at the National Archives in Washington, D.C., and Mark Thiel at the archives of Marquette University. Others are at the Houghton Library, Harvard University; Mississippi Department of Archives and History in Jackson, Mississippi; the archives of the Catholic Archdiocese of Jackson; the archives of the Methodist Episcopal Church South at Millsaps College in Jackson; the Presbyterian Historical Society in Montreat, North Carolina; the Southern History Collection at the University of North Carolina at Chapel Hill; the Federal Records Center depository, Fort Worth, Texas; and the Gilcrease Museum in Tulsa, Oklahoma.

I am particularly grateful to Dr. Patricia Galloway for her scholarly interest in the Mississippi Choctaws, her insights on the colonial period of their history, and her encouragement on this project. Robert Ferguson, director of the Museum of the Southern Indian at the Choctaw tribal headquarters in Pearl River, Mississippi, has also been helpful and encouraging. Chief Phillip Martin of the Mississippi Band has provided leadership in the period of cultural resurgence that inspired the book.

Dr. Galloway, Dr. Michael Green, and Dr. Charles Roberts have read all or parts of earlier drafts of the manuscript and offered helpful comments. I, of course, take full responsibility for any errors that may appear in the book.

The research was supported at various points by a Rockefeller Foundation Humanities Research Fellowship, a University of California Humanities Research Fellowship, a Newberry Library summer research fellowship, a Smithsonian Institution research fellowship, a National Endowment for the Humanities Cooperative Research grant, and various small faculty research grants from the Committee on Research of the University of California at Berkeley.

CLARA SUE KIDWELL

Washington, D.C.

Introduction

Old Hopankitubbee . . . was wont to say that after coming forth from the mound, the freshly-made Choctaws were very wet and moist, and that the Great Spirit stacked them along on the rampart, as on a clothes line, so that the sun could dry them.

THUS DID AN ELDERLY CHOCTAW EXPLAIN THE ORIGINS OF HIS people to an interested schoolteacher.[1] The mound is Nanih Waiyah, now a flat-topped mound some forty feet high that is the center of a state park in Noxubee, Mississippi. The contemporary Choctaw tribe occupies eight reservation communities scattered through Neshoba, Leake, Newton, Jasper, and Clarke counties, and the mound still has symbolic significance as an emblem of its identity (tourist brochures issued by the tribe tell the story of Choctaw origins there). Oklahoma Choctaws have shown a recent surge of interest in their historical roots in Mississippi, and the Choctaw Nation runs periodic free bus tours from the tribal headquarters in Durant to the headquarters of the Mississippi Band of Choctaw Indians in Pearl River, Mississippi, and to Nanih Waiyah. The trips are funded with proceeds from the Choctaw bingo gaming facility.

That the Mississippi Band of Choctaw Indians exists today as a federally recognized tribe is evidence of the remarkable tenacity of cultural identity in a country where the general perception is that all Indians died out after 1890. The Mississippi Choctaws have survived the vagaries of federal Indian policy to become a model of economic self-sufficiency while retaining their language and distinctive identity. A demographic survey of the tribe in 1990 showed that nearly 79 percent of the reservation population spoke Choctaw.[2] Choctaw Fair, held during the third week of July every year, is a celebration of songs, dances, crafts such as basketmaking, games of stickball, and in an interesting modern note, a Miss Choctaw pageant. The history of the Choctaws in Mississippi is a case study of the effects of federal Indian policy on Indian tribes in the Southeast and of the cultural survival of one tribe.

In the early 1800s, federal policy was unrepentently Christian and assimilationist in its intent, and in the face of the constitutional separation of church and state, John C. Calhoun, Thomas McKenney, and other agents of the U.S. government in the early nineteenth century sought to use Christian missionaries to mold Indians into the models of American society.

If some Choctaws believed that the Great Spirit had molded them from the moist earth of Nanih Waiya, the missionaries who came to work among them believed them to be like malleable clay, to be shaped by the Christian God into true believers. The missionaries soon found that they themselves were subject to the molding forces of Choctaw leaders, who demanded that they teach Choctaw children to read and write and do mathematics (an important consideration in an increasingly market-oriented economy).[3] They found that their incipient parishioners had their own ideas of the benefits of Christianity. Choctaw leaders saw missionaries as a means of gaining an education in the white man's way so that they could learn to deal with the forces infringing on their lives.

In the larger national arena, Christian morality and Deistic philosophy, sacred and secular, warred in debates over government policy. The noble and the ignoble savage vied for public attention. The images were part of the emerging racism of the eighteenth century, always the "other" against which an emerging nation could measure and test itself.[4]

Choctaws, like other Indians, would adopt Christianity. By the early nineteenth century, there were churches and schools throughout the Choctaw Nation.[5] They were sponsored by the government and the American Board of Commissioners for Foreign Missions, which embodied the Calvinist principles of hard work, thrift, and industry that fueled the capitalism enterprise in an expanding nation. The missionaries came, with profound spiritual intent, to convert Indians to Christianity. But their teachings meshed with the government's intent—to meld Indians into American society as productive landowners or cast them into the wilderness west of the Mississippi River where they could pursue pagan ways of hunting.

Government policy fed white land hunger and finally led to a policy of separating Indians entirely from white society, and from their lands. If missionaries could not teach them to act like Americans, then the Indians must move. Andrew Jackson's Indian Removal Act reflected both his own nationalistic idea that Indian nations could not remain within the boundaries of the United States and the public sentiment that saw Indian nations as impediments to the development of American lands.

The failure of the civilization policy was not for want of faith or effort on the part of the missionaries. It was a result of political and economic forces already well established in the nation, and of the magnitude of a task undertaken with far too few resources.

The history of the Choctaws after 1830 generally tells of their acculturation. John Swanton declared in 1931 that the Choctaws had become "poor subjects for ethnological study but successful members of the American nation." When Angie Debo published *The Rise and Fall of the Choctaw Republic* in 1934, she declared, "The merging of tribal history into the composite life of the state of Oklahoma may be said to have ended the separate history of this gifted people."[6] But acculturation theory in anthropology has given way to debate about the sources of ethnicity. The current vigor of Choctaw tribal governments in Oklahoma and Mississippi belies Swanton and Debo, but it raises important questions about what constitutes culture for American Indian tribes. Bingo and bus trips show how old paradigms of acculturation in anthropology are giving way to new questions of ethnicity.[7]

Anthropologists continued to work in Choctaw communities, even after Swanton and even as culture became Clifford Geertz's "web of meanings" rather than a collection of artifacts and culture traits. More recent scholarship in ethnohistory has shown that dynamic change over time does not necessarily mean the loss of culture. Acculturation theory in anthropology has given way rather dramatically to theory building around ethnicity. What are the boundaries that mark an ethnic group as distinctive? What are the outside forces that constrain individual and group identity? Ethnicity theory reopens the "emic\etic" concerns of anthropology.[8]

Certainly Choctaw culture has changed over time. Native population centers shifted and changed in the twelfth and thirteenth centuries, and they continued to do so after the Spaniards arrived in the sixteenth century. The Choctaws probably did not emerge as a historically identifiable tribe until after Hernando de Soto's *entrada* of 1540–43.[9] The introduction of European diseases changed forever the ways in which Indian societies were organized. Large, densely populated groups gave way to dispersion because of contagious organisms. The Choctaws' traditional yearly cycles of hunting, harvesting, and social activity were overwhelmed by the linear forces of change.

In the eighteenth century, traders introduced cloth, new weapons, livestock, and whiskey. In the nineteenth century, the U.S. government pursued policies to assimilate Indians east of the Mississippi River into American society and to move those who would not assimilate to lands west of the Mississippi. Christian missions became major agents of this policy of assimilation, but even as the Choctaws tried to adapt to religion and a market economy, they lost their land base in 1830, and most moved west. About five thousand, ancestors of the current Mississippi Band, remained in the East. In the late 1800s, missionaries arrived once more, this time drawn by pity over the desperate economic plight of landless people. Schools and churches returned to Choctaw communities, where they became new agents of Indian identity, and missionary advocacy helped the Choctaws gain federal recognition and the beginnings of a reservation in 1918. Thus the role of missionaries and Christianity moved full circle in shaping the lives of the Choctaw people.

CHOCTAWS AND MISSIONARIES IN MISSISSIPPI, 1818–1918

1 / In the Beginning

THERE ARE TWO VERSIONS OF THE CHOCTAW ORIGIN STORY. ONE IS that the Choctaws were created under Nanih Waiyah. In the other, they migrated from the East. Two brothers, Chata and Chicksa, lived somewhere in the West until Chata had a vision that told him to lead a march that was guided by the *fabussa*, a sacred pole. Every night Chata planted the pole in the ground, and every morning it leaned toward the East until one morning it finally stood upright near a hill. They carried the bones of their dead ancestors, which they buried in a large mound near where the pole stood upright.[1] The variant origin traditions suggest that the historic Choctaws were not originally a single tribe and explain the mystery of Nanih Waiyah and the three political divisions within the Choctaw tribe.[2]

Choctaw districts in the early eighteenth century centered on the watersheds of three major river systems, the Tombigbee in the East, the Pearl and Big Black in the West, and the Chickasawhay and Pascagoula in the South. The Choctaws in the Northeastern District (east of the Tombigbee) were probably descended from the prehistoric culture centered at Moundville in western Alabama. The Choctaws on the Pearl probably originated west of the Mississippi River. They hunted in the West in the early nineteenth century and warred with the Osages. They were also allied linguistically with a number of small tribes west of the river.[3] The upper towns or Southern District, along the Chickasawhay, were called the *okla hanali*, or Six Towns people. They and their immediate neighbors were distinguished by certain unique aspects of language and by their long hair. They also tattooed blue lines around their mouths, a custom that suggests a connection with Indians called "Blew mouths," west of the Mississippi, who were "in amity" with the Choctaws. The distinctions of the Six Towns people were so great as to imply that they had a different origin and were less fully integrated into the tribal identity.[4]

What bound the Choctaws together were social structures, based on a dual division that followed geographical divisions. In the eighteenth century, people west of the Pearl River identified themselves as *okla falaya* (Long People) and those east as *okla tannap* (People of the Opposite Side). A third group, the *okla chito* (Big People), occupied the Kunsha towns near the head of the Pearl and were supposedly the principal chiefs of the nation.[5] Geographical separations were mediated by the duality of the traditional *iksas*, or moieties, of Choctaw social structure. According to Choctaw tradition, The Great Spirit divided the people whom he created at Nanih Waiyah into two groups and placed one on the north side of the mound and the other on the west side. These groups were the two *iksas*—the *kashapa okla* or *imoklasha*, and the *okla inholahta* or *hattak inholahta*—that regulated marriage. Children belonged to their mother's *iksa*, and a person had to marry into the opposite *iksa*. Political power passed through the woman's line, since a chief's nephew, his sister's son, generally inherited his power.[6] The dual division also served as a mechanism to integrate disparate groups of people into the entity that became the historic Choctaw tribe. The *inholahta* were called the "elder brother" group, and the *imoklasha* were the "younger brother" group. The terminology implies a chronological sequence whereby an existing group was joined by another.[7]

The Choctaw tribe identified by Europeans was not a homogeneous group. Its three political divisions in the early nineteenth century probably had different geographic and cultural origins. They were bound together by customs based on duality and reciprocity, bonds that proved fragile in the face of social and economic changes introduced by European colonizers in the eighteenth century and American agents in the nineteenth century.

On May 29, 1539, Hernando de Soto, the Spanish governor of Florida, landed on the gulf coast of the Florida peninsula, probably somewhere near present Tampa, with a party of some six hundred Spanish soldiers. He sought to establish the claims of the Spanish government to the rich interior of southeastern North America. His *entrada* introduced major changes into native life, one of the most significant of which was disease. In the province of Cofitachiqui (near present-day Augusta, Georgia), he sent the natives messages of peace and requests for food. They accepted his declarations of peace but could not fulfill his request for food "because a great pestilence with many consequent deaths had ravaged their province during the past year." Such pestilences could well have been introduced by earlier Spanish explorers along the Gulf Coast and could have traveled rapidly among native populations.[8]

Warfare followed disease. At Mabilia, a town probably near the juncture of the Alabama and Cabaha rivers in northern Alabama, de Soto met heavy resistance from the natives. In a pitched battle, the Spaniards burned the village, killing many of the inhabitants. They rested in the vicinity for about a month before moving on into the province of Pafallaya (the Choctaw word for "long hairs").[9] It is intriguing to speculate that the *pans falaya* were the ancestors of the historic southern Choctaws, but since hairstyles change, they remain problematic as historical evidence.

In June 1542, de Soto died, and his body was committed to the Mississippi River. Explorers, after all, were no more immune to native germs than natives were to European germs. The people of the central Southeast had no further direct contact with Europeans for a century and a half. The Spanish colonial government in St. Augustine, Florida, had only a ripple effect as native populations along the Atlantic and Gulf coasts entered into new trading relationships, resettled into new lands, and suffered the effects of new diseases.

In 1682, however, René-Robert Cavelier, Sieur de La Salle, a French nobleman, appeared at the mouth of the Mississippi, and the Choctaws were confronted with French colonial ambitions. In 1699 Pierre Le Moyne, Sieur d'Iberville, established Fort Maurepas, near Biloxi. Henri de Tonti, who had been La Salle's chief lieutenant and now accompanied Iberville, established contact with the tribes along the lower Mississippi Valley, including the Choctaws and Chickasaws, in 1702.[10] From New Orleans (founded in 1718) and Mobile (1702), the French sent their traders into Indian territory.[11]

But French colonial policy was not purely for commercial interests or military diplomacy. As minister of a deeply Catholic country, Cardinal Richelieu saw religion as integral to colonizing efforts. The Company of the Isles in America (established in 1635) was bound by its contract with the French government to maintain priests to convert "the savages" to Catholicism. The French saw two ways to subjugate the Indians—"arms or religion."[12]

Slogging through floods and swamps and facing hostile natives, French Jesuits went forth to convert the Indians. If their mission was dangerous (three Jesuits were killed), their physical torment was extreme. "The greatest torture—without which everything else would have been only a recreation, but which passes all belief, and could never be imagined in France unless it had been experienced—is the mosquitoes."[13]

It took more than mosquitoes, however, to deter Jesuits, and by 1727 there were ten in New Orleans, and Father Mathurin le Petit established a mission among the Choctaws. The Jesuits were both keen observers of the customs and mores of the Choctaws and military intelligence agents. Michael Beaudouin succeeded Le Petit in 1729 and established a mission near the southern village of Chickasawhay, where he became an active participant in the politics of colonialism.[14]

The Choctaws were the most numerous of the tribes that the French encountered. French estimates of the number of warriors varied wildly, from as low as 1,466 to about 5,000, but the total population was probably around 15,000 people.[15] They were a relatively peaceful group of village farmers. Their towns were widely scattered and varied in size anywhere from half a league to four or five leagues. By one account there were forty-two villages, "so many little republics in which each one does as he likes."[16]

Men did what they liked because they believed that spirits controlled nature. There was a transcendent power, *ishtahullo chito,* which manifested itself "in dreams, in thunder and lightning, eclipses, meteors, comets, in all the prodigies of nature and the thousand of unexpected incidents that occur to man." The term applied both to unusual occurrences in nature and to witchcraft and is probably as close as the Choctaws came to conveying the idea of religious awe or anxiety in the Christian sense.[17]

The sun was the supreme being, and fire, its mate, gave the sun information about human activities. The sun guided warriors on the successful warpath. It had the power of life and death, which explains its importance in the funeral customs of the Choctaws. A dead body was exposed to the rays of the sun on a raised platform and allowed to decay, thus giving itself back to the supreme power. After the flesh had decayed, the bone picker was summoned to clean the bones and to preside over a village feast after "only wiping his filthy, bloody hands on grass," as one horrified Frenchman observed. The bone picker's role in funeral rites and feasting thus reinforced the integral relationship of life and death. The cleaned bones were placed in a basket and taken to the village bone-house. When it was full, a procession of the families of the dead carried the baskets to a designated place, piled the bones up, and covered them with a mound of earth. The dual division of the tribe held sway in death: each *iksa* was responsible for burying the bones of the other.[18]

After death, a person's *shilombish* (the life force visible in his or her shadow during life) remained on the earth like a ghost, and the *shilup,* or inner shadow, went to an afterworld, a very beautiful and pleasant land. Only the ghosts of murderers could not find the path and had to spend eternity in a barren place.[19]

Choctaw beliefs were very "this worldly." Individual spiritual power came from the belief that humans and each variety of animals and birds had "a great King or presiding Deity" possessed of "great power & wisdom." These spirits could endow men with the capacity for "the most extraordinary works," and men sought that capacity through vision quests. Having established a relationship with a bird or animal spirit, a man carried the stuffed skin of its earthly counterpart as a sign of power.[20] Bernard Romans reported that when men traveled, one usually carried an owl skin, which he fed bits of food and placed with its head pointed toward the destination. If the owl turned in the opposite direction, it was "an absolute order to return."[21]

Other spirits lurked in the woods in small, human-like form to surprise the unwary traveler. The *kashehotapalo* was a hybrid man-deer. The *okwa naholo* dwelt in deep pools and had white skin like trout. These spirits could also be sources of personal power. The *bohpoli* or *kowi anukasha* startled people by throwing things and making unexpected noises, but they could also give power. The *nalusa falaya* had small eyes and long pointed ears and might give a person the power to harm others. Anyone who had acquired power from these beings dared not mention it for fear of losing his or her life when any major misfortune happened in the community. This belief in "witchcraft" remained a powerful force in Choctaw society throughout the nineteenth century. Positive use of spiritual power, on the other hand, allowed men to cure sickness, control rain and storms, and promote the growth of crops.[22]

Spiritual power was a very personal thing for the Choctaws, and they had little in the way of major ceremony beyond funerals. They were noted farmers, and they had some yearly celebration of spring, at which, since they were also noted singers, they "made new songs for every *busk*."[23] The other major event in Choctaw life was the ball game *ishtaboli*. It may be hard to imagine that one or two hundred men, naked except for a sash with a horsehair tail trailing from it, flailing at a ball with sticks, could play an important role in mediating social relations and village conflicts, but such was the case. The game was played in deadly earnest, and with a good deal of violence that often resulted in broken limbs, cracked skulls, and occasionally, death. Winning was not merely a matter of skill and brute force. Villagers danced and implored the favor of the spirits on their respective teams. The players rubbed their bodies with sacred medicines. Four medicine men smoked to the spirits so that they could judge impartially between the two sides. Gambling, an important part of the game, was an act of faith. Betting was sometimes carried to extremes; men who had lost everything else might "wager their wives . . . and wager themselves for a limited time."[24]

The very personal nature of religious beliefs was reflected in the loosely structured political organization of the tribe, the Frenchman's accusation that "each one does as he likes." Although there were district chiefs and leading men in villages, they still by the nineteenth century "considered themselves equal."[25] Rampant individualism was constrained, however, by a stratified system of leadership and responsibility in the social realm. National and village leaders were *mingos*. The *tichou mingo* of a town directed public events, assisted by the *task-anangouchi*, his spokesman. Some towns had a *soulouche oumastabe* or *mingo ouma* (red shoe killer), whose presence may indicate a distinction between peace towns and war towns. The *hopaii mingo* (prophet chief) was presumably a clairvoyant. The function of the *fanimingo* (squirrel chief), is not clear.[26] The *atacoulitoupa*, or Beloved Men, were older men respected for wisdom. The *tasca* were warriors, and the *atac emittla* were young men who had not "struck a blow in battle" or who had killed only a woman or a child. Young men were reluctant to attack enemy villages for fear that the men would flee and only women and children would remain to be killed in battle. They much preferred to be attacked, a custom that probably accounted for the Choctaws' reputation as a peaceful people.[27]

When necessary, however, they would go to war, and their warriors had a reputation for bravery and cunning. They generally attacked in the evening, taking care to conceal their advance over the forest floor, which was "covered with dry leaves which make a noise in walking." The Choctaws had "patience enough to remove them, one by one, with their toes." When the nimble-toed warriors returned to their villages with scalps after a successful battle, they were feted with a dance.[28]

The advent of the French, however, upset the balance of power within the Choctaw homeland and between the Choctaws and their neighbors, and it introduced new ideas in the forms of trade and diplomacy. The French created their own image of centralized leadership among the Choctaws where none had existed before. The relations between the Choctaws and the French were problematic because of their differing perceptions of political power. The "grand chief" of the Choctaws had power that was "absolute only so far as he knows how to make use of his authority." The French soon learned to undercut even that authority by giving presents to the principal chiefs of the villages. One observer noted, "Those who receive them directly from the French concern themselves very little about the Great Chief of their nation."[29] In awarding medals, Frenchmen attempted to establish a ruling elite with whom they could conduct diplomatic relations. In those relations they adopted the position of fathers and protectors of the Choctaws, a stance that was puzzling in a society where men inherited power from their maternal uncles rather than their fathers.[30]

As the French tried to establish an empire in the Mississippi Valley, they encountered competition from the English for the Indian trade, and they soon became embroiled in and learned to exploit intertribal tensions. The Choctaws, on the other hand, learned arts of bargaining with competing powers. English and French governors made Indian allies and used them against each other. The Chickasaws sided with the English in both trade and war, and the Choctaws allied themselves with the French. Chickasaws raided Choctaw towns for captives to sell to the English as slaves. Sporadic skirmishes were a fact of life for both tribes, and they often escalated into major conflicts during the colonial period. About two thousand Indians died in the wars, and about five hundred Choctaws were sold as slaves between 1690 and 1723.[31] The Choctaws gave a de facto explanation in the story of Chata and Chicksa, the brothers who had led their westward migration, noting that the two quarreled at some point in the journey and that each went his own way with his followers.[32]

During the 1730s, the French were increasingly hard-pressed financially to maintain the Indian trade. They established Fort Tombecbe (on the Tombigbee River) in 1736, but English influence among the eastern Choctaws and the Chickasaws was a threat. Jean-Baptiste Le Moyne, Sieur de Bienville, the French governor, led two unsuccessful campaigns against the Chickasaws in 1736 and in 1739–40, which only drained French resources. Their failure to dislodge English influence contributed to growing conflict within the Choctaw Nation. In 1746 the Englishman James Adair began to trade in the eastern district of Choctaw territory. The French were more skillful in diplomatic relations, but the British had superior trade goods and lower prices.[33]

The conflict of European powers exacerbated the basic divisions within the Choctaw Nation. War between England and France in 1744 gave the English navy cause to blockade French ships and choke off supplies of trade goods. Red Shoes, the war leader of Couechitto, negotiated trading relations between Choctaws and the English, and by 1747 only four towns remained loyal to the French. But the English were not able to supply the goods the Choctaws wanted, and the towns split into two factions, an eastern one that remained loyal to the English and a western one that returned to the French. A bloody civil war broke out in 1746, and by 1750 the French faction, aided by French soldiers, was victorious.[34]

The outbreak of the French and Indian War in 1754 and its ultimate settlement in the Peace of Paris in 1763 destroyed French trade and political power in the Southeast. In 1759 Edmund Atkins, the chief British agent to the southern tribes, moved into the vacuum created by declining French power to negotiate a peace treaty with the Choctaws. Throughout the first half of the eighteenth century the Choctaws had been in a position to play both ends against the middle, but now they had to deal with the British.[35]

In 1763 the governors of North and South Carolina and Virginia, in a message to the leaders of the southern tribes, stated,

"Our friendship will last as long as the sun shall shine, or the waters flow." The treaty that followed established friendship, and a subsequent treaty in 1765 defined the southern and eastern boundaries between the Choctaws and the English, but the terms of the second treaty angered the Creeks, who claimed part of the territory the Choctaws had ceded. The result was a decade-long period of war between the two tribes, war that largely destroyed the Choctaw towns near the Tombigbee River.[36] The Choctaws were still a "powerful, hardy, subtile and intrepid race," but war and disease were taking their toll. Smallpox was common, and the use of sweathouses for treatment killed more often than cured.[37]

The Choctaws remained largely neutral during the Revolutionary War, although the Americans enlisted their aid to patrol the Mississippi River (the tribe had sold a part of its territory along the Mississippi to the English in 1777). Although some served with the American army, the Choctaws, like other tribes, considered the war a quarrel among white men.[38] But the quarrel was not just between American colonists and their British masters. Spain declared war on England in 1779, and the English found themselves fighting on three fronts: in Europe, in northeastern North America, and in southeastern North America. The Choctaws and other southeastern tribes were once more able to play competing colonial powers against each other. Spanish forces under Bernardo de Gálvez attacked British posts at Mobile, Pensacola, and Natchez in 1779, and in 1781 Britain surrendered West Florida to the Spanish.[39]

The Spanish colonial government was already familiar with the Choctaws who had moved westward into Louisiana to find deer to supply the skin trade. In fact, it had come to view them as a nuisance because conflicts between Choctaws, Caddoes, Kansas, and other western nations threatened the stability of Spanish trade and settlement. Spanish officials tried, largely without success, to restrict the Choctaws to areas east of the Mississippi.[40]

But Spain was also anxious to block the expansion of American interests in the South by building a barrier of Indian trading

alliances, and in the summer of 1784 a group of southern Choctaws signed a treaty at Pensacola putting themselves under the
protection of Spain and agreeing to exclude all but Spanish-
licensed traders from their territories.[41] Among those who ultimately profited most from this arrangement were the Scotsmen
William Panton and John Forbes, whose trading firm of Panton
Leslie, established in Pensacola in 1783, transcended national
politics in the transition from British to Spanish rule in West
Florida to become a prime beneficiary of the Choctaw trade.[42]

The Spanish government carried out diplomatic relations
from Fort Nogales, established near the conjunction of the Mississippi and the Yazoo rivers (at present-day Vicksburg) in 1791.
In 1793, Spanish agents signed a treaty with leaders of the Choctaws, Chickasaws, Creeks, and Cherokees. The Treaty of Fort
Nogales formalized an alliance among those tribes as well as
between them and the Spanish. In a separate treaty signed at
Boucfouca on May 10, 1793, the Choctaws agreed to cede several
areas on the Tombigbee River, including thirty "arpents" around
the site of the former French fort Tombecbe, where the Spanish
built Fort Confederation and established a trading post.[43]

The Choctaws were busy diplomatically on other fronts as
well. In 1783 some of the eastern towns sent emissaries to Georgia
to establish trade relationships with the colony. The Georgians
agreed, provided that the Choctaws could persuade the Creeks to
permit Georgia traders to cross Creek territory to reach the Choctaw villages. Given the traditional enmity between Choctaws and
Creeks, the success of this venture was doubtful, but Georgia's
leaders evidently saw trade with the Choctaws as a way of putting
pressure on the Creeks for land cessions.[44]

In 1786 Choctaw leaders signed the Treaty of Hopewell with
the new U.S. government, placing themselves under its protection (although who was protecting whom was a question). They
gave the government the right to establish three trading posts in
their territory and confirmed the old British boundary line of
1763 as their eastern boundary with the United States.[45]

In a period of approximately three years, Choctaw leaders had managed to place themselves under the exclusive sovereignty of both the Spanish and the Americans. Although such actions may be viewed as expediency, they are more a result of the important geographical divisions of the tribe and the assumptions of European and American governments that they were dealing with a unified nation. The agreement with Georgia and the Treaty of Hopewell affected the eastern district, and the Treaty of Fort Nogales affected the western district. Different leaders signed different treaties.[46]

Spanish influence in the Southeast waned in the face of European conflicts, as had that of the French and the British. In 1795 Spain gave up its claims to the disputed territory above the thirty-first parallel to the United States, and on April 7, 1798, Congress created the Territory of Mississippi. In 1800, Spain ceded its claims to Louisiana Territory to Napoleon Bonaparte, although Spain retained control of Florida (its territory below the thirty-first parallel) until 1819. In 1803, however, Napoleon sold Louisiana Territory to the United States, thereby resigning his North American ambitions in favor of his European ones.

As the Choctaws entered the nineteenth century, the contest for empire among the European nations was over, and the Indians could no longer play the role of allies, mediators, or middlemen. They now had to deal with the U.S. government and with the changes that were going on in their own lives.

2 / Civilization and the Choctaws

IN THE LATE 1790S HARDY PERRY INTRODUCED CATTLE INTO THE eastern part of the Choctaw Nation, and Louis and Michael Leflore and Louis Durant (white settlers) brought cattle into the western part, on the Yazoo River. Domesticated livestock marked major changes in the subsistence and geography of the Choctaws. For many, it meant a change of traditional roles. Men became herders (although the cattle generally ran semiwild in the woods), and women became spinners and weavers. Deer were increasingly scarce under the pressure of hunting for trade, and cloth replaced deerskins for clothing. The eastern areas of Choctaw territory were abandoned because of warfare with the Creeks and the decline of deer populations. The Scottish firm of Panton Leslie, influential among tribes throughout the Southeast, brought in new goods for the Indian trade, and Indians learned the meaning of debt.[1]

As hunting declined, the population centers of the nation shifted toward the Northeastern and Western districts. Old towns were abandoned, and populations dispersed. Rich prairie areas west of the Tombigbee provided grazing land for cattle, and families, primarily those of mixed-blood farmers, moved there. Only in the Six Towns in the South did population centers remain relatively stable.[2]

Many Choctaws moved west of the Mississippi to live permanently where they could continue to hunt. According to their traditions, they had always hunted there. By 1801 there were "a considerable number" of Choctaws in the western lands who had "not been home for several years." They had established several villages, and in at least one place, on the Washita River, they had also begun to farm. For the most part, however, they roamed lower Louisiana Territory in numerous hunting parties.[3]

Diseases, mainly smallpox and measles, were a constant

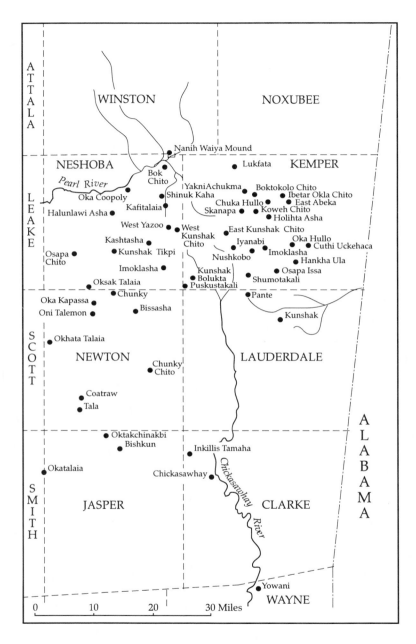

Choctaw Villages in Mississippi during the Nineteenth Century

threat.⁴ Whether because of increased death rates or the influence of white settlements, funeral customs underwent a significant change. Sometime around 1800, the Choctaws had given up the custom of exposing the dead body to the sun and had taken to burying the corpse in a sitting position. Seven poles, painted red and decorated with hoops of grapevine, were placed around the grave. The soul climbed the hoops to the top of a pole to reach the spirit world. Each month for thirteen months, relatives would go to the grave to wail loudly. Then a final mourning ceremony was held at which the poles were pulled up, and a feast was held. As the body returned to the spirit world, people ate the produce of the human world, and the cycle of death and regeneration went on. Although the form changed, funerals continued to be a major time of social and ceremonial gathering, bringing together kin groups and remaining a distinctive source of Choctaw identity throughout the nineteenth century.⁵

Despite changing politics and population shifts, however, the boundaries of the three divisions of the nation remained stable. Puckshanubbee was chief of the Western District, Homastubbee (succeeded in 1809 by his son Mushulatubbee) was chief of the Northeastern District, and Pushmataha was chief of the Southern District.⁶

Among these leaders, Pushmataha was to be the strongest ally of the Americans. His story is almost archetypal of the changing situation of the Choctaws. An extraordinarily charismatic figure, he was born on the headwaters of Buckatunnee Creek, some two miles above the site of the contemporary community of Macon. Most of his family died in wars with the Creeks and Osages, and he was left an orphan. The lack of family connections left him with no position in the social structure of the tribe and certainly no grounds to assume leadership. He gained recognition, however, through a remarkable incident. During an important council held to elect a leader, lightning struck the tree under which the participants sat, killing many of them. Pushmataha then stepped forth from behind the tree, and when the amazed survivors asked where he came from, he replied, "From the Great Spirit."[7]

If the story has legendary qualities, it nevertheless sanctioned the notion that Pushmataha was spiritually ordained for leadership, and it explained how a man of no apparent family connections could be recognized as a leader. His personal bravery in battle proved his leadership for both Choctaws and whites. He led Choctaw troops under Andrew Jackson in the War of 1812 and the Creek War. He was welcomed at Fort Madison in 1813, wearing the full military regalia of the U.S. army—dress uniform, gold braid and epaulets, and silver medal. He joined the evening promenade of officers with his wife on his arm. Pushmataha personifies the forces acting on the full-blood Choctaws of his time. He fought with the valor of a traditional Choctaw warrior, but on the side of the white leader, Andrew Jackson, against the Creek tribe. He became a hero in white society, and he would ultimately succumb to the vices of that society in the form of alcohol.[8]

The major agents of change in the Choctaw homeland were white traders—Louis Leflore, Nathaniel Folsom, and John Turnbull, among others. They established their posts, married Choctaw women, and reared mixed-blood children in homes that became important trading centers. Folsoms, Leflores, Pitchlynns, Perrys, Nails, Juzans, and Brashears became important intermediaries in relations between the Choctaws and the U.S. government and Christian missionaries. As they and their offspring intermarried, the complex relationships of blood and marriage created a group of leaders who stood on the crux of two worlds.

Nathaniel Folsom (born in North Carolina on May 11, 1756) and his brothers Ebenezer and Edmund, descendants of several generations of Scotch-Irish traders from North Carolina, settled in the Choctaw country around the 1770s. Both Nathaniel and Ebenezer married Choctaw women and raised large families. Nathaniel had two wives, cousins of Mushulatubbee, and twenty-four children. His son David was born in the Choctaw village of Bok Tuklo on January 25, 1791. Nathaniel moved his family to Pigeon Roost on the Natchez Trace sometime around 1803 and opened a tavern. David was sent to school in Tennessee for about six months and then was tutored at home. He served with Pushmataha under Jackson in the Creek War in 1812–13.[9]

David married Rhoda Nail, daughter of the Revolutionary War hero Henry Nail and his Choctaw wife. Nail and his son Joel were influential in the Southern District.[10] Ebenezer Folsom's daughter Rhoda married John Pitchlynn, the son of a British officer. He was probably born in the West Indies around 1756. John's father had been on his way to the Choctaw territory at the request of George Washington, a personal friend, when he died, leaving John to be raised in the territory. There John became a trader and interpreter. After Rhoda's death, he married Sophia, the daughter of Nathaniel Folsom. She bore him a son, Peter, on January 30, 1806. Peter later played an important role in the politics of the Choctaw Nation both before and after the removal west of the Mississippi.[11]

The Leflores descended from Jean Baptiste LeFlau, a French soldier who was in Mobile by 1735 and married Marie Jeanne Girard. Jean Baptiste's son, Louis, was born on June 29, 1762. Louis married Rebecca and Nancy Cravat, who were of mixed French-English-Choctaw heritage and nieces of Pushmataha. Rebecca gave birth to a son, Greenwood, on June 3, 1800.[12]

"LeFlau" became "Leflore," and when the Choctaw agency of the U.S. government opened on the Pearl River near present-day Jackson, and the Natchez Trace became the prominent road through the Choctaw territory in 1801, Louis opened a station on the Trace. The settlement around his home became known as French Camps, and the trading station itself became the site of the distributions of annuities from the treaty of 1801.[13]

With roads, trade, and treaties, the Choctaw Nation increasingly entered into relations with the U.S. government. Trading posts and licensed traders, for instance, were a way of ensuring that Indians were treated fairly (an ulterior motive being to win their friendship away from British and Spanish interests). From its earliest incarnation, federal policy was committed to "civilizing" the Indians, a policy that had both humanitarian and pragmatic political ends.[14]

With growing white settlement, however, also came growing sentiment for the removal of Indian nations residing east of the Mississippi River. The ideology that inspired the idea of removal was an old one, with deeply religious roots—the conflict of savage hunter and settled farmer, the disorder of wilderness to be overcome by the order of God's law. The hunter, who roamed vast tracts of land and whose efforts produced little, must give way to the farmer, who ordered the land by farming and made it most productive.[15]

The Louisiana Purchase had provided Thomas Jefferson with a vehicle for an Indian policy based on this idea. Jefferson, in his belief in the perfectibility of human nature, foresaw the decline of traditional subsistence hunting before the inevitable march of civilization. He also saw that as hunters entered the new economic system of trade, the decline of their subsistence base would force them into debt. They would then be compelled to trade land, their only resource, to pay their debts. Unless they became productive farmers, they would be destroyed. It was thus a matter of humanity to find a place for those who would not or could not give up hunting for a settled existence. The Louisiana Purchase would serve as a place in which the Indians who would not adopt the white man's way of life could be removed from contact with whites and allowed to pursue their uncivilized lifestyle, subsistence hunting. Removing Indians from their homelands would also, however, open up large areas east of the Mississippi for white settlement. Thus Jeffersonian philanthropy fed land hunger.[16]

By the early 1800s many of the Choctaws had already begun to adopt a settled life-style. Government agents could report that, having "rent the shackles of prejudice," the Choctaws were "casting their eyes to the earth for sustenance and for comforts." They had already asked for "materials, tools, implements, and instructors to aid their exertions and to direct their labors." It was the hope of the agents that "the liberal and well directed attention of Government" might make them "happy and useful." If this happened, the country would be saved "the pain and expense of expelling or destroying them." In a purely pragmatic sense, civilizing the Indians was more humane and less expensive than war or forced removal.[17]

Faced with new economic conditions and advancing white settlement, the Choctaws redrew the boundaries of the Choctaw homeland in a series of treaties with the U.S. government during the early 1800s. Tribal leaders, often inspired by debt, sold off worn-out hunting territories. In 1801 at Fort Adams they ceded over two million acres of land along the Mississippi, from the thirty-first parallel to the mouth of the Yazoo River, in exchange for two thousand dollars in merchandise and a supply of tobacco. The land that they ceded would become one of the richest parts of the burgeoning Cotton Kingdom in Mississippi during the early nineteenth century. They also agreed to the building of a road through their territory (the beginning of the Natchez Trace).[18]

In 1802, at Fort Confederation on the Tombigbee River, they agreed to the survey of their eastern boundary with the United States (originally established with the British in 1763). In 1803, at Hoe Buckintoopa, they ceded 853,760 acres in southern Mississippi and Alabama, above the boundary with Spanish Florida, in exchange for cloth, rifles, blankets, powder, lead, a saddle and blanket, and one black silk handkerchief. In 1805, at Mount Dexter, they ceded another 4,142,720 acres in southern Mississippi. John Forbes, a partner in the Panton Leslie company, personally lobbied Henry Dearborn, secretary of war, for the treaty, promising to pressure the Indians to cede land if the government would pay him directly the fifty-five thousand dollars in trade debts owed by Choctaws.[19]

Jefferson was unhappy with the 1805 treaty. He was anxious to acquire more Choctaw land along the Mississippi River, which was of increasing economic value because of the potential of the cotton industry. The Choctaws, however, refused to give up free access to the western hunting lands, offering instead a stretch of land along the thirty-first parallel. Although the treaty was signed in 1805, Jefferson did not submit it for ratification until 1808 when increasing tension with the Spanish in Florida emphasized the strategic value of this tract as a buffer zone.[20]

In 1802 the government established a Choctaw trading house at St. Stephens, on the site of the old French fort Tombecbe. Regulation of trade was an important part of government policy to see that the Indians were treated fairly and thus to cement their loyalty to the United States. In a gesture unconsciously symbolic of the passing of political power from the Spanish to the Americans, the trading house occupied the storehouse of the former fort, and the officers' barracks became the trader's home. In 1805 George Gaines, of Galatin, Tennessee, arrived to become the U.S. factor at St. Stephens, thus beginning a long and influential tenure among the Choctaws. Although the Spanish taxed goods that came up the Tombigbee through Mobile, the post did a flourishing business. Bracketed by Panton Leslie in the South and St. Stephens on the East, the Choctaws were increasingly drawn into the market economy.[21]

While they consolidated their boundaries through treaties, they also confirmed their status as friends of the United States. A contingent of Choctaws scouted for General Anthony Wayne against the Northwest Indians at Fallen Timbers in 1794.[22] Pushmataha, Mushulatubbee, and a number of other Choctaw leaders rejected Tecumseh's appeal to join his alliance with the British against the Americans. Pushmataha declared that they had never shed the blood of white men in battle and had no cause to turn against the Americans.[23]

Shunning Tecumseh's Indian alliance, Choctaw leaders sided with the Americans in the War of 1812. Pushmataha offered his forces to General Thomas Flournoy at Mobile and led contingents of warriors in Andrew Jackson's attack on Pensacola and at the Battle of New Orleans (although years later some were still asking for compensation for service at Pensacola).[24]

They also rejected the Creeks' proposal to join in a war against the Americans. In fact, they joined the Americans against the Creeks. Pushmataha, Mushulatubbee, Edmund Folsom, and John Pitchlynn led a contingent of 131 Choctaw warriors at the Battle of Holy Ground in December 1813, a disastrous defeat for the Creeks.[25]

In fighting so vigorously with the Americans, Pushmataha and his Choctaw warriors unwittingly played into the outcome of larger forces at work in their world. The defeat of the Creeks relieved the fear of major Indian insurrections in the Southeast. Although a band of Seminoles retreated into the swamps of Florida and to the protection of the Spanish, large-scale Indian warfare was over. The defeat of the British in the War of 1812 both relieved the threat of invasion by a foreign power and opened up new economic opportunities for trade along the Mississippi River and development of lands in the Creek cession and Louisiana Territory.

The treaty that Jackson forced on the defeated Creeks in 1814 after the Battle of Horseshoe Bend included a major cession of their lands in central Alabama. Part of it was the territory between the Tombigbee and Black Warrior rivers, an area long disputed by the Creeks and the Choctaws. Now the United States was in a position to dictate boundaries, and in 1816, inspired by "a liberal and judicious distribution of . . . presents," the Choctaws signed the Treaty of Fort St. Stephens, giving up part of that land and establishing the eastern boundary between their territory and the United States. In exchange, they received an annuity of six thousand dollars a year for twenty years. Cash in hand would prove useful as the Choctaws adapted to new influences in their lives.[26]

The outcome of the War of 1812 had fueled a growing sense of American pride and nationalism, and now unrestrained access to the vast reaches beyond the Mississippi encouraged rapid westward migration. The first stirrings of an American manifest destiny were felt, and the concept of a transcendent American race began to emerge.[27]

The rise of American nationalism and the westward expansion of American population were accompanied by a rising religious fervor; thus it was inevitable that Indians would have to confront Christianity. Americans had rejected the godlessness of English Deism in the Second Great Awakening of 1800–1801. A new religious awareness and a revivalistic spirit swept the land. At Cane Ridge, Kentucky, several thousand people gathered in 1801 for a camp meeting that lasted almost a week. Various members of the impromptu congregation were stricken by "bodily exercises." In one case, a woman became stiff as a board and could not be revived for three days.[28]

Such religious enthusiasm was very much a frontier phenomenon. Baptist, Presbyterian, and Methodist missionaries spread throughout the land. They went to serve church members who were venturing into the wilderness rather than to convert the Indians who were already there.[29] In regions where government trading posts and agents were few, and very little governmental regulation or organization existed to enforce law and social order, churches stood for decency and order. They brought discipline and stability and social structure to congregations who found disorder and temptation at every turn.[30]

The new American missionary spirit melded into the colonial evangelical impulse toward Indians. In 1762, the American Society for Propagating the Gospel among the Indians and Others in North America had begun as a voluntary organization, and it was given legal status by an act of the Massachusetts legislature in 1787. In 1796, the New York Missionary Society was founded as a voluntary group of members of the Presbyterian, Associate Reformed, Reformed Dutch, and Baptist churches, and it soon established missions among the Chickasaws of Georgia and Tennessee.[31]

The American Board of Commissioners for Foreign Missions was established in 1810 as an interdenominational organization of Presbyterians and Congregationalists.[32] Inspired by the thought of "many millions of men sitting in darkness and in the region and shadow of death" in America, the board despaired of their salvation because missionary efforts in other countries had been "attended with so many discouragements." Nevertheless, it was to become one of the most important missionizing bodies among the tribes of the Southeast.[33]

The field for missionary work among Indians was in some danger in the early 1800s. Fearing that New England Indians were virtually extinct, the Society for Propagating the Gospel among the Indians in 1813 commissioned John F. Schermerhorn, a Presbyterian minister, to visit Indian tribes "in the remote parts of North America." Schermerhorn and Samuel J. Mills (one of the founders of the American Board of Commissioners for Foreign Missions) visited those remote parts in 1813–14 and reported back to the society at its annual meeting on May 26, 1814. They had found the southeastern Indians spinning, weaving and knitting, and raising "great quantities of corn" and large numbers of "domestick animals" (cattle, horses, pigs, and poultry). The Indians were making "great progress in agriculture and civilization" and were "casting off the Indian habit, and adopting the modes of the whites." They were leaving their villages and giving up the hunting life. The Choctaw agent Silas Dinsmore had assured Schermerhorn that the Indians were "panting for instruction" and had "earnestly requested" schools. Dinsmore did not expect them to want religious instruction, because "of this they little [knew] the advantages," but they were "anxious to have their children educated." Schermerhorn concluded that of all the Indians in the United States, "the Cherokees, Chickasaws, and Chactaws appear[ed] the most favorable for the establishment of a mission with the prospect of success."[34]

In 1816, the American Board of Commissioners for Foreign Missions proposed the establishment of a school among the Cherokees. Cyrus Kingsbury wrote to Secretary of War William H. Crawford, on behalf of the board, that it was not only a "dictate of humanity" and a "duty enjoined by the Gospel" but an "act of justice" to extend to the Indians this "distinguished blessing." The most efficient way to accomplish this end was "to begin with the instruction of the rising generation."[35]

The missionary impetus in American history was an integral part of the westward rush of American settlement. In an almost mystical way, virgin lands and heathen souls were open for the taking. The frontier moved onward as Choctaw and Creek land cessions paved the way for Mississippi to become a state in 1817. The sale of the lands ceded at Mount Dexter and St. Stephens brought an influx of white settlement on the eastern edge of the Choctaw territory. What had been a relative trickle of white population before 1817 became a river thereafter. The majority of those who arrived brought with them the values and social system of the southern plantations of Virginia, the Carolinas, and coastal Georgia. They were by and large men who fit not the model of the Jeffersonian yeoman farmer but the entrepreneurial spirit of American capitalism.[36]

Federal policy tried to fit Indians into the yeoman farmer model, and it favored religion as a vehicle. If the Christian mind glorified Abel the husbandman over Cain the hunter, then Christian values could transform the Indians in ways consistent with the aims of the government and the expansion of American society.

Christian piety and benevolence were tempered with moral obligation and not a small element of Christian guilt. In contemplating its proposed missionary efforts, the American Board declared that if the Indians were not civilized through the medium of Christianity, they would soon become extinct, and if that happened, "their blood" would be "upon this nation."[37]

Crawford responded favorably to Kingsbury's proposal for a school and promised such aid as the laws would permit. He agreed to direct the government agent to build a schoolhouse and a home for a teacher and to furnish two ploughs, six hoes, and six axes "for the purpose of introducing the art of cultivation among the pupils." For female students, a loom, six spinning wheels, and six pairs of cards would be furnished so that they could be taught to spin, weave, and sew. The school building and supplies were to remain public property. In return for this support, Crawford asked only for an annual report on methods of teaching. He suggested that if the mission succeeded, Congress, "that enlightened body," might support the undertaking "more directly and liberally."[38]

To test Indian sentiment for education, the American Board sent the Reverend Elias Cornelius, corresponding secretary of its Prudential Committee, to visit the Cherokees, Chickasaws, and Choctaws in 1817. The committee reported, "Everywhere he was kindly received, & found dispositions highly favorable to the objects of the mission." The Chickasaws and Choctaws demonstrated "not only a readiness but an ardent desire" for schools.[39]

Armed with its convictions and the promise of government support, the board established a mission named Brainard among the Cherokees in 1817.[40] In 1818, the missionaries at Brainard, at the request of the Prudential Committee, gave "prayerful attention" to the request for a Choctaw mission and selected Cyrus Kingsbury and Mr. and Mrs. Loring S. Williams as "best suited" for the work.[41]

The missionaries had their charge, and they set off on the four-hundred-mile trek overland into the Choctaw country in May 1818. They found a fine land and Choctaws with "considerable wealth" and "strong tendencies toward a civilized state." Despite the fact that panthers lurked in the woods and roads were difficult to navigate, they approached their work with faith in the power of God to transform the Choctaws into Christians. Kingsbury wrote hopefully, "O that the Lord may have a people here."[42]

Although Kingsbury expressed his faith in God's will to make the Choctaws His own, the Choctaws were not interested in altering their religious beliefs, which even with the changing circumstances of the early nineteenth century had survived relatively intact.[43] The missionaries held a strongly Calvinist belief in the absolute power of God over the human soul. They believed in the depravity of human beings, but they tempered it with the idea that God's grace had a regenerative effect. If an individual acknowledged sinfulness, it was a sign of God's power at work. If the person became anxious over the state of his or her soul, salvation was near.[44] The Choctaws, on the other hand, valued personal freedom and autonomy. Every man could seek spiritual power and encounter spirits. Although the spiritual world could convey special skills, it was also suspect. The *alikchi*, men who attempted to assert control over others because of claims to spiritual power, were suspect. The contrast between Choctaw beliefs in individual power and Presbyterian beliefs in dependency and subjection is strikingly indicative of the cultural gulf that separated Choctaws and the missionaries of the American Board.

The missionary attitude toward the Indian is perhaps best captured in the Macedonian cry, "Come over and help us!" The image was that of the savage standing on a shore with the words issuing from his mouth. The image and the words conveyed the Christian sense that pagans need only be exposed to the word of God to be saved and that they were eager to be helped.

Choctaw leaders were eager for education, not Christian salvation. Pushmataha and Mushulatubbee expressed their thanks to President James Monroe for his assistance to "the Foreign Mission Society in establishing schools" among the Choctaws.[45] They were willing to follow the civilization policy of the federal government and learn to live with their white neighbors. They were not interested in ceding their lands.

The conflicting motives of Choctaws and missionaries served to undermine the objectives of both. The Christian God might change human nature, but financial support came from a government policy still largely inspired by Deistic principles. Religious and secular concerns clashed, to the ultimate detriment of the Choctaw Nation.

3 / The First Coming

CYRUS KINGSBURY AND MR. AND MRS. LORING WILLIAMS ARRIVED
at the site of their new mission station near the Yalobusha River
in late June 1818. Captain Levi Perry, a half-blood who was the
headman in the neighborhood of the mission site, gave them a
house in his "yard" until they could find their own place. Although Williams thought the location unhealthy, he placed the
mission family in the care of the Lord.[1]

The missionary position was clear: "Civil and religious liberty,
improvement in civilization and the arts of life, and the introduction of the best social institutions admitted to be indispens-
ible to the highest well-being of a community, are still secondary
to the one primary object of securing holiness in the hearts of
individuals."[2]

As they began their work, the missionaries found themselves
the cultural Other in a strange and often harsh environment.
They were welcomed first by Perry, a mixed-blood with a Choctaw wife, someone they could recognize and deal with, and they
continued to associate primarily with white men and the mixed-
bloods of the tribe. When they held their first public worship on
June 28, 1818, it was attended by "the half-breed natives, two
white men, and fifteen or twenty blacks."[3] Kingsbury reported,
"Half breeds [and those] who understand our object appear
highly gratified." [4] This reliance on the mixed-blood element of
the tribe ultimately served to distance the missionaries both
physically and politically from the traditional full-blood population, and it contributed to the missionaries' failure to civilize the
majority of the tribe.

The physical location of the mission was also removed from
the center of the Choctaw community life, located as it was in
the most sparsely populated area of the Choctaw Nation, the
Western District. The Yalobusha River was far removed from the

major centers of settlement along the Pearl, Pascagoula, and Chickasawhay rivers, where most Choctaw villages were located. John McKee, the Choctaw agent, had recommended the site because it was accessible for river traffic to deliver supplies the missionaries needed, not because it was near Choctaws. It was much closer to the rich lands of the Mississippi Delta, which would be attractive to permanent settlement by whites. Kingsbury, probably unaware of the distance between him and the true objects of his mission, declared himself "perfectly satisfied" with the site, where he hoped to diffuse "the light of the Gospel among these benighted & degraded people."[5]

Kingsbury named the new mission station Elliot, a tribute to John Eliot, the famous missionary to the Algonquians of the East Coast in 1636. The first trees on the site were felled around August 15, 1818, and the first house (a fifteen-by-eighteen-foot structure) was raised on August 18. Soon after, Peter and John Kanouse and Moses Jewell arrived from the East.[6]

But the missionaries almost immediately had to confront the rigors of life on the frontier. Their physical hardships were severe and certainly far greater than any spiritual hardship endured by the Choctaws in their settled and peaceful communities. They fell ready prey to illnesses induced by environmental conditions to which their Choctaw neighbors were long accustomed. The weather was excessively hot in the late summer. Kingsbury and Williams were striken with dysentery and fever soon after they arrived in the country, and Williams's wife almost died of "bilious fever" in early September. Peter Kanouse was consumptive when he arrived, and he was soon ill with fever and the effects of his disease. The mission could not afford such prolonged sickness, and he left in early October.[7]

The missionaries suffered for their faith in many ways. They were sustained primarily by their belief in their God, and secondarily by the U.S. government, but in their attempts to achieve the secular objective of federal policy (to educate the Indians to a state of civilization) and their own religious objectives (to proselytize Indians to Christianity), they found themselves

stretching their severely limited resources too thin. Their emphasis on physical discipline for children and religious discipline
in preaching antagonized influential Choctaw leaders.

Although white men and their families might welcome missionaries, there were still those who looked "upon all white
people . . . with a jealous eye." Whiskey had also entered the
neighborhood, and Choctaws went on drinking binges. Kingsbury noted, "[These] bear down our spirits and sink our hopes."[8]

The missionaries were sick, the hired help (three men) were
feeble, and the tremendous labor of establishing the mission
weighed on Kingsbury's mind. The Choctaws wanted a school,
and the arrival of the missionaries raised their expectations that
they would get one. To open one by the spring, however, Kingsbury needed at least ten men, and he had only three feeble ones.
He asked the Prudential Committee for help, suggesting that
black workers would be less likely to arouse the "jealousy" of the
natives. He expected that the missionary spirit would inspire
volunteer laborers to come from the North, and he was disappointed when it did not. He was forced to hire labor, four slaves
belonging to men in the neighborhood and two "very industrious" Choctaws. Hired help and supplies shipped long dis-
tances were very expensive, and Christian piety ran up against
the reality of debt.[9]

The missionaries struggled to establish self-sufficient establishments in the wilderness, and it was disappointing that the
Lord would not bring them all the Christian workers they
needed. Their sense of who they were was modeled on the
nuclear family of man and wife. Married couples composed the
largest part of that family. The laxity of Choctaw marriage customs, particularly polygamy, was evidence of paganism.[10] Single
missionaries, male and female, generally married soon after ar-
riving at the station. Kingsbury took a wife, Sarah Varnum, his
"dear friend," to whom he had been betrothed for three years.
She traveled to New Orleans to meet him, and they married on
December 24. They and Judith Chase, Varnum's traveling com-
panion, returned to Elliot on February 1, 1819. In mid-February,

Aries V. Williams arrived at the mission, and he married Judith Chase in July.[11]

Elliot was a bastion of Christianity in the wilderness and a closed enclave of family life. It would have been unthinkable for a missionary to marry a Choctaw woman. The size and the complexity of the physical plant were impressive. The labor to create it was intense. The mission members became a family in both a spiritual sense, through union in religion, and a physical sense, through marriages between members and the birth of children. In virtually every way, the missionaries distanced themselves from contact with the reality of Choctaw life and culture.

The task of running the establishment also preoccupied Kingsbury's attention with secular concerns, a situation that he felt keenly. "Our views & labours have been fashioned too much after a worldly policy [and not] to the glory of God."[12] Kingsbury still managed, however, to preach on Sundays to a mixed audience of half-bloods, white people, blacks, and occasionally, some of the natives. The missionaries organized themselves into the first church in the Choctaw Nation on Sunday, March 26, 1819.[13]

They had made no converts, and indeed, the Choctaws around them persisted in paganism, evidenced particularly by their belief in witchcraft. An old woman living near Elliot was murdered as a witch. Twelve persons had been killed in the past three years. Intemperance and trafficking in whiskey, although not part of traditional Choctaw culture, were also sources of missionary despair.[14]

Kingsbury was acutely aware of the Choctaws' desire for schools and was concerned about his ability to start one. If the missionaries could not meet the Choctaws' demands, they stood to lose their chance to convert them to Christianity. "However faithless the Indians may be respecting their own promises, they look for great punctuality from others. And it is hard gaining their confidence where they have once been deceived."[15]

If Kingsbury recognized the importance of schools, he was still frustrated over the lack of success in conversions. "We wish we could say that as much has been done to enlighten & save the souls of these perishing people as to make preparations for the instruction of their children." But by the spring of 1819 the missionaries could report little in the way of religious instruction. "The expectation of this people has been that all our efforts would be directed toward the commencement of a school."[16]

Although the mission buildings were still under construction, some Choctaws finally forced the issue of a school in the middle of April when they traveled some 160 miles to present their offspring, "eight promising children," at the mission. They had heard that the school was ready, and although it was not, Kingsbury accepted the children rather than risk alienating their parents and other members of the nation. On April 19, the first Choctaw school officially commenced. The familiar cycles of gains and losses prevailed, however, and on the following day Kingsbury was struck with a severe illness that left him incapacitated for several days.[17]

For Choctaw leaders, education was a way of resisting pressure to cede their lands. The rich delta region above the Yazoo River beckoned to cotton growers. The sales of the Creek lands to the east of the Choctaws opened that area to white settlement.[18] President James Monroe proposed a land cession to them in 1818, but Mushulatubbee and Pushmataha replied, "Our land is small and we do not wish to part with any of it . . . we do not wish to leave our country."[19]

To force the issue in the face of Choctaw resistance, George Poindexter, congressman from Mississippi, introduced a resolution in Congress to prevent Choctaws from emigrating to lands west of the Mississippi. Although such a move might seem antithetical to government policy, it did make sense. As long as Choctaws had free access to hunting grounds in U.S. territory west of the Mississippi, they would never cede their lands in Mississippi. Poindexter proposed "confining them to the boundaries heretofore appropriated for their use," until they acquired "the right to other lands by treaty with the United States."[20]

For as long as they could remember, the Choctaws had crossed the Mississippi to hunt in the West and to make war with the

Osages, the Caddos, and other smaller tribes. As deer and other game in their eastern lands dwindled, they became more dependent on the game in the rich lands along the Arkansas and Red rivers, and some even settled there.

American settlers and traders also moved northward to settle along those rivers after the Battle of New Orleans ended British control of the Mississippi River. The purchase of Florida from Spain in 1819 settled American control of the territory north of the Red River and set the stage for the extension of the U.S. government in what became Arkansas Territory.[21] To ensure federal control of that land, the government needed to constrain the Choctaws' freedom and force cession. Choctaws were confronted with the notion that the United States owned their traditional hunting grounds and that they must buy those lands with part of their homeland in Mississippi.

Poindexter's strategy of containment was consistent with John C. Calhoun's Indian policy. Calhoun believed that Indians should be made "to contract their settlements within reasonable bounds," with the guarantee that those boundaries would mark their permanent homes. Those who did not wish to submit should be "permitted and aided" to settle "at a distance" from white communities. The policy was supported by many Mississippi citizens, who saw the potential of the cotton industry as a source of wealth in the state. The Choctaw cession in 1805 had confirmed to the United States the rich Natchez District, where cotton became the major crop during the early nineteenth century. The possibility of another Choctaw land cession held out the promise of wealth in the burgeoning and highly speculative capitalist economy.[22]

If Indians stood in the way of expansion, they must either submit to white society or get out of its way. One form of submission was cultural. According to Calhoun, "Our laws and manners ought to supersede their present savage manners and customs." They should be taught the value of individual property and "the common arts of life, as reading, writing, and arithmetic."[23] In March 1819, these beliefs were embodied in the Civilization Act, by which Congress appropriated ten thousand dollars to prevent "the further decline and final extinction of the Indian tribes" and to introduce them to "the habits and arts of civilization." The act authorized the president to employ "capable persons of good moral character," who would teach Indians "the mode of agriculture suited to their situation" and teach their children "reading, writing, and arithmetic."[24]

Indian education was to be entrusted to "benevolent societies" that had already begun schools for Indians. These were Christian missionary organizations. The Civilization Act made no specific reference to instruction in Christianity. Its intent was specifically secular, but the appeal to a moral responsibility to prevent the "decline" of Indian tribes and the concern for the moral character of teachers gave Christian organizations entrée to Indian communities. It is ironic that in a nation where separation of church and state was promulgated in the Bill of Rights, Christian missionaries were so ready to serve as agents of federal Indian policy.[25] Christianity, government policy, and civilization went hand in hand on the American frontier.

While Congress provided for the education of Indians, Mississippi congressmen pressed for their removal. Choctaw leaders were divided in their opinions concerning a land cession. Although Mushulatubbee and Pushmataha opposed removal in their letter to Monroe, Calhoun instructed John Pitchlynn and Edmund Folsom to encourage the Choctaws to move. James Pitchlynn, John's son, reported to Calhoun, "If there was a treaty held in the nation, there would be one-third or half of the nation would move in the fall."[26]

Thus encouraged, Monroe instructed McKee to find out whether the Choctaws were willing to negotiate; in case they were, he commissioned Andrew Jackson and Colonel Burnet to conduct negotiations. Jackson rehearsed with McKee some compelling arguments to use on the Choctaws. McKee should tell the Choctaws about Poindexter's bill, which was pending until the Choctaws had indicated whether they would move west voluntarily. If they would not, they would face extinction as a nation. Whites would settle their western lands, and Mississippi would take their eastern lands. If they remained in Mississippi, they could do so as citizens of the state, "protected" by its laws on a reservation of land.[27]

Jackson's proposals essentially stated his conviction that Indians should not remain as sovereign nations within the bounds of the United States. Their presence contravened the integrity of the American nation. It was nationalism, not racial hatred, that seemed uppermost in his mind. He had no concern for Christianity or education or civilization for Indians. State citizenship and private landownership must supplant the power of Indian tribes.

Jackson was encouraged in the prospect of a treaty by a report from James Pitchlynn. The headmen of the "Lower and Six Towns" districts (Mushulatubbee, General Turner, Little Leader, Pushmataha, and Red Fort) were "highly gratified" that Jackson had been asked to conduct negotiations and were willing to "hear the talk of their father," the president.[28]

McKee called a general council of the Choctaw Nation in August to propose an exchange of Mississippi lands for the western territory. Given the encouraging signs, it came as a rude surprise when tribal leaders gathered near the French Camps community and soundly rejected the president's proposal to buy their land. McKee's appeal to Choctaw concerns for their kinsmen west of the Mississippi had no effect. Mushulatubbee and Pushmataha called the western Choctaws "strangers" and declared, "The President can do what he wants with them." It was obvious that an appeal to tribal unity had no meaning when traditional divisions within the tribe ran so deeply. Pushmataha said plaintively, "We wish to remain here, where we have grown up as the herbs of the woods; and do not wish to be transplanted into another soil."[29]

The split between the eastern and western Choctaws was a result of the changes in subsistence patterns that came with trade and livestock. The rejection of a cession was evidence of growing economic divisions within the tribe, divisions that also reflected the growing but conflicting influences of mixed-bloods. James Pitchlynn accused "rich white men" of giving "bad talks" to the Indians to discourage a treaty, and he asked Jackson not to consider the decision as "the Voice of the Nation" but only as the "Voice" of "rich white men & Half Breeds" who were willing to "enslave the poores[t] part of the nation." Styling himself "cheif [sic] of Choctaws West of the Mississippi," Pitchlynn vowed that they would retain the western lands and that tribal leaders would not sell any land without sharing the profits with them.[30]

On the role of mixed-blood leaders, McKee reported to Jackson that the apparent change of heart regarding removal was due to the actions of "a few half-breeds" whose reports that the western lands were barren "misrepresented things" but still alarmed other leaders.[31] Given that white and mixed-blood traders had acquired property rights in the nation and profited economically from their activities, most had a strong stake in retaining what they had established.

With the failure to reach accord on a treaty, a group of mixed-bloods, including Isaac Brashears, Alex Hamilton, Benjamin James, Lewis Perry, and David Folsom, determined to go to Washington to meet directly with the president, although McKee discouraged them by refusing to fund the trip.[32] Jackson reported the failure to Calhoun as evidence that nothing could "be done with the Indians without corrupting their Chiefs," an act he refused to condone. He strongly advised that Congress take action to "regulate" Indians. "Circumscribe them, furnish them with instruments of agriculture and you will there by lay the foundations of their civilization."[33]

Civilization and education, as well as removal, were certainly issues on the minds of the Choctaw leaders at the August council. Cyrus Kingsbury attended the council to hear the discussion as well as to solicit financial support for schools. Puckshanubbee, chief of the Western District, had already pledged two hundred dollars of the six-thousand-dollar yearly annuity from the 1816 treaty to the support of a school and a blacksmith shop.[34]

David Folsom spoke on the need for education, and McKee, the government agent, introduced Kingsbury to the council. Addressing the assembled Choctaws as "Chiefs, Brothers and Warriors," Kingsbury appealed to their pride and urged them to give up alcohol. "You have conquered your enemies; never let it be said that whiskey has conquered you." He appealed to their desires. "The Great Spirit has sent us a good book." This book would tell the people "what is good & what is bad" and would make them "wise & happy." Schools would teach Choctaw children to read that book. He challenged them to match "King Pukshanubbee" by contributing money. He used subtle threat. "You see that you can no longer live by hunting. You must raise corn & cattle & cotton that your women & children may have plenty to eat & to wear."[35] Several men, in a rather ironic gesture, immediately pledged eighty or ninety cows and thirteen hundred dollars in cash for support of schools in their neighborhoods. The council also resolved to give the mission two thousand dollars a year for sixteen years from the tribal annuities.[36]

Education might yet be a counterweight against removal. Mushulatubbee informed Monroe of the outcome of the August council, declaring again, "We have made up our minds not to leave the country of our fathers." But he also thanked Monroe for "the school established in our nation" and assured the president, "We have made arrangements, in respect to civilization, to do better in our country than we have heretofore done."[37]

With the financial commitment from the Choctaw leaders, and with the promise of six thousand dollars from the Civilization Fund for Elliot and for Cherokee missions, Kingsbury continued his efforts.[38] By the fall of 1819 the station at Elliot had grown significantly and was on its way to being economically self-sufficient. It boasted "seven commodious cabins," a dining room and kitchen fifty-two feet by thirty feet, a schoolhouse thirty-six feet by twenty-four feet, a millhouse thirty-six feet by thirty feet, a lumber house and a granary, each eighteen feet by twenty feet, and a blacksmith's shop, stable, and three other outbuildings. Between thirty and forty acres of land had been cleared, and between twenty and thirty had been cultivated. Some nine thousand feet of lumber had been cut by hand. Mission livestock included seven horses, ten steers, seventy-five cows, seventy-five calves, and about thirty swine. Three new workers had arrived from the East in August 1819: William W. Pride, a physician; his wife; and Isaac Fisk, a blacksmith and farmer. The school served fifty-four children, bringing the population at the mission to 76.[39]

The growth of the mission is even more remarkable in light of the incredible hardships the missionaries suffered. Even as they cleared and tried to tame their physical environment, they were plagued by natural disasters, illness, and death. Although births were eagerly awaited, the pregnancies of the women at the mission slowed the work. Mrs. Loring Williams and Mrs. Jewell were both expecting babies imminently in April 1819 when it became imperative to open the school at Elliot, and they could not contribute much to the effort.[40]

The mission journal for 1819 is a record of the illnesses of missionaries and students at the school. There were thirty cases of mumps, severe colds, and pleurisy among the students. There were also earthquakes, panthers, and wolves, and a fourteen-foot rattlesnake was killed in the mission garden. Births were offset by death. Mrs. Jewell had her baby in July, but Aries Williams died on September 6, 1819, little more than two months after his marriage to Judith Chase, who died two years later, on October 13, 1821. Sickness and death were facts of life for the missionaries, but the sickness of students led the missionaries to fear that parents would take their children away if the mission was perceived as a sickly place.[41]

The need for physical labor was an ongoing problem. Kingsbury's requests for assistance were frequent. When the healthy had to spend their time caring for the sick, it took away from the mission effort, and it also caused hard feelings and dissension. Although the concept of family was important, bearing and raising children drained the energies of female missionaries.

Kingsbury began to ask for single women to teach in the schools and for "free men of color" as laborers.[42]

The work of carving this island of civilization from the wilderness had been accomplished primarily by the members of the mission family, who worked without pay. Kingsbury, in fact, declined a salary of $666 from the Congregational and Presbyterian Missionary Society of South Carolina because the missionaries had agreed that they would not have private property at the mission. The only hired help were four Choctaws and some men sent by the American Board. The mission had cost more than $9,000, over $7,000 of which came from the American Board and less than $2,000 from the U.S. government.[43]

The general public was able to form quite a favorable impression of the mission from a glowing report by Adam Hodgson, an English traveler who arrived there on April 18, 1819. He rhapsodized over "the coolness of the air, the fresh fragrance of the trees, . . . the soft light which an unclouded moon shed on the log-cabins of the missionaries." When he and Kingsbury, on an evening walk, stopped to check for the presence of wild beasts, Kingsbury pointed out a plant that was an antidote to rattlesnake bites, leading Hodgson to marvel at "the proximity of the bane and the antidote."[44]

He was also impressed with the school day, which began at daylight with the boys at farm chores and the girls at "domestic employments." The mission family and their students assembled for reading, singing, and prayer at 7:00 A.M., followed by breakfast. After a short recess, the school opened with more prayer and singing, reading of a chapter from the Bible, testing on the previous day's reading, and lessons in "reading, writing, accounts, and English grammar." For dinner, they had bread and milk "and various preparations of Indian corn," and afterward they read from the Bible and from "Scott's Practical Observations," then more singing and prayer and, finally, bed.

Although the missionaries had as their primary objective "the religious interests" of their students, they were also "anxious to put them in possession of those qualifications, which may secure to them an important influence in the councils of their nation, and enable them gradually to induce their roaming brethren to abandon their erratic habits for the occupations of civilized life."[45]

Some Choctaws were not so impressed with the mission. Despite the frugality, the caution, and the good intentions of the missionaries, the elaborate and costly physical plant at Elliot was in itself a cause of suspicion among the Choctaws. It placed the missionaries dangerously close to that category of "rich white men" of whom Pitchlynn had complained, and it led to charges that the missionaries were enriching themselves at the expense of the Choctaws. The missionaries waged a public relations campaign with Choctaw leaders. David Folsom visited the school at Mayhew and read the children a letter from "benevolent friends of the mission" and then addressed them at length in Choctaw. Puckshanubbee and Mushulatubbee also visited and afterward wrote to Samuel Worcester, a member of the American Board's Prudential Committee, expressing their approval. "Brother, our hearts are made glad to see our children improving so fast." They even approved of manual labor. "We are pleased to see our boys go into the woods with their axes, and into the field with their hoes, . . . that they may know how to clear and cultivate our land." Echoing Kingsbury's injunction to them, they wrote: "We cannot expect to live any longer by hunting.—Our game is gone." They added, "The Good Spirit points out to us now this new and better way to get our meat, and provide bread and clothes for ourselves, women and children."[46] Pushmataha, chief of the Southern District, brought his teen-aged son to attend the school at Elliot. The young man spoke English fluently and had a good knowledge of grammar and some acquaintance with geography, which he had acquired from some white men at the trading station at St. Stephens.[47]

More parents and children appeared, and by the end of the year there were sixty students. Although some of the "larger scholars" complained of the regulations of the school with regard to physical labor, Kingsbury felt that the complaints "did not excite any discontent among parents or other students."[48]

Finances were a continuing problem. On October 5 Kingsbury wrote in the mission journal: "We know not what to do;—we are here in the wilderness more than $1200 in debt, without money, without the necessary conveniences for a large family, a number of sick to take care of, provisions for 80 or 100 to procure for a year to come, & not a single cable from the Treasurer of the Board for almost eleven months. At times, we feel as tho' we should sink into the grave & no one come forward to raise the smouldering ruins."[49] In the face of Kingsbury's despair, the Choctaws were unrelenting in their desire for more schools, and they turned to another missionary group for help.

The Choctaw council had committed part of its annuity to educate its children, but not necessarily to endorse the American Board. The chiefs had committed money, and now they wanted more schools. Puckshanubbee had his school in Elliot. Now Mushulatubbee, chief of the Northeastern District, wanted a school, and Kingsbury's inability to start one led some of the district leaders to ask John Pitchlynn to approach the Cumberland Presbytery. Samuel King and William Moore agreed to visit the Choctaw and Chickasaw country and meet with Pitchlynn to discuss plans for a new school. They did not appear for the scheduled meeting, but Kingsbury, Folsom, and Pitchlynn did, and Folsom announced that he had been authorized by the chief and warriors of the district to "take the lead in this business." He had been crucial in getting the tribe's commitment to support schools, and he assured Kingsbury that the Choctaws wanted him to establish a school, but he also welcomed the possibility that other missionaries would "come forward to labor in these vacant fields."[50]

If Folsom did not cut off the possibility of other missionaries, Kingsbury tried to. When King and Robert Bell finally did get in touch with him to offer their services, he told them that there had been a "misunderstanding" and that Folsom had charged him to establish a school. Despite his constant need for assistance, Kingsbury probably discouraged King and Bell because the Cumberland Presbytery from which they came was unorthodox in its theology and had adopted the Methodist system of circuit riding. He sent them off to the Chickasaws, where they ultimately established a mission.[51]

Kingsbury faced increasing pressure to establish more schools, although the growth of the mission at Elliot was already placing severe economic strains on the American Board's resources.[52] The prospect of a removal treaty became more attractive as a source of financial support. Indeed, Kingsbury felt that the Choctaws were so committed to the idea of education that it was "the only consideration" for which they would cede land, and he thought that some of "the half breeds" favored ceding lands for schools. He believed that if he could establish a school in Mushulatubbee's district, it "would have a great influence" on prospects for a land cession.[53]

In anticipation of a new source of funds, the missionaries made plans for three new stations that would include schools.[54] In February 1820, Kingsbury set out for David Folsom's home at Pigeon Roost with a wagonload of iron utensils and two laborers to build the new school in the Northeastern District. Along the way they were drenched by "one of the most powerful rains ever experienced in this country." Kingsbury noted, "[We] were obliged to swim the Waggon over six Creeks before we reached this place" (a real act of faith considering the cargo). Folsom and John Pitchlynn then accompanied him to select a location for the new mission. They found one on Oak-tib-be-ha Creek, about thirteen miles from its junction with the Tombigbee River. The site consisted of about one hundred acres on the border of an extensive prairie, rich grazing land that was attracting Choctaw cattle owners. It was also near the white settlements springing up to the east on lands ceded by the Choctaws in 1816. It was, like Elliot, in an area on the fringes of the Choctaw homeland, one undergoing significant economic change. Kingsbury put up a temporary residence and commuted back and forth to Elliot until early April 1820, when he and his wife moved permanently.[55]

He did so "with rather a heavy heart" because he had neither formal approval nor a firm commitment of financial backing from the Prudential Committee. "But what else could we do? The Chocktaws had made the appropriation. They were anxious to have preparations making for the school. . . . A little hesitation or delay on our part might have thrown this important appropriation, & this part of the nation into other, & very different hands."[56] He, and Sarah, probably breathed a sigh of relief when the board gave its approval. Kingsbury named the new offspring Mayhew, in honor of a prominent early missionary in New England.[57]

But as Kingsbury tried to establish new schools, the Choctaws were demanding something new—blacksmith shops. The clash between Christian idealism and Choctaw pragmatism tried Kingsbury's patience. Puckshanubbee had specified one thousand dollars of his portion of the Choctaw annuity for a blacksmith shop. Choctaw farmers needed metal tools and wagons and were becoming increasingly dependent on American technology. Skilled mechanics were scarce in the Choctaw territory and nearby, and they could command premium wages. Isaac Fisk and Moses Jewell, the mechanics at Elliot and Mayhew, provided vital services for the missionaries, but Kingsbury rejected the Choctaw proposal for a free public shop, saying that services "distributed gratuitously & indiscriminately" would not result in any "good effect." Mainly, he wanted to continue to be able to trade the services of Fisk and Jewell to the Choctaws for food, but clearly the pragmatic needs of the Choctaws would not go away. They wanted their young men to learn to be scholars and mechanics.[58]

What to teach and how to teach? Did education prepare the way for the gospel, or would the gospel make civilization possible? The Choctaws had spent their money on "instruction & civilization," not on "Gospel instruction," but since they had given it to "a Christian Society," Kingsbury concluded, the missionaries could interpret "the great work of Indian instruction" as both education and conversion to Christianity.[59]

How could the government assess the effectiveness of the civilization policy? Calhoun found an agent when Jedidiah Morse, a Congregationalist minister, was commissioned by the Northern Missionary Society of New York to conduct a survey of Indian tribes. Calhoun funded his travels in exchange for a report on the "disposition" of Indians toward education and "civilization."[60]

Morse reported that the Choctaws had "made great advances in agriculture, and other arts of civilized life." They raised corn, beans, melons, and cotton, and in one year the women spun and wove ten thousand yards of cloth. They also raised large numbers of cattle and had "laid aside hunting, as a business," though some still hunted "for amusement." Their morals were still "loose and corrupt." Although they believed in a "Supreme Being," they had "no exterior worship," marriage was nonexistent, and polygamy was common.[61]

Despite Morse's encouraging report of progress toward civilization, despite the Choctaws' support for missionary schools, and despite Mushulatubbee's promise to Monroe to "do better," the Choctaws could not stave off the pressure to give up their lands in Mississippi. As Kingsbury moved to start a school in the Northeastern District, Congress appropriated twenty thousand dollars for treaty negotiations with the Choctaws. Calhoun asked Andrew Jackson to conduct the negotiations, and although Jackson stated that he "had determined never to have any thing to do again in Indian treaties," he also declared a sense of obligation to President Monroe and a debt of gratitude to the citizens of Mississippi for their help in his battles in the War of 1812.[62]

In the Choctaw Nation, John Pitchlynn, his son James, and Edmund Folsom continued their lobbying in favor of removal, but despite their efforts and McKee's assurances that the Choctaws were willing to exchange their lands in Mississippi for western lands, resistance to the idea appeared to be growing in 1820. The Six Towns were now "in complete opposition." David Folsom in the Northeastern District and Joel Nail in the Six Towns were also opposed.[63]

The situation was tense when Jackson and his fellow negotia-

tor, Thomas Hinds, arrived at Doak's Stand for the treaty negotiations in early October 1820. Jackson bargained with promises
of Choctaw control of the western hunting lands and the argument of tribal sovereignty. Since he opposed the idea of Indian
nations as sovereign within American territory, he appealed to
"the pride of a real Indian . . . in the strength of his nation."
Choctaw nationalism and U.S. nationalism were at stake.[64]

Choctaw leaders were not eager to participate in the disman-
tling of their nation. They took a long time to get to the treaty
ground at Doak's Stand. Puckshanubbee and Pushmataha brought
only seventy or eighty of their warriors, and the Six Towns
people did not come at all. Jackson, alerted by James Pitchlynn's
letters, suspected that white men and half-bloods had kept the
Choctaws away. He chided the two chiefs for the poor showing,
and he dispatched Edmund Folsom and Middleton Mackey, the
government interpreter, to fetch the Six Towns people. In the
next few days, other leaders and their followers arrived, and
Puckshanubbee organized a ball game that helped to dissipate
tensions among the men of different towns and districts.

Jackson addressed the gathering in the paternalistic tone that
Kingsbury had used. "Your father the President of the United
States is anxious to make all his Choctaw children happy." The
president promised a country beyond the Mississippi, where "his
Choctaw children" could live and be happy. Those who wanted
to remain in Mississipi could "do so, and be happy likewise." He
used reason. "For farming, you have more land than is necessary.
As a hunting ground, it has not sufficient game." But he also
threatened. "Without a change in your situation, the Choctaw
nation must dwindle to nothing." If the Choctaws did not take
the land that the president had acquired "at much expense . . .
for his Choctaw children," the land would be taken over by
white settlers, and the Choctaws would have nothing. He also
cajoled. They were being asked to cede only a small part of their
lands in exchange for a much larger western territory, and those
whose homes fell within the ceded territory could take individual
allotments and be protected by the laws of the federal govern-

ment. He promised support for schools, noting that the president had "every wish to educate and civilize his Choctaw children." Any resistance to his proposals he attributed to "the false statements of . . . white men and half-breeds" who desired "riches and Power" and wanted to "make fortunes unjustly" and from whom the president wanted to protect the Choctaws. He stated the consequences if they resisted. "You must feel the effects of your folly." The "effects" would be a move to land that was "poor and sterile, trackless and sandy deserts."[65]

As the Choctaws talked and played games, Jackson grew impatient. He promised them that a township of land in the cession would be sold to fund schools both in Mississippi and in the western territory.[66] They talked for four more days about the offer, and Jackson's impatience gave way to threats. The government would make a treaty with the Choctaws in the West. Jackson stamped his rhetorical foot, "If you will permit the obstinacy and folly of a few amongst you to work your own destruction, you cannot hereafter complain." Americans had, he said, fought the British to protect Choctaw territory (with, of course, Choctaw help) and had "preserved" them from Spanish influence (which was much less aggressive than American influence). He advised them, "Consult your best interests, and all will be well; otherwise, no foresight can calculate your distresses."[67] In the face of Jackson's challenge, the Choctaws went back to their deliberations. Puckshanubbee, whose territory was most at stake, stalked off the treaty grounds, but he was mollified by the promise of a special payment of five hundred dollars in the final treaty terms, and the Treaty of Doak's Stand was signed.[68]

Kingsbury, who had become a fixture in Choctaw deliberations, was undoubtedly relieved that the seventh article of the treaty provided fifty-four sections of the land to be sold for a school fund. He immediately presented Jackson and Hinds with an ambitious plan for building schools, arguing that Choctaw children should "be initiated in habits of industry, and a portion taught the Mechanics Arts." The plan called for immediate appropriations of $5,000 for the school at Elliot, $12,000 for building a school at Oak-tib-be-ha, and $10,000 for establishing five small schools during 1821. After that, the missionaries would establish two more major schools, serving eighty to one hundred students, and twenty-eight more small schools, serving twenty to forty students, in Choctaw communities. According to Kingsbury's plan, Choctaw schools would in the long run cost $358,500, or an average of $44,812 a year through 1828.[69] With this commitment, the American Board could meet the demands of the Choctaws for schools. Jackson looked at the plan, asked Kingsbury to sign it, and said it would be forwarded to the president, with his influence to have it carried into effect "as far as circumstances would permit."[70]

Kingsbury had been right in saying that the Choctaws would cede land only for schools. Jackson and Hinds reported that without the provisions for schools, they could not have gotten the Choctaws to sign the treaty, and Kingsbury's plan accompanied the document to the president.[71] Kingsbury was somewhat satisfied. "The Lord is continuing his gracious smiles on the work which Christian benevolence has been labouring to accomplish for this nation." But he knew that the sale of Choctaw lands would not cover all the costs of mission expansion. The plan would succeed only if "able & devoted persons," that is, volunteer missionaries, came forth to carry it out.[72]

The Treaty of Doak's Stand was ratified by the Senate on January 8, 1821. The Choctaws ceded approximately six million acres on the western edge of the Choctaw Nation in exchange for approximately thirteen million acres in Arkansas Territory. The treaty embodied the "important object" of Indian policy, "to promote the civilization of the Choctaw Indians." It made explicit the distinction between the civilized and the uncivilized, the latter being those who would "live by hunting . . . and would not work." It gave the hunters the opportunity to use the lands west of the Mississippi and provided them a blanket, a year's supply of corn, and the accoutrements of hunting—a kettle, a rifle, bullet molds and nippers, ammunition, a blacksmith, and a trader. For the civilized Choctaws, the treaty offered private property. Those who were settled in the ceded territory and wanted to stay would be granted a tract of land one mile square to include their improvement. When all the Choctaws had become "so civilized and enlightened as to be made citizens of the United States," their lands would be allotted among them. The treaty also promoted centralized authority in the Choctaw Nation. All whiskey brought into the nation was to be seized by the government agent, and two hundred dollars was provided annually for a corps of light-horse, a group of men who were given the authority to compel all men, Indian and white, to pay their just debts and to compel "bad men" to leave unless they had authority from the Indian agent.[73]

The Treaty of Doak's Stand did not require the Choctaws to leave their homes. For those who wished to maintain their traditional life-styles, it offered inducements to move voluntarily, and it encouraged those who remained to become civilized through education and private landownership. But it also opened part of the Choctaw territory to white settlement, thereby increasing the likelihood that there would be future pressure for more land. The divisions within the tribe, both geographical and cultural, were undermining Choctaw resistance. In exchange for land, the Choctaws were to get education, about which they were to become increasingly ambivalent. And the mixed-blood element of the tribe demonstrated the importance of manipulating political affairs in the nation. These were the disparate elements of the "civilization" that American policy sought to inculcate among the Choctaws.

4 / The Progress of Civilization, 1821–24

THE TREATY OF DOAK'S STAND PRESENTED THE CHOCTAWS WITH choices defined by strong notions of what constituted "civilization": private property and education in the white man's ways. As the lands from the cession came on the market, millions of acres of Choctaw land passed into the hands of white landowners, and the upper Pearl River region became the fastest-growing section of Mississippi during the 1820s. Although some cotton plantations flourished in the area, the white population comprised mainly small farmers.[1]

As white farmers settled on the new boundaries of Choctaw lands, the missionaries' work to make farmers of the Choctaws proceeded, but in the face of significant obstacles. Once again, the conflict between Christian idealism and capitalist intention in American Indian policy is evident. Christian missionaries debated the relative merits of proselytizing and teaching while they struggled to support their institutions with insufficient funds and insufficient human labor.

If Elliot and Mayhew were bastions of order and civilization in the midst of the wilderness, they also required a considerable outlay of time and money for materials, and they represented a significant financial investment for the American Board. Moreover, the management of their building and maintenance and the supervision of workers required a large amount of Cyrus Kingsbury's time and effort. There were not enough laborers, and there was no money to hire additional ones. Kingsbury not only was responsible for "the preaching of the Gospel to a whole nation, & the superintendence of two establishments," but also had to spend much of his time "Waggoning, loading boats, &c, &c." Rather than giving the Choctaws enlightenment and civilization, he had to carry on a regular trade of cloth, utensils, and beads for food and labor. Religious idealism clashed with hard, economic realities and lack of resources.[2]

The financial support that Kingsbury had expected for his school plan as a result of the Treaty of Doak's Stand did not materialize. Although Calhoun thought Kingsbury's plan was good, he did not approve it. He noted, "It will involve a greater expense, than the appropriation for Indian civilization will authorize." He offered no explanation about the sale of lands that was supposed to support the schools. Kingsbury had hoped for at least $8,000 for the American Board schools after the treaty, but Calhoun promised an amount not to exceed $2,275, which, as Kingsbury noted, was "not the half" of what was needed. It was certainly not enough to fulfill Pushmataha's request for a school in the Southern District. Kingsbury stated, "To make promises to Indians which we cannot fulfill is the direct way to destroy our influence & usefulness."[3]

The financial constraints of the American Board compounded the problems of the missions. The War Department in its policies and the slowness of communication and disbursement of funds compelled the missionaries to assume debts because they had to spend before they could be reimbursed. Not only did Calhoun not approve Kingsbury's plan because of financial exigencies, but he issued a directive that payment for the construction of mission buildings be made only after the work had begun and that only two-thirds of the cost be paid initially, with the other one-third to be paid on completion of the building and on certification that the improvements or buildings were as "above described" and that they "actually cost the amount charged."[4]

The financial situation was becoming desperate. The establishment of Mayhew had put the missionaries in debt some five thousand dollars, and Kingsbury issued an ardent appeal to the readers of the *Missionary Herald*. "Will the Christian public see those, who have volunteered to wear out their days in a sickly climate, sinking under a burden, which *alone* they cannot sustain—but which, *with the assistance of their brethren throughout the country,* would be easily borne? Shall we be hurried to an untimely grave for want of that friendly aid, which might so well be afforded?"[5]

Kingsbury's letter represented both the plea of a man deeply committed to carrying out his mission to the Indians and the importance of the financial obligation that the board was undertaking. The missions were a sizable investment, and the balance of financial and spiritual concerns was to be an ongoing problem for both the board and its missionaries.

The lack of communication stemmed from the fact that the American Board was experiencing its own financial crisis in 1820, word of which reached Kingsbury inadvertently when he opened a letter addressed to Cephas Washburn, one of the board's missionaries to the Cherokees. Kingsbury was dismayed by the news. He wrote, "We are indeed brought into difficulty,— and know not what to do." But he expressed the hope that "the present embarassing circumstances" would make them "better missionaries"—"more economical, more willing to conform to any circumstances."[6]

Whether Kingsbury's plan to build schools throughout the Choctaw Nation was too elaborate, or whether the federal government was too niggardly in its appropriation for civilizing the Indians, the progress of education was slow. The sixty children at Elliot by the end of December 1820 were a very small number of those who might be educated. And the government did not sell the lands to provide the financial support for schools promised in the treaty. The Choctaws' concessions, the missionaries' efforts, and the government's own policies were being thwarted by the government's failure to act.

Even under the burden of debt and financial uncertainly, the missions continued to expand. Mayhew grew considerably. Its setting was idyllic—the edge of an extensive tallgrass meadow, where herds of cattle, horses, and wild deer grazed peacefully together. Flowers of all hues were "scattered, by a bountiful God, in rich profusion, and in all the beauty and innocence of Eden."[7] By March 1821, there were ten buildings in various stages of completion and three more for which materials were ready. About seventy acres had been fenced and partly ploughed. A school was scheduled to begin in the autumn.[8] But more workers were needed for a school, and Kingsbury waited anxiously for new arrivals from the East Coast.[9] Finally, a group reached the Walnut Hills, and at last, on March 3, Calvin Cushman and his family and William Hooper reached Mayhew.[10]

At Elliot, reinforcements had arrived to keep the school there in operation. Cyrus Byington reached Elliot in April 1820 and took over Kingsbury's role as superintendent. If Kingsbury was the spiritual leader of the Choctaw missions and the man most singularly responsible for the secular concerns of hiring laborers and dealing with the government agents, Byington was the teacher whose influence on the Choctaws was the most lasting. He was preaching in Massachusetts when the group of missionaries assigned to the Choctaws passed through Stockbridge in the summer of 1820. He was assigned the task of fund raising for the new mission. "It was supposed he might add much to the comfort and expedition of the journey." He was the advance man for the group, making arrangements for their accommodations, preaching about their goals, and soliciting money, which he did "with great cheerfulness and alacrity." He finally arrived at Elliot in April 1820, where he assumed the superintendency of the station after Kingsbury's departure for Mayhew.[11]

Of all the missionaries to the Choctaws, Byington had probably the greatest impact on the tribe's future identity through his efforts to learn the Choctaw language and translate the texts that promoted literacy among the natives. Perhaps his early training in Latin, Greek, and Hebrew influenced his interest in learning Choctaw. His library included John Heckwelder's account of the Delawares, with a word list of the language, Roger Williams's vocabulary of Narraganset, Josiah Cotton's vocabulary of Massachusetts, and John Pickering's Cherokee grammar.[12]

In their respective roles, Kingsbury and Byington represented the conflicts that the missionaries of the American Board faced in dealing with both their spiritual responsibilities and the secu-

lar forces of tribal and federal politics. Kingsbury was the strongest advocate of preaching and conversion, but he was also the person most visible as the spokesman of the missionary effort in the national political arena. As superintendent of the mission, he was the person most sensitive to the demands of the Choctaws for schools. Byington was concerned that the Choctaws be educated, particularly in the reading and writing of their own language, but that was so that they might better learn the word of God and be converted. He came to object strongly to what he felt was Kingsbury's preoccupation with the schools. The issues of preaching and teaching, and the balance of sacred and secular obligations, were to be of continuing concern to the missionaries and their leaders.[13]

The initial enthusiasm of some of the Choctaws began to wane in 1821 when it became obvious that the curriculum at the schools was not what they had expected. Manual labor and physical discipline were foreign to Choctaw child-rearing practices. Choctaw children learned by example, by emulating their parents in their daily chores, and the ethics and values of the tribe were passed down by grandparents, who sat the children down in the evening for lectures about what was right and what was wrong. Children had a great deal of freedom in their own society because they were constantly involved in the world of adults, observing and copying their behavior. Discipline was enforced by teasing or ridiculing children who were acting inappropriately.

The discipline and the requirement of manual labor in the mission schools ran counter to traditional Choctaw child-rearing practices, and although it met the missionaries' needs for sustaining the missions and inculcating the Christian virtues of hard work and industry, it inspired harsh criticism from at least one Choctaw leader. Robert Cole, Puckshanubbee's "speaker" and potential successor, became a vocal critic of the practices at Elliot. Although Puckshanubbee supported the school financially, sent his nephew to attend it, and visited him there, Cole became increasingly outspoken against the mission.[14] He complained that the school at Elliot was in session only two or three hours a day and that the missionaries "made little boys work with heavy axes & when they had lame feet."[15] Part of his disgruntlement stemmed from the fact that Kingsbury had refused to accept one of the children of Cole's brother-in-law, James McCurtain. McCurtain already had five children in school, and when Kingsbury would not admit another, McCurtain withdrew all his children. Cole, as maternal uncle (a role that in traditional Choctaw custom gave him greater power than the children's father), interceded with Kingsbury to take the children back. He expressed regret that the children would not have the benefits of education.[16]

The episode with McCurtain's children brought Cole into the role of ongoing critic of the mission schools. He objected to the emphasis on farm labor and thought the Choctaws should learn "mechanical trades so that they might be useful" to the nation. He visited the school and criticized it before the students. Such criticism undermined the hard-won gains of the missionaries, and Kingsbury complained that it weakened "government over the children."[17]

Student labor was a significant dilemma for the missionaries. They needed it to supplement their own meager forces. If they shifted the curriculum to "mechanical trades," that is, blacksmithing, they would lose the benefit of student help and lessen their ability to teach the students to speak English and read so that the students could understand the word of God. Cole's criticisms made quite apparent the discrepancy between what the Choctaw leaders wanted from mission schools and what the missionaries were prepared to give.

Kingsbury's patience was tried by the criticism of the discipline at the schools. He complained that some of the Indians seemed to feel that the missionaries were obligated to educate the children because they were paid by the government. "We need much wisdom to know how to help this people without doing them harm," he wrote.[18] He appealed for assistance from David Folsom, who visited Elliot and gave the scholars "a good talk."[19] Although Kingsbury met with Cole twice during the winter of 1822–23, Cole continued to criticize the missionaries, now for taking money from Choctaw families, to which Kingsbury retorted that families came to visit their children and remained for extended periods of time, taking advantage of missionary hospitality.[20]

Despite the criticism of Elliot in the Western District, Kingsbury still felt that the establishment of a school at Mayhew in the Northeastern District was crucial. As he wrote, "The Natives, perishing for lack of knowledge, . . . are expecting a school in the fall; & our word is pledged to put it in operation at that time."[21] If a school could not be started, the missionaries would lose more credibility with the Choctaws. The Lower Towns council had committed its financial support, and Kingsbury had been charged by Folsom with the responsibility of providing schools. Kingsbury feared the reaction if the missionaries did not start a school at Mayhew. "We cannot retain our present standing."[22] He also noted: "Some ill disposed half breeds are beginning to say that we have not fulfilled our promises. And some have even gone so far as to say that if we do not get a school into operation . . . we must quit the country." Once more, however, he was assisted by Folsom and Pitchlynn, who "nearly silenced these murmurings." Kingsbury added, "*They* are well satisfied with our proceedings."[23]

Plans for the proposed school were not going smoothly in terms of finances. Kingsbury had requested $8,000 from Calhoun, but the government's appropriation for the year of 1821 totaled only $5,000, $4,000 for Elliot and Mayhew and $1,000 for a school to be established in the Six Towns area.[24] Kingsbury complained to Calhoun that it would take at least $10,000 to build an adequate school in the Six Towns.[25]

In the face of inadequate funds and lack of sufficient labor, the missionaries changed their strategy. Rather than building more large, permanent stations with boarding schools, they decided to start day schools in Choctaw communities, as Kingsbury had proposed in the plan that he had presented to Calhoun in 1820. Large boarding schools were a significant financial burden.

In day schools, the children could live at home and be supported by their parents, and the local stations could be small because they would house only the mission family.

Day schools held out the prospect that missionaries could live in the more traditional Choctaw communities and be in closer contact with the people they also sought to convert. That, however, was not the result. In the spring of 1821, Loring Williams, who evidently felt very confined by life at Elliot, went traveling through the Choctaw Nation for the sake of his health, and Kingsbury and the other missionaries charged him to explore the possibility of local schools. At French Camps in the Western District, Williams presented the idea to Louis Leflore and Samuel Long, and he was somewhat surprised to find them "so animated at the thought of more schools and near them too." He should not have been particularly surprised at this reception, since the local community was comprised of "mostly white men old settlers, of property and influence, who have Indian families." Their homes were scattered along a thirty-mile stretch of the Natchez Trace, the major conduit of white influence in and out of the Choctaw Nation. They were already part of the process of acculturation. After hearing Williams's proposal for a local school, the leading men of the community agreed to furnish the buildings and board for the teachers and students, labor for caring for the sick, cooking, and cleaning, and land near the Upper French Camp, on high ground between the Pearl and Big Black watersheds. This first school thus came about at the behest of white men and mixed-bloods and were in communities that were marginal to the mainstream of Choctaw cultural life. They paid due deference to Puckshanubbee, chief of the district, by asking his approval for the school, which he gave readily. Despite some concern that "these gentlemen had not counted the cost of such an undertaking," the missionaries agreed to appoint Williams as the teacher.[26]

Williams named the new establishment Newell, in honor of a recently deceased missionary, but the Board of Commissioners ultimately named it Bethel. Williams's wife did the actual teaching.[27] The Williams family did not have an easy time at their new post. Their infant daughter died shortly after their arrival, and Mrs. Williams and their surviving children suffered from ague and fever. They were also isolated from the support and companionship of the mission family, but Williams stoically quoted Psalms, "It is good for me that I have been afflicted."[28]

The school began on December 11, 1821, but despite the initial enthusiasm, the results were disappointing. By January there were only twelve students. Williams lamented, "Had this disappointment been foreseen . . . it would have been thought hardly worth while for us to occupy this field for the sake of so few." The school served mainly mixed-blood children who were already bilingual.[29] Williams still hoped to serve as many as twenty-five to thirty children, and by February, the enrollment had increased to fifteen, but nine of those had transferred from Elliot.[30] Both Williams and his wife became so sick that they had to suspend the school in April and return to Elliot to recuperate. Although one of the missionaries from Elliot tried to maintain the school in their absence, the effort faltered.[31]

Despite financial uncertainties and the rocky start for the school at Newell, Kingsbury put on a brave front in his annual report to Secretary of War Calhoun. "The schools are more flourishing than at any former period." The total enrollment was seventy-five, about twenty of whom were "full blood natives." An additional five children from white families attended.[32]

Another day school was opened near David Folsom's home at Pigeon Roost. It served a community of about one hundred Choctaws who had settled there. These people were marginal in Choctaw society: they had no clan affiliation and hence no villages of their own and no claim on the tribal annuities. They settled near Folsom on his promise to use his influence to obtain annuity payments for them. He also encouraged them to give up drinking and to lead a settled life, and he invited Alfred Wright to explain to them "the attributes of God, the Creation of the world, the fall of man, & the plan of redemption." After hearing

Wright, the community requested a school, and Kingsbury appointed Wright as missionary and William Pride as the teacher.[33]

The notion of community schools created a dilemma for the missionaries. They were reluctant to move into the heart of Choctaw territory. It was not only a practical matter of distance and the expense of building far from major rivers. It was also a matter of significant cultural distance. The spiritual terrain in Choctaw country was not promising. Those communities with large-enough concentrations of population were, Williams presumed, "composed wholly of Indians whose minds" were "not prepared for the thing."[34]

There was also implicitly an element of spiritual fear on the part of the missionaries. To leave the mission and live among the "heathen" meant that they must "leave their Brethren" and go "alone" to face all the "inconveniences" of living without contact with the other missionaries.[35] Such comments echo the themes of early Indian captivity narratives in which the Christian captive fears not death or physical punishment but the despair that comes from being deprived of civilized company and God's grace in a totally alien land.[36] Particularly for the mission families of the American Board, contact with their fellows sustained them in an environment extraordinarily different from that of Protestant New England, where they had their roots. To isolate oneself from that family was emotionally hazardous indeed. The problems with the local school at Bethel certainly did not offer any encouragement.

On the other hand, the missionaries came increasingly to realize how distanced they were from the people they most wished to influence. The large physical plants of the missions, with their contingent of laborers, had already aroused the suspicions of Choctaws and were far from any Choctaw villages. William Pride advised his brother-in-law that the latter would be better able to serve Christ by practicing charity in his own hometown in Connecticut than by coming to Mississippi.[37] Byington also complained that the location of the stations was too far from Choctaw villages. "Thereby the assistant missionaries are stationed & kept at such a distance from the heathen that they can exert but little influence upon them."[38]

The missionaries finally fulfilled their commitment to the Northeastern District when the school at Mayhew opened on April 30, 1822. There were twelve students, eight Choctaws and four children of missionaries. The Indian children's native dress was exchanged for clothing that had been donated to the missions with the fervent wish that "these previous little immortals" could "be clothed *in robes washed, and made white, in the blood of the Lamb.*"[39] By December, a new school building, "constructed on the Lancastrian plan," was inaugurated. In a fit of optimism, Kingsbury wrote that the building was "sufficiently large for 100 scholars." As an appropriate role model, McKee Folsom, David Folsom's brother who had been sent away to the mission school at Cornwall, Connecticut, spoke at the opening of the new building.[40]

In June, David Folsom and Pitchlynn visited Mayhew and "expressed their approbation" of the way the school was conducted. Mushulatubbee arrived on June 30 with fifteen or twenty captains and two of his own sons and a nephew to enroll in the school. The next day he witnessed a demonstration of the skills of the students, who "read & spelt in various places in the spelling book; & several of them in the hardest part with promptness & accuracy." The students' skills gave Mushulatubbee hope for the future of the Choctaw Nation, hope that he would "live to see [the] council filled with the boys . . . now in school" and that they would "know much more & do much better" than his generation.[41]

Kingsbury, however, was not so happy with the Choctaws' response to the school. Students did not always return from vacations, and absenteeism was an ongoing problem. To solve the problem, he asserted his own and federal authority at an assembly of Mushulatubbee and his captains at Mayhew on August 1, 1822. He pointed out that the Choctaws themselves had contributed $4,000 toward the school, the president of the United States had contributed $1,275, and the American Board had contributed $8,000. He explained that "the white people prospered & became numerous" because they "listened to the instruction of the great Spirit, & taught their children to read the good book." The Choctaws, meanwhile, became "few & feeble and poor" because they did not have the "good book," had "never been taught the good way," and had not "educated their children." Parents must be punctual in returning their children to school, he insisted. They must not stay too long when they came to visit. The children must not take away the clothing they were given at the school. And above all, he scolded, if the Choctaws wanted schools, they "must expect them to be managed in all respects, not according to their own views, but according to the views of the President, and the good people who established them."42

Kingsbury's condescending tone and paternalistic message obviously did not endear him to the Choctaw leaders. They were determined to have schools, but on their own terms. Puckshanubbee and Mushulatubbee had schools in their districts. Now Pushmataha wanted his. He had contributed the Southern District's share of the annuity money, and Moses Jewell visited the Six Towns in the summer of 1821 to investigate the possibilities for a school. Although he returned with "intelligence . . . of a very interesting and promising nature," the promise was not immediately fulfilled. The people of the Six Towns agreed to establish a local school and support Jewell and his wife, but they had not done so by October when Kingsbury wrote rather anxiously to Jeremiah Evarts, the secretary of the American Board, asking "to know the mind of the Pru[dential] Com[mittee] on this subject, & how far they could make appropriations towards the support of local schools." The schools already in operation needed more support. "And yet there are reasons for Br. J's taking a local school soon."43

The matter languished until the spring of 1822 when Kingsbury attended the council for payment of the tribal annuity. The chief men and warriors of the Six Towns district wanted a school "as soon as practicable," and they agreed to let the missionaries choose the location, since "if it were left to them, they should not be agreed." Kingsbury was skeptical of their support, however. "The impression on the minds of the natives is generally favorable towards schools and civilization. But, like the rest of the world, they give good talks, but conduct very badly."[44] Nevertheless, he proposed that not one but two community schools should be established, if the board approved.[45] Although Jeremiah Evarts hoped for an enrollment of at least fifty, the missionaries planned on about twenty-five students.

Kingsbury and Jewell went to the Six Towns to look for a site for a school in the fall of 1831. The terrain was heavy forest interspersed with rich prairie lands, but it was sparsely inhabited. Kingsbury attributed the lack of population to a shortage of water and implicitly to the failings of the natives. "It is probable there are many springs concealed under the rich alluvial soil, which, if the country should be inhabited by civilized people, would be easily found by a little digging." They finally reached an area called Long Prairies, near the intersection of the southern boundary of the Choctaw Nation and the Mississippi-Alabama state line.[46]

A white man named Henry Nail lived in the area with his "quadroon" Choctaw wife. His son Joel, who was captain of the local company of light-horse and "influential with the local captains," lived nearby. Kingsbury and Jewell found the Nails "very friendly" toward their objective, and they chose a location for a school about half a mile from the Nails' residences, on the east side of Buckatunnee Creek about twenty-five miles from the nearest major river landing on the Tombigbee and fifty miles from the government trading post at St. Stephens.[47]

The site would provide fairly easy transportation of supplies and the support of an influential mixed-blood family. It would also avoid the costs that a school in the interior of the nation would entail. Although the proposed site was rather far removed from the major Choctaw settlements in the district, which were anywhere from twenty to sixty miles away, this was an advantage for the missionaries because the children at the school could be taken from their parents and from the influences of their own cultural milieu.

Kingsbury and Joel Nail announced plans for a school to a crowd of about five hundred Choctaws from the Chickasawhay and Huwahnee villages, whom they found gathered for a ball game near the Chickasawhay River. The village leaders were pleased with the prospect of a school and "expressed themselves satisfied with the scite [sic]" that Kingsbury had selected. Not everyone was happy, however. When Kingsbury and Nail arrived in the Six Towns district, Hwoolatahoomah, the leader, was "much rejoiced" at the prospect of a school but was "very sorry that it could not be in his clan." Kingsbury promised to write to the American Board to have "good persons" sent to open a school for his people.[48]

The shifts and changes of population within the Choctaw Nation, the result of ongoing forces far beyond the control of the missionaries, affected their ability to reach significant numbers of people. Communities were no longer where they had been. Where Kingsbury had expected to find "compact towns" among the Six Towns people and to locate a missionary and teacher in each, he found instead that the Choctaws were now scattered over an area of about six hundred square miles "for the convenience of wood, water, & agricultural pursuits."[49] The settled, civilized, agricultural life of the yeoman farmer now dictated separation rather than village life for the Six Towns.

Pushmataha was not pleased with the proposed location of the new school. He wanted a school at a more central site on the Chickasawhay River, and he made his displeasure evident. Kingsbury, sensitive as always to criticism from the people he was working so hard to accommodate, was frustrated, and tension grew. In November, Kingsbury pointed out to Pushmataha and his captains and warriors the effort involved in establishing a school on the Chickasawhay. It would require that a road be built, that a ferry, a sawmill, and a blacksmith shop be established, and that supplies be transported some thirty to fifty miles through the wilderness. It would take a year longer and an additional expense of one to two thousand dollars to build a school on the Chickasawhay.[50]

Pushmataha, the noted friend of the Americans, pointedly cited his war record and his understanding that the school would be built near his home. He, of all the Choctaw leaders, had been most involved in the affairs of the U.S. government. Since he had helped the white men who had come into his land, they should accommodate him. He wanted a school, and he gave Kingsbury a choice of three locations. He threatened to withdraw his portion of the annuity if Kingsbury did not accept one of his choices.

Kingsbury, ignoring what he might have known of Pushmataha's role in American history and concerned about the limited finances of his effort, retorted, somewhat inaccurately, that Pushmataha could not withdraw the annuity because "it was confirmed by treaty," although the treaty made no specific provision to the American Board. The redoubtable warrior, not stymied in warfare, was evidently taken aback. He and his captains withdrew for "further consultation on the subject." They did not come back with a reply, and the talks ended inconclusively.[51]

The mission station established in the Southern District was located at the site that Kingsbury had originally selected, near the mixed-blood Nail family. Moses Jewell and his wife, their departure delayed by illness, left Mayhew and took up residence in the Southern District in January 1823. The station that they established was eventually named Emmaus.[52]

The grandiose plans for boarding schools that Kingsbury had laid before Calhoun in 1820 were largely abandoned by 1823, together with the hope for self-sufficient missions that would draw the Choctaws so that they might be easily saved. The missionaries had chosen to shift "the burden of boarding" to the parents of students. The decision was a deliberate trade-off of objectives. The students could not "be brought forward" as quickly in the "various branches of a civilized education," but the missionaries could reach a greater number of people, particularly the adult population, by going out into the towns of the nation.[53]

The three Choctaw chiefs, each with a boarding school in his district and now taken with the plan for local schools, endorsed the missionaries' educational plans at a council in May 1823. Mushulatubbee lectured Kingsbury on appropriate discipline in the boarding schools—"it would do to whip the small scholars, but not the large ones"—and on priorities. He was "willing they should work some, but wanted them to attend school more than they worked." He then announced that he wanted a teacher for his children. Pushmataha also requested a teacher to live at Pierre Juzan's, near his home in the Cooncha district, and Puck-shanubbee wanted a school at his home just east of the Pearl River.[54]

Although the notion of civilization was a matter of government policy, the Choctaw leaders nevertheless wanted to keep control over the missions, since it was Choctaw money that was largely funding them. The leaders drew up a formal agreement with the missionaries and spelled out their mutual obligations and responsibilities. The board had the right to establish schools and mechanical shops, cultivate land, and keep stock as long as it maintained the schools. Teachers who established schools in Choctaw communities would be boarded free of charge, and parents were to provide board for their children at the school and assist in furnishing the schoolhouse.[55]

The first American Board venture into an authentic Choctaw community was at Mushulatubbee's home in the summer of 1824. Aden Gibbs arrived on June 4 and began teaching five students on the fifth. From the missionaries' point of view, a major advantage of his presence was that the situation would allow him to "improve himself" in his command of the Choctaw language. After a month, he proclaimed that he was "contented with his situation" but had only six pupils, although there were prospects of three or four more.[56] Mr. Haddon, a "pious young man" from Kentucky, was hired to teach the school that Pushmataha had requested at Juzan's, and he soon had nine students. Brother

Anson Dyer was sent to run the school at Puckshanubbee's home.[57] Hwoolatahoomah, chief of the Six Towns, finally got the school that he had requested in his neighborhood. It was located at a village called Yokena Chukamah ("good land") "in a high healthy country," about 115 miles southwest of Mayhew and 50 miles northwest of Emmaus. The population within a ten-mile radius of the site was "perhaps more dense than in any other part of the nation." It presented an ideal situation for missionary efforts, both because of the concentration and because the people were "in great darkness" and lived "very miserably." Alfred Wright, who had begun to master the Choctaw language, was the missionary, and Elijha Bardwell was the teacher.[58]

In October, however, Robert Cole, always a critic of the schools, was denouncing them as "bad things for the nation." He told Kingsbury to leave "my District."[59] Kingsbury, seeing opposition as evidence of lack of civilization, attributed Cole's feelings to "ignorance, & prejudice, & enmity of the natural heart."[60] The criticism may well have had political rather than cultural implications. Puckshanubbee, who was in his early eighties, had given Cole reponsibility in matters pertaining to the school, but the old chief had been consistent in his financial support of the schools and had sent his nephew to attend the school at Elliot. Cole, whose heritage was Chochumma and white, had emerged as Puckshanubbee's "speaker," and it is quite possible that as the chief's political heir apparent, he was criticizing the school to establish his leadership.

The school at Mushulatubbee's was also faltering badly, evidence once more of the large gap in expectations between traditional Choctaw families and missionaries. Mushulatubbee's ideas about discipline did not conform to Gibbs's, and the chief refused to "permit the scholars to be governed in a proper manner." Gibbs now felt himself "unpleasantly situated," and the missionaries concluded that Mushulatubbee's conduct was "insufferable." Nevertheless, they encouraged Gibbs to make one more attempt "to overcome the ignorance and prejudices of this poor people." The attempt failed. Gibbs's situation became "more & more unpleasant, & even critical," and the missionaries called him back to Mayhew.[61]

Mushulatubbee, expecting the service from the missionaries that other leaders had gotten, was upset by Gibbs's departure, and he threatened to "break up all the schools in the nation" if the missionaries would not send the teacher back. The chief appeared at Mayhew with William Ward, the agent, in tow to demand Gibbs's return, but Kingsbury did not give in to his threats. After some negotiation, Mushulatubbee signed an agreement concerning the running of the school, although he objected to Kingsbury's demand that whiskey be banned from the chief's house. Mushulatubbee said that the leaders of the district had agreed that they should have "a little whiskey" at the close of councils and that he could not prevent it, but he assured Kingsbury that "they should have but little" and that they would not interrupt the school. Kingsbury agreed to start the school again on September 1.[62]

Despite Cole's opposition and Mushulatubbee's demands, the missionaries were able to expand their school system during 1823, and by the end of the year there were six schools. Sickness was still a major problem. The school at Elliot had been "much broken." There was an outbreak of measles in the spring of 1823, and as a result, a number of other students did not return after the summer vacation. Robert Cole had withdrawn twelve students on learning that a number of other students were sick. Although the enrollment at Elliot was thirty-four boys and ten girls, the enrollment would undoubtedly have been higher had it not been for illness.[63] Choctaw beliefs in witchcraft also undermined the school when rumors circulated that one student had been killed by a witch and when a woman living in the neighborhood of the school became suspect.[64]

At Mayhew the enrollment was sixty-eight students (although attendance averaged only fifty-four). The average enrollment at Bethel was twenty to twenty-five, including eight full-blood children added during the year. Emmaus had ten students, although the school was in operation only two weeks and then closed because of illness. There were ten students at Juzan's. The school at Yokena Chukamah in the Six Towns was still in the planning stage, although the projected enrollment was about fifteen to twenty students.[65]

Despite criticisms of their educational practices, suspicion about their economic motives, severe illness, and personal loss, the missionaries had persisted, and although their gains were small, they still had faith that God would reward their efforts. Some Choctaws, on the other hand, had gotten the schools they wanted as a way of dealing with their white neighbors and their need for skilled mechanics, but they had done so at the expense of their lands. For most Choctaws, education had had little or no impact because the mission schools were far removed from their villages.

5 / Conversion and Change

THE FEDERAL POLICY OF CIVILIZATION HAD A PURELY SECULAR
objective. The American Board of Commissioners had a spiritual
objective. In giving over its policy implementation to a "Christian benevolent organization," the U.S. government thrust the
American Board and its missionaries into the moral dilemma
between these secular and spiritual objectives. The government
intended that Indians learn agriculture, reading, writing, and
arithmetic. The missionaries taught those things, but as a means
to their major objective of Christian salvation. They were constantly faced with conflicting priorities between their sacred
concerns of preaching and their secular concerns of teaching
and maintaining their schools and stations. The government
also compounded an already formidable task by imposing financial restrictions and providing inadequate resources, and the
American Board was unable to give enough financial support.

If the annual school reports to the commissioner of Indian
Affairs could cite statistics on the number of Choctaw children
who were learning to read and write and spell, they could not
report a significant number of Christian converts. As the missionaries struggled to establish schools, they also felt the strong
need for churches, partly to meet their own religious needs and
partly to provide congregations for the soon-to-be-converted
natives. Their first church opened at Elliot, in March 1819, and
their second, at Mayhew, was established on May 6, 1821.[1] In
November 1822, a church was organized at Bethel, a joyous
occasion for the Williamses, who had been for several months
isolated from their brethren and "deprived of the stated ordi-
nances of the Gospel."[2]

The faith of the missionaries was being sorely tried by harsh
reality and practical need. They needed financial support, spiritual sustenance, and physical labor. In the spring of 1821 a heavy

storm washed away the bridge on the road between Elliot and Mayhew. In June the crew of a boat bringing supplies to Elliot became sick, stranding the boat, and fallen trees made it impossible for the men from the mission to land the boat at the mission dock. In the face of such circumstances, simple events of Christian faith sustained the families. The Elliot journal for July 2, 1821, reported: "Monthly concert, a joyful day to the missionary in the bosom of this great wilderness. We were much refreshed by intelligence in the Herald for May."[3] There was sorrow as well. On July 6, 1822, the Cushmans' eldest child died at Mayhew "after a day of great pain and distress."[4]

A joyous occasion frequently reported in the mission journal was the arrival of boxes of clothing and household articles donated by "pious Females in different parts of our country." The donations clothed the mission family and the students in the school. They were welcome because they "manifested . . . attachments to the Redeemer's cause, & . . . compassion for the neglected, perishing Indians."[5] But there was a more practical and secular reason for gratitude. Clothing, a major trade item for the Choctaws, became a primary medium of exchange for the missionaries, who received virtually no cash from the American Board.[6] As Choctaw clothing styles changed from traditional buckskins to American dress, the Choctaws were dependent on the missionaries. Cyrus Kingsbury noted, "There is hardly any thing the Indians will take more readily in exchange for what we buy of them." Twelve yards of cloth would buy a day's labor from an Indian.[7]

But the cloth trade also led to criticism. A letter in the *Charleston Courier* on August 16, 1821, charged that the missionaries were selling the clothes to the Indians and that the Indians in turn were selling the clothes for money to buy whiskey. The writer implied that the missionaries were inadvertently feeding the Indians' "known habits" of drunkenness. In response, a lengthy editorial in the *Missionary Herald* denied any wrongdoing.[8]

The missionaries were certainly involved in the changing economy of the Choctaws. They were dependent on local supplies of food when they could not grow enough to sustain themselves or when weather conditions prevented deliveries of goods, and given the vagaries of the weather, that was fairly often. On occasion, when Choctaw crops failed, the missionaries provided food to Choctaw families. Choctaw families expected hospitality from the missions when they visited their children, which put an added strain on mission resources. The farmers at the missions were licensed to trade in the Choctaw Nation by the Indian agent. Since the granting of licenses evidently required the payment of a bond, it appears that the missions had some economic investment, or at least liability, in the trade. As of August 26, 1826, Calvin Cushman had capital of $1,000, Moses Jewell $500, and S. B. Macomber $2,000.[9]

In the midst of these secular concerns, the missionaries were constantly alert to and sustained by evidence of conversions. Such evidence was of necessity long in coming. The missionaries believed that Christ had died for the sins of all mankind but that true faith and salvation came through the operation of the Holy Spirit on the human soul, which was indicated in the anxiety of the individual. The first sign of conversion, then, was concern about the fate of one's immortal soul. The missionaries looked long and hard at anxiety before accepting it as proof of salvation. Their own rigorous standards denied them the bounty of souls for which they might hope.

The signs could be faint. Reports came from Elliot about "a general seriousness in the minds of the children" at the school there.[10] The problems of conversion among Choctaw adults were great. "The moral condition of this people is truly deplorable & must cause every benevolent heart to weep." There were no words in Choctaw for concepts such as sin and guilt and redemption, and although some of the Choctaws had "some confused notion of a great Being above," they did not know "his character" or "what he require[d] them to do." Indeed, many had "not the least idea of a superior being."[11] The signs of conversion that did appear were generally among whites or slaves. At Mayhew, two black women who worked there displayed "serious impressions."[12] And at Newell, after Kingsbury had preached for two Sundays in May 1822, there was a general outbreak of religious feeling. "A glorious work of grace has commenced. A few are already rejoicing in hope & a bit more are pricked in the heart, & anxiously enquiring what they must do to be saved."[13]

The largest number of potential church members were blacks. Williams reported "the happy fruits" of the interest at Bethel when ten adults gave "evidence of piety": four white men, five slaves, and one free mulatto. He noted, "The seriousness is now pretty much confined to the negroes." Students and Choctaws nearby were not interested in Christian preaching, although Williams noted that two or three Choctaw women had begun "to enquire into these things."[14] At Elliot, "more than a usual number of the black people" attended public worship on February 18, 1821, and on September 2, two slaves and Mrs. Levi Perry, the Choctaw wife of the mixed-blood chief of the district, expressed interest in joining the church.[15]

The most visible anxiety among the pupils in the school was experienced by John Long, a student at Elliot, who was discovered in his room weeping bitterly. He wrote in a letter: "I feel that I am a sinner and every thing that I do is displeasing to God. I wish that the missionaries would pray for me in case I die and go to hell and be tormented forever."[16]

John Long's experience is evidence of the long road to be traveled by Choctaw converts from traditional value systems to Christianity. The transition from a world of personal relationships with spiritual beings to one of complete dependency on an omnipotent god was extreme. Choctaws believed in their abilities to control spiritual powers through their visionary experiences, whereas converts had to accept the absolute power of the Christian God to control their lives and destinies. John Long's anxiety was an event of great joy to the missionaries because it confirmed their belief in the power of their God. The sense of powerlessness and anxiety that the boy experienced was totally antithetical to traditional Choctaw beliefs.

But John Long was not from a traditional Choctaw family. His father, Samuel Long, was a white man, one of those who supported the establishment of the school at Newell. After the father received "a solemn admonition from his Son," he too began to have "serious impressions" and "commenced family prayer . . ." and was "very active in every good work."[17] John Long's good influence was cut short rather dramatically, however, when he died on October 19, 1821.[18]

Choctaws who had heard of the missionaries' activities sometimes came to express their interest. The *Missionary Herald* reported a very interesting conversation between a missionary and a young Choctaw man who had previously been denied entrance to the school because of his age. In part, their dialogue went as follows:

T. Can you tell who made the world?
C. God.
T. Where is God?
C. Above.
T. Can you tell where people go when they die?
C. They go above.
T. What becomes of bad people?
C. They go to a bad place—to a great fire.
T. Who are bad people?
C. People who get angry—drink whiskey—take knife and kill one another. I have heard about these things:—how, when all people are dead, the world will be burnt up, and bad people will go to the great fire, and stay there for ever. Now I want to come to school, and learn to pray, and be a good man. I want to be like the missionaries. I have heard I have a bad heart. I know I have a bad heart . . . I believe what the missionaries say. I am willing to work, and do any thing you tell me. . . . I want to learn good things. Choctaws cannot tell me good things. Some Choctaws don't believe what the missionaries say. I believe what they say.[19]

In February 1822 a man named Tuscamiubby and his son visited Elliot to learn about Christianity.[20] Tuscamiubby, a man of about seventy, told the missionaries how his father had thrown him away and he had "lived on the ash heap" until he was old enough to talk and run about. He had then lived with a Frenchman who had treated him as a slave. Finally, the missionaries came, and they were like fathers and taught him useful things.[21] For Choctaws who, like Tuscamiubby, had been isolated or alienated from traditional Choctaw life, the paternalism of the missionaries was attractive.

For Choctaws who still lived in their own communities, Christianity had few if any attractions, and traditional beliefs persisted. Kingsbury tried to disabuse an elderly Choctaw man of his belief in witches by questioning him closely about what they were and where they lived. Although the old man kept replying that he did not know, he would not deny their reality, and a frustrated Kingsbury compared the conversation to "pouring water on a rock."[22]

Religious anxiety was largely confined to whites, blacks, and mulattos. Although Williams could report thirteen people who gave "pleasing evidence of piety," and three or four who seemed to be "anxiously inquiring," there was virtually no interest among the "scholars or the natives." Williams cried out in frustration: "Wherefore O Lord? How long?" He attributed the Choctaws' "unbelief & hardness" not to the failure of missionary efforts or to the power of Choctaw beliefs but to the "pernicious examples" and the "Deistecal" or "diabolical" principles of some of the white settlers in the neighborhood. Although he did not name names, it is likely that some of the men who had so enthusiastically supported the establishment of Bethel were also more concerned with "Deistecal," that is, secular and pragmatic, concerns than they were with spiritual ones.[23] Kingsbury lamented to Jeremiah Evarts, "We cannot tell you of that which is most of all things desirable, the conversion of the souls for whom we are labouring unto God."[24]

When widespread evidence of conversion came, it did so from an unexpected and not altogether welcome quarter. In December 1823, Kingsbury noticed that some of the girls at Mayhew displayed "an unusual spirit of inquiry" concerning religion, and he instituted weekly prayer meetings to encourage "the influences of the Holy Spirit."[25] The hopeful signs resulted, however, not from American Board efforts but from the appearance of Wiley Ledbetter in the Choctaw Nation and the new appeal of Methodism. The appeal was not doctrine, but Methodist style. Ledbetter, who was officially appointed by the Mississippi Conference of the Methodist Episcopal Church in December 1823 to ride the Choctaw circuit, arrived with a Mr. Hensey at Mayhew in March 1824 and preached "several interesting & animating discourses," which produced "an unusual excitement." Methodist missionaries had established circuits in areas surrounding the Choctaws by 1820 and intended to start schools, and they had been welcomed at Mayhew and Elliot and had preached there before, but they had not made major inroads into Choctaw territory.[26] After Ledbetter's sermon at Mayhew on the evening of March 7, however, many of the audience exhibited "an unusually great anxiety . . . for the salvation of their souls." By the following week several seemed "deeply sensible of their guilt & danger," and two hired men were saved.

The sudden surge in religious interest was probably as much a function of Methodist style as it was of profound religious conversion. Ledbetter's effect at Mayhew was dramatic, but although most of the female students exhibited "religious impressions," Kingsbury soon feared that the impression had worn off without leaving any "permanent change of feeling or conduct." Only two or three students gave serious evidence of having been "born into the kingdom of the Redeemer," and Kingsbury attributed the girls' behavior to "the very great excitement of animal feeling" produced by Ledbetter's sermons. It was the effect not of "apprehension of divine truth" but of "mere vehemence" in preaching style. It did not "arise from a view of divine truth," and their behavior was not "attended with a proper sense of guilt, or desert of punishment." Nor did it reveal conviction of the need for "persevering prayer."[27] Animal passion could in no way substitute for Christian anxiety. The "natural heart" was proving remarkably resistant to the work of the Christian God.

Ledbetter's inspiring sermons might have intrigued an emotional interest among the young women and hired hands at

Mayhew, but Kingsbury was disdainful of the effects. If Kingsbury held Ledbetter and Methodism in low esteem, Methodist opinions of American Board missionaries were equally low. William Winans, the bishop of the Methodist Conference, described the efforts of the board missionaries as "if not quite unprofitable," at least as of "little value."[28] Such competition and disparaging remarks seem to have been fairly common in virtually all missionary efforts.[29]

Despite Kingsbury's opinion, Ledbetter was still "flourishing greatly" in his efforts among the Choctaws by the summer of 1824, although he, like Kingsbury, needed money.[30] By December he produced tangible evidence of his work when he introduced some Choctaw converts to Bishop Joshua Soule at a session of the Methodist conference in Tuscaloosa, Alabama. Soule's soul was "deeply stirred within him. Standing erect in all his imposing stature, eyes filled with tears of joy, he cried out; 'Brethren, the Choctaws are ours. No, I mistake; they are Christ's.'"[31] Whoever laid claim to the Choctaws—the Methodists, Jesus Christ, or the American Board—it appears that Choctaw souls were viewed as trophies by competing denominations.

If widespread religious change was not taking place among the Choctaws, political change was, and it was attributable to the desire for schools. In the Six Towns district, Mingo Hwoolatahoomah and his captains passed a number of laws. They banned the importation and use of whiskey and also forbade stealing hogs or cattle. Other laws intruded more directly into the family lives of the Choctaws. These included laws against infanticide, which Kingsbury characterized as a "horrid practice" that proved "the heathen" were "without natural affection," and laws against polygamy and adultery. The new order provided for punishments as well. A woman and her husband were publicly whipped for infanticide. Those who went to Mobile and New Orleans and neglected their crops were to have their corn burned.[32]

Hwoolatahoomah's laws were passed to demonstrate that his district was ready for a school. After he found out that the proposed school in the Southern District was not to be located in his district, he declared to the American Board that he and his people had made laws because they wanted "to follow the ways of the white people" and hoped that those people would assist them in getting their children educated. The sentiments may well have been those of Hwoolatahoomah and his followers, but the handwriting in his letter to the board was David Folsom's, and it is quite likely that the influence behind the laws was Folsom's as well.[33]

Hwoolatahoomah's code is striking for its presumption of authority by a Choctaw captain over the private lives of his followers. The code is indicative of the cultural changes going on in the nation. Choctaw leaders had taken action to regulate alcohol by law because they recognized its dangers. These laws were thus an attempt to destroy one influence of white "civilization." Mushulatubbee and his captains gathered at Pigeon Roost in August 1822 and "unanimously resolved" that if anyone tried to sell whiskey in their districts, they would take "prompt & effectual measures" to destroy it. They "acknowledged they had all drank too much" and feared that whiskey was "destroying their country." Little Leader went so far as to declare that if whiskey selling did not stop in his district, he would "take off heads."[34] At a council near Mayhew, Choctaw leaders asked all white people in the nation, including the missionaries, to "abstain from the use of spirits altogether."[35] Although the missionaries certainly preached against the evils of alcohol, their own invoices showed shipments of brandy and Madeira (used, presumably, for medicinal purposes). Yet the Choctaws had already experienced the nonmedicinal effects.

Hwoolatahoomah's laws extended to traditional marriage customs, sexual practices, and the regulation of work habits, and they went far beyond traditional rights to chiefly authority. Tradition was, however, changing rapidly. The establishment of a light-horse company in the Treaty of Doak's Stand was only the beginning of increasingly centralized authority in the nation.

The Choctaws wanted education, and they were adapting to certain conventions of white society to get it. If the missionaries were to capitalize on evidence of the kind of civilization that law making provided, they needed to expand their efforts. But to do so, they needed more laborers to sustain their efforts. The American Board could not supply their needs with money to hire laborers or with volunteers to do the work. In the antebellum South, slaves were the only alternative to free or paid laborers, and slavery was an ongoing source of moral and philosophical conflict for the American Board. Once again, the spiritual and secular concerns of the missionaries placed them on the horns of a dilemma. It they did not have sufficient labor, they would lose the opportunity to bring the Choctaws to Christianity. If they used slaves for that labor, they would condone an immoral institution.

Kingsbury's letters to the board are full of pleas for volunteers. The financial constraints of the American Board made it impossible for him to hire enough laborers. In the Calvinist theology of the American Board, it was also clear that missionaries were to labor both spiritually and physically to be assured of their rewards in personal salvation and in the salvation of other souls. They were to do the physical work of building and maintaining the stations as well as the spiritual work of preaching. In his sermon at the inauguration of the church at Mayhew, Samuel Worcester, infusing the secular with the sacred, declared that although "husbandry" was "secular business in common life," the mission farm was "the farm of the Lord." Since the missionaries were servants of the lord, they should "shew cheerfulness" in their labor. Worcester had forewarned that hired labor could only be a source of secular concern (a situation of which Kingsbury had become painfully aware). Instead, he envisioned men and women, white and Indian, working together at the mission "according to God's plan" and "His will." Farming as religious activity thus justified the unremitting labor of missionaries and the use of student labor as well.[36]

The rationale may have been inspiring, but the work was still backbreaking. Students could be used for a certain portion of the labor in the cause of teaching them the ways of civilization, but they could not meet all the needs. Indeed, the requirement that the male students work in the fields was one of the major complaints of Choctaw parents about the schools.

Worcester's Christian ideal was also far removed from the reality of the missionaries' situation. Missionary volunteers were not readily forthcoming, and those who did come were often in poor health when they arrived (Peter Kanouse) or became sick shortly afterward (Aries Williams). This lack of volunteers from the North was particularly distressing. At Elliot, Byington was "pained in the extreme" because money "from the Treasury of the Lord" would have to be spent to hire laborers.[37] Ten men had to be hired to help build the mission at Mayhew. By the following year, Kingsbury was requesting more missionaries and assistant missionaries. Although he acknowledged the desirability of having mission work done by "consecrated hands," nature intervened. The health of the missionaries and its "uncertainty . . . in this climate" left many of them unable to "render efficient aid," and Kingsbury was forced to hire help.[38]

The specter of illnesses introduced by Europeans had long affected the Indians of the Southeast, and the missionaries still reported outbreaks of sickness among the Choctaws, even as they feared that similar outbreaks among their students would affect the stability of their schools. Illness among the members of the mission families, however, undermined their efforts in a different way. It was particularly a drain on human resources because those who remained in good health spent a good deal of time caring for those who were sick.

Missionaries died like flies, particularly missionary wives, who worked from early morning until night in the kitchens, laundries, and sewing rooms of the stations. Judith Chase died in October 1821, and Sarah Kingsbury died shortly after giving birth to her second child in September 1822. The deaths of members of the mission family were a tragic reminder of human frailty, a cause for rejoicing that the deceased had been received by the Lord, and a blow to the needs of the missions for physical labor.[39]

The obvious solution to the problem of labor was a problem in its own right—the use of slaves. By 1820 the issue of slavery had already become a national issue in the Missouri Compromise. The arbitrary physical division of the nation into slave territory and free territory marked the growing intellectual division between abolitionists and proponents of slavery.

Slavery was a fact of life for a certain group within the Choctaw Nation. A number of whites and mixed-bloods owned slaves. John Pitchlynn farmed two hundred acres with fifty slaves, and his son Peter had ninety acres and ten slaves. David Folsom had ten slaves, and William Ward, the federal agent, owned seven slaves. Of the full-blood leadership, only Mushulatubbee (who had ten slaves for his thirty acres of farmland), Captain Little Leader, and Appasawintubbee held slaves.[40] For the most part, Choctaw farms were too small to warrant slave labor, but more important, Choctaw customs mitigated against it. Captives taken in warfare were either killed or adopted. The Choctaws had certainly learned from Europeans that captives were valuable for labor. In the colonial period, they had captured Chickasaws to sell as slaves to the French. But they did not use slaves themselves.[41]

The vast majority of Choctaws probably had little interest in the American debate over the question of slavery. For Kingsbury and the American Board missionaries, it had significant moral and practical considerations. They could hire slaves from mixed-blood families like the Turnbulls. To use slaves, however, appeared to condone the institution of slavery.

At Elliot, the missionaries decided, after "agitated" discussion, not to hire two slaves, although it would cost twelve to fourteen hundred dollars to hire white laborers for the year 1821. Obviously hoping for some relief from an ambivalent American Board, they appealed to the Prudential Committee for a decision on "the propriety of employing slaves in the service of this mission." They made it clear that they abhorred slavery and considered it "unauthorized by the word of God & contradictory to some of its most glorious truths."[42] Despite Byington's deep-felt personal convictions against slavery, slaves—hired from Anthony Turnbull, a mixed-blood neighbor—were working in the fields and in the kitchen at Elliot by April 1822.[43]

The hiring of slaves was especially problematic because they constituted the largest single category among the participants in the meetings for worship. If slaves were hired to work around the missions, they stood a greater chance to be saved than the Choctaws. If they came, however, their presence contravened Christian doctrine.

Despite moral qualms, the missionaries saw very pragmatic reasons to hire slaves. The board was not able to fill the need for laborers, and without them, the missions could not operate. Cash was scarce, and slaves could be had for barter rather than for cash. They cost less than white laborers to hire, and most important, they could endure the heat much better than whites. Balanced against these considerations was the missionaries' responsibility as role models. Byington noted, "Many effects which may result from this mission by our labors & our example are yet unknown, but still may deserve our serious attention."[44]

In the final analysis, the missionaries faced the contradictions of sacred and secular in early-nineteenth-century America. In microcosm, they reflected other political and moral agonies of the nation. If they used slaves, they condoned an immoral institution. If they did not use slaves, their missions might fail, and any hope of civilizing or converting Indian nations might be lost.

The American Board itself was ambivalent about the question of slavery. The Presbyterian Church, one of its sponsoring institutions, would confront the issue head on, deciding to view slavery as a civil issue with which it would not interfere. The issue would, however, split the church in 1837 into the Old School and New School factions.[45]

On a local level, the question of slavery was causing concern within the missions. Evarts requested that a formal response be ready by the time he visited the nation in the spring of 1824. Byington took the initiative and, in a letter to Evarts, vigorously declared, "To a man born in the land of freedom, & rocked in the cradle of liberty beneath the Sun of Righteousness, the bare thought of holding one of his fellow men as his slave, whether bought or hired of a master is revolting to all the good feelings of his heart." He declared that he could not submit to "the control of any man or body of men on earth" who would require him "to sanction slavery."[46] Loring Williams wrote more moderately, asking, "If we admit that slavery is an evil, and we do not actually bear testimony against it by every prudent means—how are we guiltless?"[47]

After his visit to the missions, Evarts agreed with the need to hire slaves. Byington was surprised by the decision.[48] He, however, had been released from his duties at Elliot to live with the family of David Folsom in order to learn the Choctaw language, and he did not have to face the immediate problems of sustaining a large missionary establishment. Kingsbury, as superintendent of the entire Choctaw mission effort, was directly responsible for meeting the demands of maintaining the missions, and after Evarts's decision, he suggested that the mission at Mayhew buy slaves. His arguments were persuasive. The purchase price would offset the cost of hiring. "We give $220 a year & clothe them. They could be bought for $1000." The slaves could then earn their freedom, and with that knowledge they would be more faithful workers.

Those responsible for running the farms, notably Brother William Hooper, the farmer at Mayhew, approved of using slaves.[49] The moral justification was clear. In Jewell's words, "Would not the service that would be done to the cause of humanity & the evils it would remove from our present practice, be sufficient to warrant it[?]" If slavery made it possible for the missionaries to continue their work, then slaves could be bought.[50]

The debate over slavery, with its profound moral implications, also focused attention on Kingsbury's preoccupation with the management of all the affairs of the mission at Mayhew. It evidently led to friction between him and other members of the mission family. The situation required a written set of resolutions, in which it was agreed that Kingsbury would "lay aside all anxiety and interferance" with the secular concerns of the mission and turn them over to "the prompt and efficient prosecu-tion" of the lay members of the group.[51]

Despite Evarts's decision that slaves could be hired, the anti-slavery sentiment among the mission family carried the day. In 1826 the missionaries decided to "diminish" the schools by the end of the year rather than continue to use slave labor. For some, the decision may have represented a welcome relief from secular concerns, but its results were left "with him, whose wisdom is unreachable & his ways past finding out."[52] It may now remain for the historian to assess the outcome.

The problem of balancing sacred and secular concerns emerged in another arena in the ongoing debate between teaching and preaching. Was education necessary to conversion, or vice versa? Byington focused on the extent to which the Choctaws' de-mands had superseded the objectives of the missionaries when he complained: "The education of children is made the grand & leading object of attention. . . . The preaching of the gospel should be our great object."[53]

The question of whether to preach first or teach first raised the next question: in what language should either be done? Was it more important for the missionaries to teach the Choctaws the English language so that the Indians could hear and read the gospel and be saved or for the missionaries to learn the Choctaw language so that they could translate the gospel, preach to the people in the Choctaw language, and teach the Indians to read the word of God?

If language is a basic aspect of cultural identity, the transfor-mation of an exclusively spoken language into a written one is one of the most profound changes that its speakers experience. Literacy objectifies the words and their meaning and gives them permanence. Attempts by missionaries to reduce native lan-guages to written systems is testimony to a profound Christian belief in the metaphor of Logos, the word made God.[54] Oral traditions give the spoken word a life and power of its own. It is difficult, if not impossible, to assess the impact of literacy on individual Choctaws and their understanding of the world. Nevertheless, the work of Byington, Alfred Wright, and others to produce a written version of the language was to have significant historical consequences.

Some Choctaws wondered whether the Christian God understood their language. After being instructed about salvation and the need for prayer, the parents of several children at Elliot asked whether they could pray in their own language.[55] One earnest young man announced, "I never knew that I had a bad heart as I do now." In response, Brother Joel Wood encouraged him to pray in Choctaw and told him that God would understand.[56]

Although God might understand Choctaws, the missionaries did not. If they were to get out of the missions and into the communities of their potential converts, they would have to learn to speak the language. The use of native languages was, however, controversial in federal and mission opinion. Although Byington and Williams were committed to mastering Choctaw and using it to teach and preach, their efforts contravened the opinions of both the American Board and the federal government regarding the usefulness of native languages.

The American Board had begun its first missions with encouragement for "imparting the Holy Scriptures to unevangelized nations in their own languages" and "the translation and publication of the Bible in languages spoken by unevangelized nations." It had provided funds for these activities. The time and difficulties attendant upon learning those languages, however, led the board to withdraw its support. In 1816 the board concluded, "The obstacles which have been supposed to be in the way of teaching [the Cherokees] in *English* are rather imaginary than real." The policy became to make the Indians "English in their language, civilized in their habits, and Christian in their religion." Even if the Bible were translated into native languages, it would be of no use to people who could not read. It would be easier to teach them to read it in English, and in the process, "the sources of knowledge and means of general improvement" would be "incomparably greater and more various" than anything they could learn in their own language.[57]

The rationale for the use of English was the missionaries' general presumption that Indian languages were very limited. Indeed, the lack of specific terms for such concepts as sin, guilt, and salvation made it difficult to convey some of the basic tenets of Christianity. Byington knew, however, that there were six or seven villages within a day's ride of Elliot where congregations and local schools could be established. He had confidence that preachers could "go around among these people, learn their simple & easy language & talk to them of the Redeemer."[58]

In January 1823 Byington went to David Folsom's home for help with his studies, and by the end of the month, he was able to converse with Levi Perry's widow, "a hopeful subject of converting grace." Although she was "uncommonly intelligent," she could not speak English and was "much gratified" that Byington could converse with her in Choctaw.[59] Folsom was supportive of the missionaries' attempts to learn the Choctaw language. He welcomed Byington and later Wright into his home at Pigeon Roost.[60] In April 1823, Byington was permanently released from his duties as superintendent of Elliot so that he could spend time in Choctaw villages. Although the mission family could ill afford the loss of any laborer, it felt that he was "called, in the Providence of God," to study Choctaw so that he could preach to the people without the aid of an interpreter.[61]

By 1824, Loring Williams felt that he knew Choctaw well enough to teach in it at his school at Bethel. When that school failed because the Choctaws in the neighborhood moved away, Williams moved to Goshen, in the Southern District, so that he could study Choctaw with Joel Nail, the mixed-blood leader in the district.[62]

Byington strongly believed that the way to reach the Choctaws was through their own language and, moreover, that the written word could ultimately reach a far wider audience than the spoken word. With Folsom's help, he and Wright compiled an alphabet, a system of vowel sounds and accents, a spelling system, and a dictionary of some one thousand words. They still confronted the problem of dialectical variations among Choctaw speakers, but they were able to acquire "some facility in speaking this strange language."[63] When Byington finally established a permanent mission station in conjunction with the school near Folsom's home, he named it Aikhunna, from the Choctaw word that he translated as "a place of knowledge."[64] His first attempt at preaching in Choctaw occurred when Folsom was gone temporarily and Byington was without an interpreter. He wrote out his own sermon in Choctaw. "And to my surprize [*sic*] [I] found my people understood me quite well."[65]

Other missionaries were also studying the language, and by the end of the year Loring Williams, John Wood, Anson Dyer, and Aden Gibbs had made some progress in learning Choctaw. William Pride, the physician stationed at Mayhew, studied it so that when he tended the Choctaws' "bodily complaints," he could also direct them to God "as the only physician of the soul."[66] Byington was doing the majority of his preaching in Choctaw.[67] He had also translated ten hymns, a few of which "many of the Choctaws" had "learnt to sing." Despite the initial interest in sermons in Choctaw, however, the novelty soon wore off. Byington described the attendance at his services as "thin."[68]

The missionary efforts to learn the language did not meet with unanimous approval from the Choctaws. At least one mixed-blood, "partially intoxicated," confronted Kingsbury in 1824 with the accusation that the missionaries only wanted the Indians' money. As Kingsbury reported the Indian's words, "Instead of learning the Choctaws to talk English, we ourselves were learning to talk Choctaw & . . . we had better leave the country soon."[69]

Despite such opposition, Byington committed most of his efforts after 1823 to preparing materials in Choctaw for the mission schools so that students could learn to read and write their own language. Although the board had opposed translating the gospel into Cherokee, Evarts sent Byington a copy of John Pickering's Cherokee grammar to help him find a way to develop a writing system and translate materials into Choctaw. Byington ultimately adopted Pickering's method of writing because it re-quired fewer letters than any other system.[70]

The first book published in Choctaw was a spelling book, which appeared in 1825.[71] It was soon revised as Byington's vocabulary grew to some four thousand words. Language was thought to be a tool of civilization; however, the objectives of its wielders were different. Byington saw written Choctaw as "an instrument in the hands of the Lord of communicating . . . a knowledge of his salvation." Folsom, on the other hand, felt that "if his warriors could read thus he could introduce laws among them to much better advantage."[72] Christian ideals and Choctaw pragmatism could both be served by literacy, but the tensions between them would not be resolved.

Alone in the wilderness, speaking primarily to themselves despite new language ability, the missionaries found the opportunity to speak to others of their kind through the establishment of an organization of the missionaries to the Choctaws, Chickasaws, and Cherokees. An initial meeting at Mayhew on May 6, 1825, led to a second at Monroe, in the Chickasaw Nation, and to a statement of objectives, "to promote mutual edification & to strengthen each other by counsel & prayer & to concert measures for the advancement of the cause in which we are engaged."[73]

The importance of native languages as tools of conversion became a major concern of the organization. At a subsequent meeting, two questions arose: "How much importance shall be attached to the acquisition of the native languages?" and "What can we do for the great mass of the Indian population, not white men or their children, but the real Indians?"[74] The first was addressed when the Choctaw missionaries resolved to provide schoolbooks in Choctaw, with English translation. The group also gave Anson Dyer free time to study Choctaw at the station at Goshen.[75]

The controversial aspects of language surfaced once again when Thomas McKenney, head of the Indian Office, wrote to Kingsbury. He stated, "The plan of teaching Indians to read in their own language is not the best way to proceed with them." He advised, "Learn them first our language, and they will read their own as a matter of course." McKenney was quite explicit in his educational philosophy. "It is in man's nature to be idle. Labor is painful. Education and habit alone can reconcile him to it."[76]

Kingsbury assured McKenney that education in the mission schools would go on as it had and that the teachers would continue to teach "English first." The purpose behind the effort to learn Choctaw was not to teach it to the children but to reach the adult population. Kingsbury pointed out, however, that the impact of education in English was not what the government had hoped. At Elliot and Mayhew, much time had been spent in educating children and supplying farm implements, but "no corresponding effort" had been made "to preach the gospel." The enrollments at the schools had dropped off, and the neighboring population was spending its money on whiskey. At Byington's school and mission at Aikhunna, by contrast, whiskey was kept out. The difference was due in part, but not wholly, to the effect of Byington's preaching. Although Kingsbury did not explicitly tell McKenney that Byington preached primarily in the Choctaw language, he noted that "previously to the reception" of McKenney's letter, some of the missionaries had decided that if they could not "be in a situation to acquire the language of the natives, and instruct [the natives] through that medium," they did not feel a duty toward the Choctaw missions.[77]

To circumvent McKenney's opposition, the Prudential Committee of the American Board took under its immediate supervision and funding the missionary activities devoted to studying the language, preparing books, and teaching or preaching in Choctaw.[78] In 1827, Byington and Dyer taught in Choctaw and English. Byington reported that of twenty-four children in his school at Aikhunna (twenty-two of whom were full-bloods), seven could "read write and spell both in Chahta & English with tolerable correctness, and 6 others [could] read both languages." In the school at Folsom's, where Dyer was the teacher, were twelve students, five of whom were instructed principally in their own language.[79]

The association of missionaries to the Choctaws, Chickasaws, and Cherokees (which was ultimately recognized as the Tombigbee Presbytery of the Presbyterian Synod in 1829) took upon itself the responsibility for the training and ordination of new ministers, and it actively promoted the use of Choctaw in preaching. In conjunction with the Monroe meeting in 1826, two services were held in the Choctaw language, one at Monroe itself and one at an Indian village. When Loring Williams sought ordination, he was advised to study theology and learn Choctaw, and when he had become "competent to give religious instruction in Choctaw," he could seek a license to preach.[80] When he was finally ordained at Aikhunna on March 26, 1830, he had to prepare a written lecture on the parable of the sower in both Choctaw and English and preach a sermon in Choctaw. The first native Choctaw preacher was Joseph Dukes, from the Mayhew mission, who was trained as a catechist in 1831.[81]

Despite Kingsbury's disclaimer to McKenney that written Choctaw texts were used for adult education, they were part of the school curriculum for children, and the American Board continued to support their publication. Many were indeed intended for Choctaw adults. Folsom expressed an interest in having one of the Gospels translated and printed, and he translated into Choctaw one missionary tract with the remarkable title "Wonderful Advantages of Drunkenness."[82] Wright and Byington published a catechism in 1827 and a book of Choctaw hymns in 1829.[83]

By June 1829, there were a number of texts in Choctaw being used in schools—three spellers, some portions of scripture, and brief stories of the lives of two Cherokee children who had been converted to Christianity. A school had been established near Emmaus, "for the sole purpose of teaching the natives, adults and children, to read and write their own language," and about fifty people had attended, taught by "a young man of their own nation." At Goshen, a number of adults and children had been taught to read in their native language, and twenty captains of clans in the Six Towns district had solicited teachers to instruct their people to read Choctaw. The schoolbooks that Byington and Wright had worked on so diligently were having an effect.[84]

But the missionaries' attempts to give the Choctaws "the inestimable word of God in their own tongue" met with limited success. Perhaps the attempt to introduce widespread literacy failed because the writing system was still an alien introduction. The Choctaws never undertook the remarkable adoption of writing that the Cherokees did after Sequoyah devised his syllabary in 1821. Byington's writing system was based on the English alphabet. After Sequoyah's achievement with the Cherokee language, Loring Williams proposed a system of writing Choctaw "with Characters denoting Sylabic Sounds," although he emphasized the dissimilarities of the two languages and of his system from Sequoyah's. Nevertheless, he claimed that with his system, a Choctaw could "learn to read & write his own tongue in six weeks."[85]

Not many did. The skills of reading and writing Choctaw were introduced to the relatively small number of children who attended the schools at Aikhunna, Goshen, and Emmaus and to adults in the neighborhoods of those schools.[86] With so many other aspects of Choctaw culture undergoing change during the early nineteenth century, the introduction of literacy to a new generation was only a small part of the process. Subsistence was changing. Stock raising was replacing hunting (although Choctaw cattle essentially ran wild in the woods and generally had to be hunted down). Bodies of law represented a centralization of authority previously unknown in Choctaw society. Traditional funeral customs of platform exposure and bone pickers had been replaced by interment and pole-pulling rituals.[87]

The changes were the result of complex factors of economy and politics. Christian ideals played little if any part in the change. Funeral rites were still distinctively Choctaw, and the pole-pulling rites that ended the period of mourning served to distance Indians from missionaries because the events were often the occasion for drinking binges.[88] Most Choctaws still thought that the soul of the deceased wandered in the woods.

Choctaw souls were quite different from the entities that the missionaries were used to. Ideas about salvation and the eternal persistence of personal identity were probably quite puzzling to Choctaws. Whatever "civilization" the Choctaws were gaining was largely from their white neighbors' example, which was often less than exemplary.[89]

6 / Years of Crisis, 1824–26

WHILE THE MISSIONARIES STRUGGLED TO BREAK THE INVISIBLE
boundaries of language that separated them from the Choctaws,
the Choctaws struggled to maintain the boundaries that separated their land from that of their white neighbors. That struggle
sharpened the growing division in the tribe between the rising
young mixed-blood leaders and the traditional full-blood chiefs.
It undermined both attempts by the Choctaws to preserve their
lands and efforts by the American Board missionaries to carry
out their work. The apparent failure of the American Board to
"civilize" significant numbers of Choctaws, coupled with a growing desire for Choctaw land, contributed to pressure to force the
Indians west.[1]

The Treaty of Doak's Stand, which had satisfied some of the
demands of citizens of Mississippi for land, had caused a furor in
Arkansas Territory. Many white citizens of the state of Mississippi expected the Choctaws to move peacefully to the west,
whereas some residents of Arkansas feared the Choctaws would
do exactly that. There were reported incidents of Indian depredations in Arkansas, and one angry letter to the editor of the
Arkansas Gazette described the prospect of Choctaw emigration
as "a death blow to the territory."[2]

Although some Choctaws drifted over the river to settle in
the western territory, the majority were not interested in moving, either because of reports such as Pushmataha's that the land
was poor and sterile or because of reports that there were white
men living in parts of the territory. Edmund Folsom was appointed by the government to lead an emigration, which largely
failed to materialize. It was true that white settlers were en-
sconced on lands that now belonged to the Choctaws by treaty.
Either the government could move the whites, or it could move
the boundary. John Calhoun chose to do the latter.[3]

Calhoun, who was actively campaigning for the presidency, hoped to gain political advantage for himself in Mississippi by persuading the Choctaws to cede their land in the state.4 In May 1823 he appointed Thomas Hinds and William Woodward to hold treaty negotiations with the Choctaw Nation to adjust the western boundary. Hinds never received the appointment letter, and there was some suspicion that William Ward, the Choctaw agent, had deliberately misdirected it. In any event, it was not until December that the situation was discovered, and Calhoun decided not to pursue the matter "for the present." Instead, he approved the Choctaw leaders' request that they be allowed to go to Washington to negotiate a treaty, and he instructed Ward to make arrangements for their journey, "having regard to the strictest economy."5

There were individual Choctaws who had reason to favor negotiations for a new treaty. Their claims were based on the new economic situation in which they found themselves. The issues were now about pay for goods and services. Subsistence and barter no longer mattered. Choctaw warriors who had fought with Jackson at Pensacola in 1814 had not been paid.6 Pushmataha and Mushulatubbee owed personal debts to traders, and a rumor circulated that they favored ceding some of the Arkansas land to pay off those debts. Opposition to a treaty came from Louis Leflore, John Pitchlynn, and David Folsom, who objected to the two chiefs' plan to turn their personal debts into national ones.7 Puckshanubbee, whose district had lost the majority of its land in 1820, was also opposed to a land cession, perhaps fearing that once again he would be most vulnerable.

It was late September 1824 before the Choctaw delegation finally set out for Washington. Its members were Puckshanub-bee, Pushmataha, Mushulatubbee, David Folsom, Robert Cole, Captains Daniel McCurtin, Talking Warrior, Red Fort, and Chi-letchoma, and James McDonald, who served as interpreter.8

The trip to Washington and the subsequent stay had momen-tous consequences for the tribe. Puckshanubbee (who was eighty-five years old) stepped off a cliff along the Ohio River at

Maysville, Kentucky, and died.[9] This passage of one of the staunchest supporters of mission schools would elevate Robert Cole, one of the strongest critics, to the position of chief of the Western District.

The remainder of the party arrived safely in Washington in the last week of October, although several were suffering from colds. Calhoun began the negotiations on November 9 with a proposal for a Choctaw cession in Mississippi, which the delegates firmly refused. They did accept his proposal for a cession that would move the eastern boundary of their Arkansas territory to a line running from the Arkansas to the Red River (approximately along what is now the eastern boundary of Oklahoma), with the proviso that white settlers remaining in their territory would either move or be moved by the government. The question was, how much would the government pay the Choctaws for the land?

Calhoun sent an offer of $65,000 in annuities, which the delegates rejected as "entirely inadequate." The Choctaws had, however, learned the value of a dollar and how to bargain. They wanted education so that they could deal with the demands of white society. They countered President Monroe's offer with a proposal for $30,000 in gifts, $9,000 annually for twenty years for "mechanical institutions," the same amount for the education of Choctaw children in "colleges or institutions out of the nation," and $3,000 annually for twenty years for education for the western Choctaws. Although the sum was large, it would go primarily for education. The Choctaw delegates wanted their own "rising generation" to be educated, and they flattered Monroe that by acquiring "a knowledge of literature and the arts," the Choctaws would be able "to tread in those paths" that had conducted white people "to their present summit of wealth & greatness." Monroe ignored the flattery, however, and found the Choctaw proposal "wholly inadmissible." Negotiations ground to a halt.[10]

Undeterred by the failure of larger philosophical issues to hold the day, Folsom and McDonald pressed specific claims of individual Choctaw warriors arising from the Treaty of Doak's Stand.

While the delegation waited for Monroe's reply, Pushmataha died of what was probably pneumonia on Christmas Eve.[11] Alcohol may have played some role in the death of the chief, who had fought so valiantly on behalf of the United States. Despite Calhoun's directive to Ward about "strict economy," the bar bill for the delegation totaled $2,149.50.[12]

The government gave the delegates ample time to drink. It was almost a month before Calhoun finally responded to the delegation, citing "the press of business" for the delay. He informed them that Monroe asked them to reconsider their earlier demands. They asked how much he was willing to give. Monroe raised the offer to $90,000 in annuities over ten years; the Choctaws demanded settlement of their claims from Doak's Stand and $6,000 a year in perpetuity, and Monroe agreed. The treaty was finally signed on January 22, 1825.[13]

The Choctaws gave up more of their western lands, a process that was becoming increasingly inevitable. Their negotiators were now primarily mixed-blood men—David Folsom, Robert Cole, James McDonald—very much aware of the demands of white society. They bargained for guarantees of boundaries and education. What they wanted in the way of education was very practical, "instruction in the mechanic and ordinary arts of life." To fund these services, the government agreed to survey and sell the fifty-four sections of land that had been set aside for the support of schools in the Treaty of Doak's Stand.[14] The treaty of 1825 also confirmed the entry of the Choctaws into a cash economy. They were to receive their annuities in cash rather than in goods, with power to spend the money as they wished.

But more important, the deaths of Puckshanubbee and Pushmataha now brought new leaders to the fore. David Folsom, advocate of the American Board missionaries, expressed his disdain for the dead chiefs. "God has seen fit to take those men away so that better men may be raised up in their places."[15] Although Folsom thus set himself above the old order of clans and families and men who were recognized by right of family and personal qualities of leadership, he spoke only for a highly acculturated element of Choctaw society. Who the "better men" of the future were to be was still problematic.

The treaty of 1825 turned the fate of the Choctaws and the attention of their leaders toward the West. The Choctaws had always lived and hunted west of the Mississippi. They had warred against the Osages. But the majority of their followers still lived in Mississippi and adapted their lives to those of their white neighbors. They raised cows and hogs (relatively new introductions) and planted corn, as they had always done, and potatoes, a new crop. The Choctaws were adaptable. They had come into the Southeast over the years, amalgamated, subsisted, and survived. They would remain.

But the treaty provisions for schooling gave hope to the American Board missionaries for expanding their schools in Mississippi, which were languishing.[16] While the Choctaw delegation negotiated in Washington with the express intent of encouraging education, the board's schools faltered. The school at Bethel was in trouble early in 1824 because most of the neighboring white families had moved, probably because the government had moved the Choctaw agency to a new location on the road from Columbus to Natchez. Those who remained were "much disaffected," and Louis Leflore took back two of his slaves who had been helping there and forbade his other slaves to attend church. He also took eight of the "most promising & forward scholars" out of the school and hired his own teacher. His disaffection stemmed from the fact that one of his sons had been suspended from school for "obstinate incorrigible behaviour."[17]

The situation was disillusioning. Loring Williams noted, "We are by this providence forcibly taught to trust not in man." It was also frustrating. "The vast expense incurred—for what? only to teach about a dozen Indian boys with little or no prospect of benefitting their parents." The early promise of success in the northwestern area of the Choctaw Nation now foundered on the issue of discipline.[18]

And suddenly, competition appeared. The school that William Pride had started in late 1824 at Robert Cole's house, Bethany, was appropriated by Wiley Ledbetter, the Methodist missionary. Ledbetter approached Cole with an offer to operate the school and provide free board and clothing for the children. He was evidently encouraged by a white man named Riley, Cole's brother-in-law and a persistent critic of the American Board schools. Cyrus Kingsbury suspected that Cole's previous dissatisfaction with the American Board may also have been inspired by Riley.[19] The first inkling that Pride received of the situation was when one of Cole's captains (Cole had left for Washington for the treaty negotiations) came to tell him that his services were no longer needed.[20]

Kingsbury complained strongly to Bishop William Winans about Ledbetter's actions. The American Board had invested over one thousand dollars in the school. Kingsbury pointed out that the school was under the patronage of the U.S. government and that he had suggested to Bishop Robert Richford Roberts that the Methodists establish small schools in neighborhoods different from those served by the American Board. Although he considered "the salvation of sinners" far more important than "the predominance of any particular sect or party," he complained to Secretary of War Calhoun about the situation.[21] Calhoun wrote to the Choctaw delegation in Washington, pointing out that Bethany had been built by the American Board and placed under Kingsbury's supervision and that there appeared to be no cause for complaint against Dr. Pride, the teacher. Calhoun concluded on a chastising note. "You must be sensible that the Government has no object, other than that which relates to your own good, and that any other course in relation to the schools than that which is laid down in this letter would tend to the subversion of the whole system."[22]

Obviously, competing objectives were at work. Cole wanted a school that would not cost him anything. Kingsbury wanted a school that would carry out the work of salvation for the American Board and save its investment. And Calhoun saw the school as an object of government policy for the Choctaws' "own good."

Despite the importuning, Ledbetter retained control of the

school, but he failed to fulfill his promise to board and clothe the pupils. The school was finally abandoned altogether, and Led-better's career among the Choctaws came to a rather abrupt end when the Methodist Conference noted that he had failed to convert a single Indian, and he was "located" to a different post.[23]

In spite of the commotion over Bethany, the American Board had eight schools in operation by the end of 1824: Elliot, Bethel, Mayhew, Aikhunna, Captain Harrison's (near Puckshanubbee's home), Captain Charles Juzan's (near Pushmataha's home), Em-maus, and Goshen.[24] There were churches at Elliot, Mayhew, Bethel, and Goshen.[25]

Although the missionaries were reaching out to the Choc-taws, Kingsbury complained that the prospects of the missions were "very gloomy." He added: "We can place no dependance on the promises of parents & guardians. In several cases of late where we thought the prospect was most promising, we have been disappointed."[26] Yet despite setbacks and gloomy prospects, the treaty of 1825 gave Kingsbury incentive to propose a "higher school" to be located at David Folsom's house at Pigeon's Roost. Such a school would keep the annuity money in the nation, the expense would be less, and the "conspicuous standing of its pupils" would encourage younger students. Choctaws educated in the nation would "be exposed to fewer vices and retain a fair moral character." Improved education would increase the desire of the Choctaws for schools.[27]

Education in at least one American Board school was not improving. The school at Mushulatubbee's house was not having the desired effect. Gibbs reported in June 1825 that very little "evangelical labor" was being accomplished. Although the na-tives came to the school frequently, "particularly on the Sab-bath," they came "to hear singing and a good talk."[28] Singing and talking, activities very familiar and dear to Choctaw people, were attractive, but the Choctaws in the neighborhood were also drinking heavily. Given the situation, Kingsbury decided to close the school at Mushulatubbee's once again.[29]

Some of the men in the district petitioned the American Board to open a school in a different location, an action that undercut Mushulatubbee's leadership.[30] On hearing of the situation, Thomas McKenney issued a sharp rebuke to the Choctaw chiefs and threatened to close all the schools in Mushulatubbee's district. "Your great father has seen with pain that the doors of the school at Mushulatubbee's are shut! He approves of what the teacher of that school has done. He was sent there for your good, and for the good of your children. If you will drink and quarrel, and make it impossible for these good people to carry on their plan of education, you must bear the evil of your own doings."[31]

The threat backfired. Just as Kingsbury was sending off his proposal for the "higher school" to Calhoun, he received the dismaying news that Mushulatubbee had committed the whole annuity, six thousand dollars a year, as well as the proceeds of the sale of the fifty-four acres of land, to the Baptist Mission Society for the establishment of a school in Kentucky. Mushulatubbee's decision operated at several levels. He was stung by McKenney's criticism and threat, and he resented Kingsbury's closing of his school.[32]

More important, he was also asserting his authority over that of the chiefs of the other two districts in claiming the whole annuity. In this respect, his decision to locate a school outside the Choctaw Nation was probably as much a function of his changing political position within the nation as it was a rejection of the American Board schools. The deaths of Pushmataha and Puckshanubbee had shifted the political balance within the tribe. Robert Cole became chief in Puckshanubbee's Western District, and Pushmataha was succeeded in the Southern District by his nephew Tapenahomah, who was a virtual political nonentity.[33] In Mushulatubbee's Northeastern District, David Folsom was an increasingly powerful person, one very much in favor of the American Board's schools. Mushulatubbee had many reasons, then, to reject missionary and white influences in the nation.

Mushulatubbee had also favored the cession of the Arkansas

land in 1825, a position seemingly based on self-interest. He and his "old queen" had harassed Aden Gibbs to the point of driving him away from the school at his house. He had allowed drinking in his district, a reversal of previous laws. As he struggled to maintain his position in the nation, the missionaries and their schools were caught in the middle of the escalating confrontation between Mushulatubbee and Folsom. The issues were not religious but political.

Folsom strongly opposed Mushulatubbee's action, and James McDonald wrote to the War Department concerning the "singular and unheard of manner" by which the entire Choctaw annuity of $6,000 had been "diverted to the almost exclusive benefit of one district."[34] Not only had Folsom been deprived of having a school at his house, but more important, Mushulatubbee had preempted the rights of other district leaders. For Mushulatubbee, the move was a power play that both asserted his position of leadership and undermined the efforts of the American Board. For the missionaries, their already precarious position in the Choctaw Nation was further threatened by the influence from outside the nation and from another denomination, the Baptists.[35]

The Choctaw Academy in Kentucky ultimately played an important role in the politics of the Choctaw Nation in Mississippi. Its origins were religious, but its curriculum and its methods were almost completely secular. It represented a new era in Choctaw education. Its forerunner had been established by the Baptist Mission Society of Kentucky at Great Crossings in 1818. The society declared, "The aborigines of our beloved country, inhabiting the wilderness and the forest, appear to have a peculiar claim on our humanity." The school admitted its first class of eight boys in the spring of 1819.[36] If it seemed a potential threat to the American Board's efforts in the Choctaw Nation, its initial success was short-lived. Missionary contributions dropped off during 1820–21, and the society decided to close the school.[37]

But when Mushulatubbee and other "Choctaw chiefs and headmen," dissatisfied with the American Board and seeking to find an alternative, asked William Ward to write to some "missionary society distant from the nation," Ward contacted the Baptist Mission Society about starting a school. Ward's brother-in-law, Richard Johnson, was a prominent member of the Baptist Church in Kentucky. Johnson was also a flamboyant military man and politician whose political fortunes rested in part on his claims that he was the man who had killed the great Shawnee leader Tecumseh at the Battle of the Thames in 1813.[38] He was deeply in debt when he received Ward's request, and he agreed to house a school in buildings on his property and to provide room and board and clothing for students for a flat fee of two hundred dollars per student.

Johnson recruited Thomas Henderson, "a Teacher of uncommon merit—a scientific character, and in the habit of Teaching from the ABC," to head the school. Henderson, who was also a "preacher of the gospel," was appointed by the Board of Managers of the Baptist General Convention as superintendent and missionary. Obviously, with his "moral character," "industrious habits," and "dignified manners," he was an ideal choice to carry out the civilizing mission of the school.[39]

The Choctaw Academy began classes on November 1, 1825, with thirty-six students: twenty-six Choctaws and ten young men from Johnson's neighborhood.[40] Although Johnson and the society were designing the school, funding for its students came from the Choctaw annuity, and Thomas McKenney set up government rules: the school day should begin at sunrise the year round, and the duties of the day should be finished by sundown, except on Saturday when they could end at noon.[41]

One of the most important of McKenney's rules was that each student must have a certificate from a school in the Choctaw Nation. The academy thus functioned as the "higher school" that Kingsbury had planned, but it was outside the nation, and it was totally beyond the control of the American Board. It became the Choctaw "prep school," a training ground for a new generation of leaders. Its curriculum, despite its Baptist affiliation, was totally secular. Instruction included reading, writing, arithmetic, grammar, geography, astronomy, vocal music, and on a rather ironic note, considering the future outcome of Choctaw land claims, practical surveying. The school's equipment included a pair of "elegant artificial globes," a variety of atlases, an orrery, an octant, a quadrant, a telescope, and two surveying compasses.[42]

The academy's first contingent of students was from Mushulatubbee's district.[43] The old chief had preempted not only the annuity but the student body as well. He was determined to create a cadre of young men who were educated in the white man's ways and who could serve the practical ends of the nation, rather than the religious ends of the American Board. It is not surprising, then, that over the years, its students were mainly the offspring of the mixed-blood element of the tribe, the politically ascendant group. McKenney insisted that the student body represent all the districts of the nation, and the other districts of the nation agreed to send an equal number of students (twenty-one) to the academy.[44] By 1827, the list of students in the school contained the names of most of the prominent mixed-blood families in the Choctaw Nation—Folsom, Pitchlynn, Nail, Juzan, Harkins, Garland, Perry, Durant, Leflore. It also included the names of Alexander Pope and Samuel Worcester, students who were probably full-blood Choctaws, since the missionaries often replaced the Choctaw names of their students with those of contributors to the missions or with those of their own predilections.[45]

Mushulatubbee and his captains sent their young men to learn practical mechanical and economic skills that would prepare them to deal with white society. McKenney saw, in addition, that the school could promote the government's policy of Indian removal and foster Mushulatubbee's interest in moving west. McKenney instructed Henderson to "encourage the boys to write home" but to "examine and correct their letters" so that they would "tend to the great objects of the Government"—that the Choctaws would take the western lands, set up a recognizable government, and adopt laws. He suggested that Henderson knew how to "advise" the students to appeal "to the prejudices of their parents" to achieve these ends of government policy.[46] The usual parental injunction to college-bound children to "write home" thus resulted in political missives.

The Choctaw Academy was a major experiment in the federal government's civilization policy. For McKenney, the school provided the possibility that students could advance in education beyond the elementary levels of the American Board schools. If the students at the Choctaw Academy did well, Kingsbury was eager to take credit, since the academy drew the "most forward scholars" from the American Board schools. If they did not learn, it was because the academy lacked discipline. The students' "peculiar alacrity" Kingsbury attributed to the fact that they were not required "to labor with their hands," as they were at American Board schools.[47] The academy was quite different from the schools of the American Board in the nation, with quite different objectives. The teaching of skills that the Choctaws themselves saw as practical replaced the Christian sense of discipline in the cause of civilization.

Kingsbury was frustrated and angry over Mushulatubbee's defection.[48] Robert Cole and James McCurtain had also begun accusing the missionaries of being "cheats & liars" who were "encroaching upon the rights of the nation," and their charges were heard as far away as Marietta, Ohio.[49] By 1827, the academy was "in high repute," and American Board missionaries and their schools in the nation were "in very low estimation among the people generally."[50] Missionary education was losing its credibility. The American Board school at Cornwall, Connecticut, a training ground for native preachers, was also suffering. Although Israel and McKee Folsom had been educated there and had returned to preach to the Choctaws, by 1826 there was "no disposition, either among the Cherokees or Choctaws, to send their young men to Cornwall."[51]

Reports of the Choctaw schools in the *Missionary Herald* dwindled from glowing monthly notices to two brief notices during 1826.[52] In 1830 Sarah Tuttle, author of an inspirational book for young people entitled *Conversations on the Choctaw Mission*, alluded delicately to the lack of reports in the *Mission-*

ary Herald, attributing the problems of the missions to "too strict regulations in the schools" and to rumors, spread by white men, that discredited the schools.[53]

The Choctaw Academy became the preparatory school of the Choctaw Nation. Choctaw leaders Greenwood Leflore and Charles Juzan visited the school and endorsed it enthusiastically.[54] Although the expense was relatively great, Leflore expressed himself "perfectly Satisfyed" with the school. "Although it is probable that we could get our children Taught Something cheaper yet we do not wish to put out their Education to the Lowest Bidder."[55]

The school was not without its critics, however. The American Board teachers had been very reluctant to enroll "older scholars" in their schools, having discovered that older boys were troublesome to manage. At the Choctaw Academy, whose student body was exclusively older male students, Peter Pitchlynn, one of the students, charged that, among other things, the food was bad, the linen dirty, and the coffee weak. Johnson and Henderson vigorously defended the school in letters to David Folsom and John Calhoun. Among those cosigning Henderson's letter were Pierre Juzan, Geo. W. Harkins, Saml. Garland, and Robert Jones, scions of the most prominent mixed-blood families in the Choctaw Nation.[56]

Education as a means of civilizing the Choctaws, whether through the Choctaw Academy or through the American Board schools, did not produce wide-scale or highly visible results throughout the Choctaw Nation, and all the efforts could not forestall the complaints of citizens of the state of Mississippi about the Choctaw presence. Congressman Christopher Rankin wrote to James Monroe on behalf of his constituents, noting that they were "very interested in the removal of the Choctaw from Mississippi." Rankin urged Monroe to implement the removal provisions of the 1820 treaty and to drive white squatters from the western lands in Arkansas so that the Choctaws could take possession. These things should be done, he stated, before crops were planted.[57]

Rankin had a receptive audience. Even as the Choctaws negotiated the treaty of 1825 to consolidate their Arkansas territory
and remove white settlers from it, Monroe prepared to articulate
a removal policy that undercut the guarantees of possession of
the eastern lands in the Treaty of Doak's Stand. Maintaining
that it was "impossible to incorporate them . . . into our system,"
he called on Congress to give each tribe "a good title to an
adequate portion of land" and provide it "a system of internal
government" to protect it from invasion and promote "the regular progress of improvement and civilization," thus preventing its
"degeneracy." He requested an appropriation to appoint commissioners to explain the benefits of removal to Indian tribes.[58]

This first major statement of a removal policy was inspired by
several forces. One was the demand by the state of Georgia that
the government carry out its promise of 1802 to remove all
Indians from its territory. Another was the voice of a Christian
missionary, Isaac McCoy, a Baptist whose work among the Potawatomis and Ottawas in Michigan had convinced him of the
pernicious influence of white society on Indians. McCoy was
inspired with the idea of "colonizing" Indians in their own state,
with their own civil government, well removed from white communities. McCoy presented his idea to the Board of Managers of
the Foreign Mission Society of the Baptist Church in 1824 and
to John C. Calhoun. It reinforced a growing feeling in Washington that Indians could and should not live with whites.[59]

The idea of an Indian colony grew in McCoy's mind as he
observed the effects of alcohol on the Potawatomis and Ottawas.
He feared that they would be ruined by "whiskey sellers," and he
observed the "ruinous effects" of white settlements near the
Indian villages.[60]

The removal policy was not a dramatically new idea but was
the evolution of many different and often conflicting ideas concerning Indians. Jefferson envisioned the assimilation of civilized
Indians and the separation of those who would not be civilized.
He had faith, however, in the ability of Indians to learn to live in
new ways. McCoy, from his firsthand observations, concluded

that Indians would never work for their own best interests but would always be swayed by the influence of whites.

According to one white citizen of Mississippi, the Choctaws around the Six Towns and Chickasawhay villages in the Southern District were practitioners of "heathen ways" such as "cruel and inhumane murders" of people suspected of witchcraft and "pretensions to the art of conjurations" of the *alikchi*. They were also "the greatest ball players." Missionary influence extended to only a few captains and was actively resisted by most other Choctaws.[61]

The American Board missionaries could certainly report their despair and ample evidence of Choctaw resistance and continuing cultural practices. Meanwhile, McCoy actively proposed a plan of removal, Georgia pressed for the government to carry out its commitment to remove the Indians, and the Indians themselves gave evidence of a lack of civilization. In addition despite Monroe's policy, the settlement of the boundaries of the Choctaws' western territory early in 1825, and the wishes of the citizens of Mississippi, the leaders of the tribe stood firm against further land cessions in Mississippi. Having established their position and gotten guarantees of more schools, relief from their debts, and a steady income from the government, they were prepared to stay where they were.

The plantations and slaves held by several mixed-blood captains undoubtedly contributed to their desire to remain in Mississippi. A small but thriving Choctaw landed aristocracy— David Folsom, Greenwood Leflore, John Pitchlynn and his son Peter, and Joel Nail, among others—had vested interests sufficient to sway their political opinions (see table 1). Cole and Tapenahomah were "very much against parting with land" and spoke "lightly of any Indian" who appeared to favor a cession.[62] They and several other leaders declared, "We will sell no more land on any terms."[63] David Folsom wrote to McKenney: "I am sorry the President hears the Chahtas wish to sell land. I only can say he hears more than the Chahta people know anything about."[64]

But there were certainly Choctaws who were willing to move west. Although the Choctaw lands in Mississippi were held in common according to tradition and custom, Choctaws were becoming increasingly aware of the notion of private property. John Pitchlynn, Jr., would take his warriors and move if paid for his "improvements" in Mississippi. Pressure from the surrounding white population also influenced decisions. John McKee reported, "Many are willing to emigrate but are unaware of the route."[65]

A willingness to move west cannot be taken to imply a willingness to give up tribal lands in Mississippi. Moving back and forth across the Mississippi River had been part of the Choctaw life-style for generations and would continue to be. The ability to move was increasingly constrained as white settlement surrounded the Mississippi homeland and encroached on the western lands, but freedom to move was a fact of life. Nevertheless, any large-scale voluntary resettlement of Choctaws would increase the chance of their losing the homeland permanently.

Just as tribal opinion about moving west was not unanimous, missionary opinion was also divided. Kingsbury, discouraged by constant criticism and the lack of success of his mission stations, wrote, "All things considered, we are not sure but it would be well for a great part of the Indians if they were over there." Although Choctaw leaders still requested schools for their followers, others, in their opposition to the missionaries, seemed "determined to be their own worst enemies."[66]

The pressure for removal precipitated increasing political turmoil that revealed the depth of the divisions both among and within the three districts of the Choctaw Nation. The first major incident occurred in the spring of 1826 when a council in the Northeastern District elected David Folsom as chief, thus deposing Mushulatubbee.[67] Rumors circulated that the old chief was in favor of selling the homeland, but Folsom stated, as "the truth on the subject," that it was because of Mushulatubbee's "intemperance, tyrannical disposition, ignorance and his manner of disposing of the annuity," as well as "many other charges" that it

Table 1: Owners of Land and Slaves in the Choctaw Nation

Name	Acres	Slaves	
Nitakechi District			
Capt. Jas Gardner	32	1	
John Garland		2	
Allen Yates (white)	140	12	
J. H. Nail	140	8	
Charles Juzan		20	
Rebecca Bond (widow)		2	
Westly Train		3	
Z. Breshears, sen (white)	50	14	
Mushulatubbee District			
Robert Folsom	30	2	
Capt. Jos. Kinkade	22	1	
John Pitchlynn (white)	200	50	
Samuel Garland	60	7	
Peter Pitchlynn	90	10	
John Jones	8	1	
John McKinney (half)	50	2	
Andrew Kincade	12	1	
John McIntosh (white)	30	5	
Alexander Brashears	30	8	
William H. Buckes (white)	25	4	blacks
Stanmore H. Johnston (white)	12	1	
Zad'k Brashears, Jr.	25	2	
Delila Brashears	50	16	
(married David Wall)			
Turner Brashears	40	7	
Sampson Moncrif (white)	60	19	
John Walker (white)	40	8	
John Jones, sen.	20	3	
Samuel Jones, sen. dec.	40	4	
Sally Tom (a free woman)	10	1	
John Coleman	50	3	
Capt. Little Leader	12	2	
Mingomushulatubbee	30	10	
Col. David Folsom	150	10	
Col. William Ward	80	7	blacks
Grabile Linscomb	30	5	blacks
Jessee M. Fields	8	1	black
(blacksmith at agency)			

Name	Acres	Slaves	
Leflore District			
Green. Leflore	250	32	
[*note* Zekiel Roebuck in Armstrong Roll, p. 89, dist. 3]			
Capt. Shields	21	7	
Ned Perry	20	4	
Charles Hays	20	2	
[*note* Jacob Thompson dist. 3, 5 acres near Yello Busha, p. 93]			
Samuel Foster	40	12	
David Oxberry	30	1	
James Perry	50	30	
James Davis	20	6	
Perry (widow)	30	15	
Joseph Perry	80	21	
Charles Frazier	9	4	
Appasawintubbee	2	4	
Eli W. Crowden	15	1	
Edon Ward	20	1	
Nelly Beans		11	blacks, free, her children born in the nation
Jerry Nearney	30	20	
Mrs. Wilson	200	11	
George Turnbull	30	9	
John Cafry (white)	30	3	
Mary Harrison	40	4	
Martha Milton	6	1	
Capt. William Hays	30	2	
Benjamin Leflore	100	10	
John Ellis (white)	14	1	
Cornelius Kearney (half)	70	12	
Widow Burris	15	5	
Benjamin Batiest	30	1	
Joseph Anderson	3	1	
Daniel Anderson	30	1	
Winney Batiest	20	2	
Tobias Ward	30	1	
William Crevatt	20	2	
Capt. Chatametaha	40	4	
William Leflore	50	6	

Figures are taken from the Armstrong census roll compiled in 1830–31. 23d Cong., 1st sess., S. Doc. 1230, "In Relation to the Location of Reservations under the Choctaw Treaty of the 27th of September, 1830," April 11, 1834, in *American State Papers*, vol. 2.

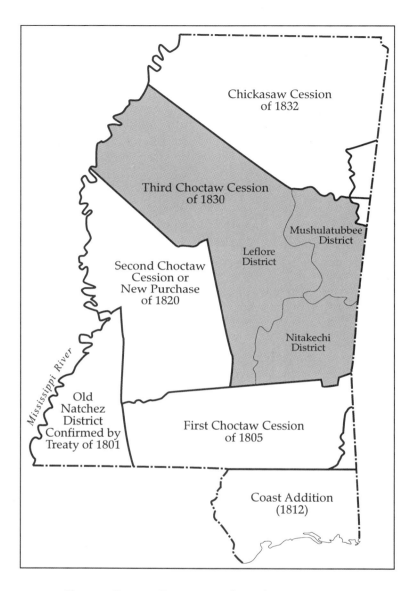

Choctaw District Divisions and Land Cessions, 1830

was "not convenient" for Folsom to note. Thus did Mushulatubbee sow the seeds of his own destruction in his action against the
American Board schools. He had, indeed, overreached himself
in committing the whole annuity from the 1825 treaty to the
Choctaw Academy.[68]

Power shifted in the Western District when a council, on June
21, elected Greenwood Leflore, the twenty-six-year-old son of
Louis Leflore, as chief, thereby deposing Robert Cole. The council invested Leflore with "constitutional powers," thus introducing a new element into Choctaw politics. The captains and Leflore moved to form themselves "into a legislative body," which
then enacted a set of laws.[69]

The establishment of a constitution and a legislature in the
Western District gave new form to traditional ways of governing.
The form in some respects represents not a drastic departure
from, but an evolution of, the old system of chiefs, speakers, and
warriors, a system in which men of certain social rank based on
achievements were entrusted with decision making. The new
system did, however, limit the number of men who exercised
power. Each captain was to bring together twelve warriors as a
court. He was also to appoint three people to enforce the laws, a
change from the companies of light-horse whose peace-keeping
functions had been formalized in the Treaty of Doak's Stand.
The most dramatic change from tradition was in the formation
of laws regarding private property. Property of a deceased man
was to be divided between his widow and children. In the traditional matrilineal society, women owned their own property,
inheritance was through the mother's line, and a man's property
would thus devolve on his maternal relatives rather than his wife
and children.[70] The new law dramatically marked the changes
that were taking place in control of property among mixed-
blood families and that were spreading to the rest of the Choctaw population.

Following the lead of the Western District, Leflore, Folsom,
and Tapenahomah met in August to form a national constitution. The constitution and laws should be read not as an accep-

tance of the white man's modes of civilization but as an effort to present a united front against the U.S. government's pressures for land and its attempts to play factions within the tribe against each other. The three chiefs acted primarily in response to Mushulatubbee's preemption of the annuity. They stated firmly that Choctaw land was the "common property of the whole nation." Despite the long-standing division of leadership and the different nature of the three districts of the nation, the three leaders reaffirmed the unity of the Choctaw land base. No district could sell or cede any portion without the "full and fair consent" of the other two districts, and no one chief could make a contract that involved annuity money without the consent of the other two chiefs. The autonomy that the district chiefs had previously enjoyed was now formally constrained. "Having felt the evils of a want of proper regulations among themselves," the chiefs had seen "the necessity of entering into some definite compact" and of passing "a few general laws" for "the whole nation."[71]

The constitution provided for a general council, composed of the three principal chiefs, the captains of each district, and a warrior from each district to be selected by the chief. The council was to meet twice a year. Any law passed by a majority would be law throughout the nation unless it was disapproved by at least two of the chiefs, in which case a two-thirds vote of the council could override the disapproval. The laws passed by the general council would override any conflicting law of a particular district. A National Committee was established "to watch over the welfare of the whole nation" by reporting depredations of white men against Choctaws and establishing a force to prevent "disorderly and improper conduct at councils and annuity distributions."[72]

The power of consensus gave way to law as the older generation of leaders was replaced by mixed-blood leaders. They were now bound by a written document to act for the good of the nation as a whole. Ultimately, the constitution was a step to protect the nation. But it was also held up by the mixed-blood leaders as proof that the Choctaws were indeed becoming civilized so that they could live with their white neighbors.

The mixed-blood leaders mounted a public relations campaign to convince the U.S. government that the Choctaws were adopting the ways of white society. James McDonald praised the missionary stations at Mayhew, Elliot, and Goshen, and David Folsom wrote to McKenney, "The mission schools are in a more prosperous state then they have been heretofore." He added, "There is a great deal of improvement made in many real Chahta families and . . . an increasing thrust for learning among many of them."[73] The missionaries had the support of John Pitchlynn, who had "the most general influence in the nation," of Charles Juzan, who was influential among the Coonshas and Yannahys and was "under the guidance" of the missionaries, and of Joel Nail, who was the mixed-blood leader of the Chickasawhays and "a friend to education for the Indians."[74]

For the Christian public, the *Missionary Herald* carried on its public relations efforts with two specimens of composition from students at Mayhew. One was a letter addressed to a group of Choctaw leaders who had come to Mayhew to observe the school in July 1826. It opened with a statement to David Folsom: "We rejoice to think that we have a chief who is a friend to his people, and wishes their good, and favors the schools in the nation. Had it not been for you and the friends of mission, we think we should have been wandering about in the wilderness. We have heard people say the missionaries have done us no good; and now is the time for them to see if we are in the same situation that we were eight, or even four years ago."[75]

The second composition, by a young female student, was a letter addressed to a clergyman. She wrote: "I do not know that one adult Choctaw has become a Christian. We all pray for them, but we cannot save them; and if they die where will they go? I do not want any one to go to hell. May the Lord pour out his Spirit upon the poor Choctaw people. They do not know who made them, and they drink and kill each other. God is very good to send the missionary here to teach the poor Choctaws."[76]

If the expressions of sentiment in the first composition were real, and one can assume that they probably were, since they came from a student who had boarded at Mayhew for three years, they indicate the extent to which Christian beliefs and morality were inculcated into some students at the school. The second composition, however laudatory its message, also revealed the lack of effect of missionary teaching and preaching on adults. The positive aspects of such essays nevertheless served as very effective propaganda pieces, to uphold the cause of the missions to supporters and to counter expressions of native discontent.

The glowing picture that the Choctaw leaders and the *Missionary Herald* painted did not match either the missionaries' perception of their progress in civilizing the Choctaws or the reality of the situation. David Folsom, who before his election as chief was reported to be "completely governed by Mr. Kingsbury," changed his position afterward.[77] As an elected chief, Folsom was undoubtedly aware of the feelings of his constituents. Kingsbury heard that Folsom had "feelings unfavorable to the plan of the Mission, to the station at Mayhew," and to him "in particular." Kingsbury and Calvin Cushman visited with Folsom, who was quite cordial and complimentary of the school at Mayhew. But Folsom thought, "as there were objections & prejudices," that Kingsbury should resign.[78] Kingsbury could not believe that Folsom objected to him personally but rather to "the *plan* of the Mission."[79]

The continuing criticisms by the Choctaws, and by fellow missionaries, plunged Kingsbury into despair regarding his abilities. He felt he could not "meet the expectations of [his] brethren, or of the Pru. Com. as it respects preaching the Gospel,"[80] and he offered to have his acts examined by "an impartial and competent committee" to be appointed by the president of the United States, the board, and the Choctaw Nation. If it was recommended, he would "consider it a privilege to be released from present responsibilities and labours" and to go to one of the Choctaw villages to learn the language and "be useful in teaching some to read the word of God, & perhaps eventually to communicate to them, the truths of the Gospel."[81]

However, the *Missionary Herald* put a brave face on the situation and published a glowing report of the accomplishments of the schools in the Choctaw Nation by the end of 1826. A total of 186 children (including children of the missionaries) attended eleven schools. At Mayhew, 54 native children had been taught. The boys also did the chores of clearing land and harvesting crops, for which they were paid five dollars a month. The girls were engaged in sewing, and they had made thirty-five shirts, six pairs of pantaloons, four coats, one cloak, fifteen vests, seven hunting frocks, sixty-nine dresses, sixty-five aprons, thirty pairs of stockings, a variety of smaller articles, sixty dozen candles, and three barrels of soap. They were also learning to read, write, and recite the rivers, capital towns, soil, climate, and major products of the United States. At Aikhunna, Byington preached to his congregation in Choctaw and taught his students to read the scriptures in the Choctaw language.[82]

But as Choctaw children learned the skills of civilized life, and as Choctaw leaders touted the advances of the nation in law making, farming, and education, Mississippi politicians and white citizens looked at Choctaw lands and saw not civilized people but the potential of wealth. Civilization was not the salvation of the Choctaw Nation.

7 | The Final Stand

EVEN AS THE CHOCTAWS ATTEMPTED TO DEMONSTRATE THEIR AD-vancing state of civilization, the pressure for Indian removal intensified. It took many forms: the benevolence of Thomas McKenney, who feared the extinction of Indians surrounded by white society and who would "take them firmly but kindly by the hand, and tell them that they must go"; the despair of Cyrus Kingsbury, who believed that the Choctaws were their own worst enemies because they failed to accept Christianity and that they would be better off "over there"; the fervor of Isaac McCoy, the Baptist preacher who envisioned the creation of an "Indian Canaan" where Indian nations could be gathered to-gether to be saved without white interference; and the national-ism of Andrew Jackson, who saw Indian nations as threats to the integrity and security of the sovereign United States and as of necessity subjects of the country's laws.[1]

Racism pitted Indian against white in the language of hea-thenism and civilization, and growing numbers of white settlers demanded Indian land. The issue of removal was joined on several fronts. The Choctaws, of course, had their reasons for resisting. Many were attached to their homeland on religious grounds. Although many were willing to take up residence west of the Mississippi, they were not necessarily willing to give up their claims to their lands east of the river. The federal govern-ment, on its part, had reasons to balance its relationships with and obligation to the states in order to assert its own power—hence its acquiesence to Mississippi's power over the Choctaws while it asserted its power over the western lands and promised to protect the Choctaws if they would move there. The mission-aries, with yet another set of motives, saw removal as a gross injustice to the Indians, and they also feared that they would lose the gains in moral improvement and Christian conversion

that they had made, as well as their significant financial investment in buildings and fields so laboriously carved out of the
wilderness.

The issue of removal coalesced the conflict in the Choctaw
Nation between the old guard and the new into opposing political factions, variously labeled by Kingsbury as the "Pagan" and
the "Christian" and by Mushulatubbee as the "Republican" (his
followers) and the "Despotic" (David Folsom and Greenwood
Leflore and their followers).[2] It drew the missionaries deeper
into the fray as religious persuasion aligned political divisions
within the tribe. Their painstaking efforts to bring the nation to
a full realization of Christian salvation were disrupted. Anxiety
over land and political power was stronger, and white land hunger was more powerful than Choctaw "civilization."[3]

In 1827 Secretary of War James Barbour sent Thomas McKenney on a trip to the Choctaw and Chickasaw nations to persuade
them to sign removal treaties.[4] The Choctaws had already made
their opposition known. Indeed, Folsom and Leflore had been
elected "on the express grounds" that they would resist "*any and
every proposition* . . . for a sale or exchange of territory."[5] McKenney presented such a proposition to the Choctaws at a council
on October 17, 1827. The tribe had to give up its attachment to
its ancestral homeland. "The ancestors are dust, but the future
generations of the tribe must have land." If they wished to remain in Mississippi, they would have to be subject to its laws.[6]

The Choctaw leaders did not accede. Late that night, Leflore
visited McKenney and told him that the chiefs "could not even
seem to accede to removal" for fear that they would be removed
from office, but he admitted that he personally favored removal.
He suggested that the Choctaws be allowed to examine the proposed western lands before negotiations for a treaty proceeded.[7]

Leflore's public persona and his private opinions epitomize
the dilemma of the Choctaw people, faced with the prospect of
giving up forever their claims to the land of their origins in order
to retain their political autonomy.[8] Leflore's ambivalence about
removal was symbolic of the greater tensions within the nation.

From his initial meeting with McKenney in 1827 to his changing statements about whether he would move west, he was torn between self and tribal interests. He ultimately remained in Mississippi and built his claims under the treaty (he was guaranteed four sections of land) into a domain of some fifteen thousand acres.[9]

But, as is true in the practical and pragmatic realism of tribal life, there was no single position or clear dichotomy within the tribe. The different factions within the districts, Leflore's election over Robert Cole, and Folsom's election over Mushulatubbee show that opinion concerning removal was not sharply divided but was shaped by many conflicting forces.

Both missionaries and federal policymakers saw little success in attempts to educate the Choctaws, who did not have "all that confidence in the advantages of education." The situation of the schools continued to be discouraging. Although the school at Elliot had "risen much" in the opinion of the Choctaws, and advancements were being made in teaching the Choctaw language, the "progress of knowledge" had not been "so rapid, as was anticipated by most friends of missions."[10] What had been accomplished was probably due in large part to the nature of the student body. Nearly half of the students at Elliot were children of "respectable white men, with native families," who had already been exposed in some degree to white society.

In the neighborhood of Mayhew there was still "much playing of ball, dancing, &c.," a situation not conducive to education. Speaking about other parts of the nation, Kingsbury noted, "Drinking prevails so much, that there is little encouragement for schools." In the face of discouragement, Kingsbury decided to drop the idea of neighborhood schools and concentrate the mission efforts at Mayhew.[11] There were no reports of conversions, and the missionaries were drawing back from Choctaw communities.

Where Kingsbury despaired, the Methodist Episcopal Church saw hope. After Wiley Ledbetter's disastrous attempt to start a school in 1825, the Methodists had retreated from the Choctaw field. However, they were eager to reestablish their presence, and in 1828, they found a willing worker in Alexander Talley, a physician who espoused "liberal" reform principles in the governance of the Methodist Church and its plans for itinerant preachers. He also supported antislavery sentiments.[12] His disaffection from the mainstream of Methodist thought made him a prime candidate for a circuit as remote and possibly unpromising as the Choctaw Nation.

Methodist theology embraced beliefs much more compatible with traditional Choctaw values than those of the American Board—freedom of the will, universal access to grace and salvation, and the importance of a mystical experience of closeness to God. And unlike the American Board, Talley and his fellow Methodists took their beliefs out to the people as they rode their circuits and preached.[13]

Talley began riding his circuit in the spring of 1828. The territory he covered was in the Western and Southern districts, and the majority of the Choctaws he encountered were "aged full-blood natives," many of whom he deemed "quite intelligent."[14] He quickly established a base of operations at Greenwood Leflore's home, a center of political activity where he could preach to a number of leaders. Three chiefs who appeared at Leflore's home on business stayed for a prayer meeting, at which "a deep seriousness appeared on every countenance." The chiefs "humbled themselves in the dust" with other potential converts at the end of the meeting and showed signs of "true conversion," along with Leflore's wife and mother.[15]

An incident at the American Board school at Bethel undoubtedly worked in Talley's favor. In June 1828 Zeddock Brashears, a prominent mixed-blood, accused Stephen Macomber, the teacher at Bethel, of seducing and impregnating his grand-daughter, Susan Lyles, a student at the school. Under questioning, the girl accused both Macomber and Aden Gibbs of seducing her. Missionaries were fallible, despite their moral rectitude, and Macomber was virtually alone in the wilderness with a wife who was a bedridden invalid. However, Leflore seemed less concerned with the morality of the situation than with the question of monetary responsibility for the child. Although traditional Choctaw customs placed no stigma on children born out of wedlock, and the matrilineal kinship system gave the mother's kin responsibility for the child, the Brashears family was mixed-blood. Support had to come from the father, and Leflore demanded that the missionaries pay five hundred dollars to the nation for the child.

Susan Lyles's child thus became a pawn in a political power struggle. It gave Leflore the opportunity to make demands on the missionaries, and to do so on behalf of the nation rather than the girl's family specifically. Kingsbury was willing to pay the family, but he refused to recognize any claim by the nation. The incident became a test of wills and also an indication of Leflore's intent to act as spokesman for the Choctaw Nation. In a sharp exchange of letters with Kingsbury, Leflore pressed his demands. Macomber was removed from the station at Bethel and ultimately dismissed from missionary service, but Kingsbury never paid the five hundred dollars.[16]

The incident caused Talley to keep his distance from the American Board. Although Leflore was finally reconciled to the board's missions, he ultimately converted to Methodism after the death of his wife.[17] Talley, for his part, was well aware that his work presaged an incipient conflict with the American Board missionaries. He had been on friendly terms with them, but he feared that this would not last as he and Robert Smith, his fellow missionary, began to "admit persons into society" near Elliot. Nevertheless, if the Choctaws wanted it, he and Smith would "go fearlessly forward." In addition, he had competition in a young Choctaw who had trained as a Baptist preacher at the Choctaw Academy and who was trying to baptize Methodist converts without telling them that he represented a different denomination.[18]

Talley's success among the Choctaws was in part due to the style of Methodism. Whereas the American Board depended primarily on large, permanent stations such as Elliot and Mayhew, which were highly labor intensive and situated near communities of mixed-bloods, Talley and his assistants rode the circuit through the Western and Southern districts, and they used the camp meeting to bring together people from remote areas.

Talley held his first meeting on August 15, 1828, at Nine Mile Creek on the old Natchez Trace. It produced immediate results. An older woman fell into "a strange condition," and "her spirit seemed to leave the body." She appeared dead for "a good while." When she revived, she said that "the Great Spirit had given her a new heart." By the end of the meeting, Talley had admitted "five or six under our care," and the next morning, "8 or ten met us for prayer, and appeared unwilling to part with us." At a subsequent meeting, Talley numbered twenty natives, two whites, and five blacks who had joined the church. He planned to baptize those who were "prepared" and to "immediately administer the sacrament to them."19

The remarkable responses to Methodist preaching were readily accepted as signs of conversion. Both Methodists and Presbyterians subscribed to a theology that stressed the operation of God's will on the individual as a condition of salvation. The Methodists, however, put greater stress on the free will of the individual to accept the saving power of God and the development of a personal and emotional relationship with God. The American Board missionaries looked for sustained evidence of anxiety about the state of one's soul as a sign of salvation. The Methodists accepted highly emotional states in the presence of the gospel as proof of God's will.

The camp meeting provided an ideal vehicle for Methodist conversions. Traditionally, Choctaw people gathered in large groups for ball games and dances, which entailed social interaction, singing, gambling, and long speeches by individuals who recited their personal exploits. The camp meetings brought people together, promoted social interaction, and included singing and long speeches by Talley and by Choctaw orators about God.

If the Choctaws were deeply moved by the preaching at Methodist camp meetings, the American Board missionaries were

impressed as well. After Loring Williams reported from Aikhunnah about "the wonderful success" of the Methodists in the
southern part of the nation,[20] Kingsbury decided that the tech-
nique might indeed work, and he held his own camp meeting at
Hebron, the new station near Robert Folsom's home. The timing
was not ideal (December), and the weather was "unfavourable."
The turnout was disappointing. Cyrus Byington was sick and
could not attend, and the Choctaws who did appear were disappointed that there was no one there to preach to them in their
own language.[21]

The results were, nevertheless, remarkable, and they spread.
Williams reported that "a still small voice" was heard around
Aikhunnah, and he could also hope that "the operations of the
Holy Spirit" had resulted in a few conversions. A man who had
been "a noted leader in heathen abominations" was now "as
active in building up the cause of Christ, as formerly in trying to
pull it down."[22] In the Southern District, Alfred Wright held a
camp meeting near Goshen in late January. John Garland, elected
chief of the district, and his followers attended. The result was "an
impression . . . in favour of the Gospel" not seen before.[23]

Talley, on his part, reported in September 1829 that some two
thousand people, most of them Choctaws, had experienced the
very emotional state associated with conversion to Methodism.
Indeed, during one meeting, the son of a prominent chief was
"so much affected" that the missionaries were "apprehensive" he
would fall into the fire by which he was standing. Talley noted,
"From these feelings we were soon relieved by his falling a different course."[24]

Kingsbury reported only three or four hundred people in the
neighborhoods of Aikhunnah, Yoknokchaya, and Hebron who
had "taken the anxious seat." Although the number represented
a sizable increase, he was skeptical of the intentions of the converts and feared that the anxiety was "more the effect of sympa-
thy & of a desire to appear like others, than of any deeply
wrought convictions through the operations of the spirit and the
belief of the truth."[25]

The Presbyterians required long periods of anxiety as proof of true salvation. The Methodists accepted immediate emotional response as a sign. There is little specific evidence from Choctaws themselves about how they viewed conversion. The most telling example is the account by "T." While looking for his horse, "T" saw a deer lying down and thought how easily he could kill it. He pondered, "Perhaps my Heavenly Father intends to present me with that animal for my use." He concluded that if the deer was still there after he fetched his gun from home, it would be a sign of God's will. When he returned with the gun, the deer was still there. "After lifting up my heart again to my Father above, I fired and killed it." Thus did "an old hunter" translate Christianity into terms that he could understand and accept.[26]

If Methodists and Presbyterians questioned each other's theology and effectiveness as missionaries, they nevertheless adopted each other's practices. Talley appreciated the value of community schools and the use of the Choctaw language as a medium of communication. By June 1829, he had two schools in operation, Siniasher under a Brother Sims and the Old Queens School under the supervision of Brother Moses Perry, with thirty-one students. He also felt that too much time and effort had been spent in trying to teach Choctaw children the English language, and he declared, "Books in the Choctaw, and Teachers of the Choctaws, and itinerant preachers, will be our principle objects next year."[27]

For the American Board, the Methodist schools had a spillover effect that was both encouraging and discouraging. Leflore petitioned the board for a school near Black Creek in his neighborhood. Talley had established a boarding school, and if the board would not start a similar school, Leflore wanted the money so that he could establish one himself. But the board could not start any new schools without more teachers, and again Kingsbury found his efforts being thwarted for lack of personnel.[28]

The evidence of widespread religious feeling in the summer

and fall of 1828 was further ammunition for the Choctaw leadership in the fight against removal, and they continued their efforts to prove that the nation was civilized. *Niles' Weekly Register,* the national newsmagazine of its day, reported that a Choctaw had entered a subscription. In his "exceedingly well-written letter," he described "with much feeling" the "progress of Improvement" in the Choctaw Nation, pointing out that "many old customs" had been abolished and that hundreds of people had "lately embraced the gospel" and were learning "the importance of self-discipline." Assuming that *Niles'* readers read the reports, the Choctaws could show proof that they were learning to live, and read, like whites.[29]

David Folsom was quick to note signs of civilization in a letter to Thomas McKenney. In the Southern District, the chief Tapenahomah had been deposed for drunkenness and John Garland put in his place. Folsom took political change and religious fervor as signs that the nation was "rising" and had already risen "so high as to look down with contempt upon dissipation."[30]

The American Board welcomed such evidence as part of its larger political agenda to oppose Jackson's policy of Indian removal. The board certainly had humanitarian grounds to save the Indians from the hardships of forcible removal. Moral grounds bade it to uphold the inherent rights of Indians to their lands (although there it acted from principles of private property rather than spiritual attachment to a homeland). The board wanted to protect the gains it had made in church membership to prove the effectiveness of its efforts. And, a more secular consideration, it needed to preserve its own monetary investments in schools and mission buildings, which were largely the investments of its contributors.

Jeremiah Evarts circulated a questionnaire among the American Board missionaries in the summer of 1828 to gather evidence of "improvements" in the status of the Choctaws. The response was very positive. Kingsbury, in a burst of extreme optimism, doubted that any greater improvement could be found "in any portion of the civilized world" than that in "the civil, moral &

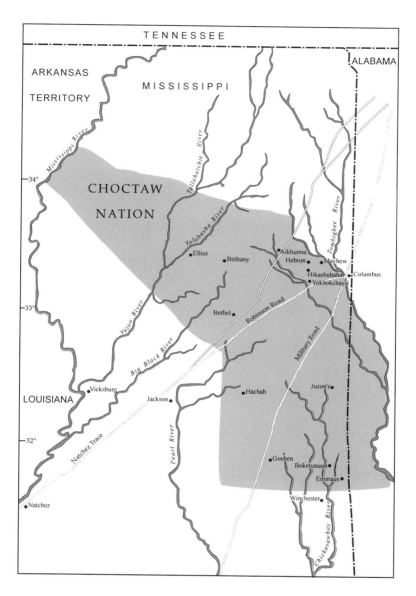

American Board of Missions and Schools, 1818–1830

religious status of the Choctaws." Although he gave some credit to "enlightened chiefs," he ascribed "whatever of good" they had done to the "enlightening and sanctifying influences of the Gospel." The Western and Northeastern districts had both passed regulations against whiskey, and there had been no sign of drunkenness among the four or five thousand people at the last annuity distribution. Kingsbury made the rather startling claim that "less ardent spirit" was now used in the Choctaw Nation than in any other part of the United States. There was also an "increase of industry" and "advance in dress, furniture and all the comforts & conveniences of civilized life." Blacksmith's shops were being established in the Northeastern District, and two hundred dollars' worth of tools had been purchased. The nation now had a constitution and laws concerning theft, murder, infanticide, marriage, polygamy, the making of wills and settling of estates, trespass, false testimony, enclosure of fields, and "other matters." The funeral rite of pole pulling had been abolished. Witchcraft was no longer punished by death. The most striking evidence of civilization to Kingsbury's mind, however, was "the reception" the Choctaws had lately "given to the Gospel," although he admitted that the Methodists had added "a new impulse to the cause." Removal would "retard & embarrass, if not entirely . . . defeat," the efforts to educate the Choctaws.[31]

Near Yoknokchaya, David Folsom's new place on the Robinson Road, the natives were raising cotton, making cloth, and operating blacksmith shops. They were now "quite temperate." Laws had been passed. The old chiefs of the nation, "ignorant, wicked & profligate" men, had been replaced by new chiefs who were "moral" and "more or less under the influence of religion." About 194 persons had sat on the "anxious seats," more than 300 were "of the spirit," and some backsliders had also been "reclaimed." The doors were "opened wide" for religion. They were not so open, however, for education. Although Kingsbury had reported enthusiasm for education in the nation, the teachers' hopes were often "blasted" when students went home "to their amusements & former follies." Attempts to give them "an English education" had not been very successful.[32]

The missionaries were most forceful in opposing the idea of removal. It was against their own interests and against those of the Choctaws. Byington painted a dismaying picture of the Indian forced to leave.

> [He] will stand & gaze on us, as long as he can. He will look once more at his home the land of his fathers & of his own birth & then turn on his heel away from the white man & all that he could offer him & fixing an eye sullen with despair on the great western wilderness would enter it no more to return, but carrying in his bleeding heart & sence of wrong & opression entirely unprovoked which he will not forget to tell his children even in death & which he will carry up in his heart to the bar of God to the Avenger of Nations, where again he will meet the white man face to face.[33]

Armed thus with evidence of the American Board's efforts and the deleterious effects of removal, Evarts carried the fight against the removal policy to the American public in the *National Intelligencer,* where he published a series of letters on behalf of the Cherokees, who were involved in a bitter conflict with the state of Georgia. He memorialized Congress.[34] He editorialized in the *Missionary Herald*:

> The Christian public should be fully aware, that these tribes . . . are strongly attached to the country, which they received from their fathers; . . . that they are extremely reluctant to leave it;—that they think it guaranteed to them by numerous treaties with the United States;—that they will not remove, unless upon compulsion . . . that they regard a removal . . . to be altogether unjust and oppressive, and that they importunately call upon the friends of justice and humanity to interpose in their behalf and arrest a course of measures, which . . . will be disastrous in the extreme.[35]

The public relations campaign failed. Despite the evidence of civilization, government policy and sentiment called for removal. McKenney, disillusioned by what he considered signs of dissolution and degradation during his trip through Indian country in 1827, asked

> *What are humanity and justice in reference to this unfortunate race?* Are these found to lie in a policy that would have them to linger out a wretched and degraded existence within districts of country already surrounded and pressed upon by a population whose anxiety and efforts to get rid of them are not less restless and persevering, than is that law of nature immutable which has decreed that under such circumstances, if continued in, *they must perish?*[36]

His disillusionment was fed by reports that missionaries often antagonized Indians with their attempts to proselytize. James McDonald, interpreter for the tribe and David Folsom's protégé, complained of the "inefficient, bigotted, or overzealous" efforts of some of the American Board missionaries among the Choctaws.[37]

The citizens and legislature of Mississippi added their voices to the chorus, encouraged by Jackson's election as president in 1828. Resentful of the failure of John Quincy Adams's administration to undertake wholesale removal of both the Choctaws and the Chickasaws, they joined citizens of the state of Georgia, which was dealing with the Cherokees, in overwhelming support of Jackson's policy of Indian removal. The Mississippi legislature memorialized Congress, "A large portion of the most valuable territory within the chartered limits of this state, is occupied by savage tribes, interspersed with disorderly whites, whose vicious and intemperate habits give the example, and afford the facility of indulging in intoxicating liquores, a practice rapidly extinguishing their numbers, and entirely hostile to the progress of civilization."[38]

The legislators called on Congress to persuade the Indians to move to a place "more congenial to their nature" and to secure their "permanent interest" by using the proceeds from sale of their lands for schools, farm tools, and other implements of "civilized life." Calling on both the "philanthropic feeling" of Congress and its "natural disposition to advance the prosperity of the new state," they asked "forcibly" that the Indians within the state boundaries be removed.[39]

John A. Quitman, a leading Mississippi politician, suggested a strategy to force removal. Tax the whites in the nation and "drive off the Northern missionaries and lawless whites" in Indian country, and the Indians could be removed. The legislature also considered but ultimately rejected a bill to extend its jurisdiction over the Choctaws and Chickasaws in 1828. The consideration, however, threatened ominous consequences.[40]

Jackson laid out his removal policy in his State of the Union message on December 8, 1829. Appealing to "humanity and national honor," he stated:

> Their present condition, contrasted with what they once were, makes a most powerful appeal to our sympathies. Our ancestors found them the uncontrolled possessors of these vast regions. By persuasion and force they have been made to retire from river to river and from mountain to mountain, until some of the tribes have become extinct and others have left but remnants to preserve for awhile their once terrible names. Surrounded by the whites with their arts of civilization, which by destroying the resources of the savage doom him to weakness and decay, the fate of the Mohegan, the Narragansett, and the Delaware is fast overtaking the Choctaw, the Cherokee, and the Creek. That this fate surely awaits them if they remain within the limits of the States does not admit of a doubt.[41]

He proposed the creation of a western territory and removal as the means to save the Indians. But Jackson was concerned with much more than national honor. The power of the federal government and the rights of states to exercise constitutional powers were compromised by the existence of Indian nations as sovereign entities in their midst. Jackson had already informed the Cherokees and Creeks that he would not countenance "their attempt to establish an independent government."[42]

Had the Choctaws inadvertently played into Jackson's hands by establishing a constitutional government with its council and its laws? Were the very acts that Kingsbury and Byington applauded as evidence of moral and cultural civilization among the Choctaws to be implicitly held against them? Such was the conundrum occasioned by Choctaw attempts to learn the white man's ways.

The government's pressure for removal continued. In September 1829, Secretary of War John Eaton, voicing Jackson's concern that Choctaw resistance to removal was inspired by "vicious white men," instructed William Ward to expel such men and to require a license of all white men who remained in the territory. The agent's right to regulate residence of whites in Choctaw territory had been established in the Treaty of Doak's Stand to protect the Indians, but now it was being used for the explicitly political ends of removal policy. Not only was Ward's authority reinforced, but Eaton also bluntly stated that the Choctaws were "within the limits & jurisdiction of a state whose laws" could at any time "be extended over them" and that the government could not prevent that extension. The constitutional power of the U.S. government to protect the Choctaws existed only beyond the Mississippi. The issue of states' rights was thus joined. Jackson would concede power to states in order to make them agents of his removal policy and strengthen his own political power base. If he could force the Choctaws and Chickasaws to move, he would gain the gratitude of the Mississippi electorate.[43]

Folsom's response to Eaton's letter was simple and to the point. "We do not wish to sell our land and remove." With disarming candor he asked: "The American people say that they love liberty. . . . Why will they take it from the red man?"[44] For Jackson, however, the issue was not liberty but the sovereignty of the American people. In October 1829, he offered the Choctaws land beyond the Mississippi, which they could live on "as long as grass grows and water runs in peace and plenty." Again, the Choctaw chiefs rejected the offer.[45]

The chiefs did not speak for all the Choctaws, as they never had. Some Choctaws were already moving west, and some were prepared to move to the Brazos and Trinity rivers if Mexico ceded

Texas to the United States.[46] There was no clear consensus, by voice or by action, on the issue of removal. If Folsom, Garland, and Leflore were committed to oppose ceding the homeland, Mushulatubbee was a potent political force who favored removal. He did not take easily to being deposed, and he still had a significant following. Voting for leaders remained a foreign concept for most of the Choctaws. Although federal officials in Washington wanted to deal with elected leaders, elections in the Choctaw Nation represented an increasing splintering of power.

Mushulatubbee actively promoted removal. He visited the Choctaw Academy in September 1829 to seek supporters. There is a certain poignancy in the picture of the old, full-blood chief among the young Choctaw men at the academy, although the picture is somewhat romanticized, since Mushulatubbee had always had his own way and was not about to give up power to the rising generation. He learned from the students that states had the power to extend their laws over individuals.[47]

With this knowledge, he proposed to Eaton that Mississippi "adopt the Choctaws as children upon equal terms" with its white citizens. Always the pragmatist, however, he saw little possibility of that happening; the only hope for the survival of the nation was to move west.[48] The students at the academy gave Mushulatubbee a letter addressed to "friends and countrymen," saying that the state of Mississippi was depriving the Choctaws of their rights and proposing that the tribe make a treaty with the government guaranteeing their rights to a territory that could be admitted to the Union as a state.[49]

The students, in a rush of idealism, did not specify whether the territory was to be in Mississippi or in the West. As the products largely of mixed marriages and the effects of boarding school education, the students were concerned with tribal autonomy, wherever it would be. For Mushulatubbee, the issue was clearly a choice between the homeland in Mississippi and a new home in the West.

The conflict in the Northeastern District escalated after Mushulatubbee returned from the academy. He called a council of his supporters in November, where he denounced Folsom for resisting removal and had himself elected as district chief.[50] He used his election to bargain with William Ward for a promise that the government would recognize him as a chief in the West if the nation moved.[51]

Leadership of the district was now openly contested, and the issue of removal was overt. The Choctaw leaders were feeling the pressure. David Folsom complained to Ward that Middleton Mackey, the government translator, was promoting removal, and Ward summarily ordered Mackey to leave the nation. Mackey in turn complained that he had encouraged the Indians to move but that the missionaries, acting out of self-interest, influenced them to oppose emigration.[52] Ward accused Loring Williams of working to stir up resistance to removal, together with Peter Pitchlynn and a member of the Folsom family.[53]

In the midst of charges and countercharges and contested elections, the state of Mississippi abruptly preempted the matter. The state legislature first extended its jurisdiction over areas of Indian land that adjoined Wayne and Covington counties, and on January 19, 1830, it extended its laws over "the person and property" of all Indians resident in the state. Tribal governments were abolished, and it became a crime for anyone to claim to be a chief of an Indian tribe.[54] If the government could not force the Choctaws to negotiate a treaty, the state of Mississippi would.

The Choctaws saw the legislation as a mortal blow to their nation. They could no longer exercise their own autonomy without threat of punishment. Mississippi citizens saw it as a way of getting rid of the Choctaws. One hailed the legislation as "a noble piece of policy" and declared, "Abrogating the powers of their own government, will be as sure a way of getting rid of them, as if we were to shoot them."[55] The editors of *Niles' Weekly Register* saw the legislation as a benevolent action on the part of the state to integrate the Choctaws peacefully into its population and to extend to them the benefits of private property. Benevolence and malevolence joined to deprive the Choctaws of land and nationhood. What the "civilization" policy had not been able to accomplish with education and Christianity, Mississippi would accomplish with individual property rights.[56]

Mississippi's action provoked an immediate outcry among missionaries. Although it made the Choctaws subject to state laws, it did not give them suffrage. Bishop William Winans denounced it as "a most violent invasion of the *Rights of Man*—a most iniquitous breach of *treaty obligations*—an assumption upon the clearest and most unquestionable *rights of property*—a wanton disregard of the *claims of humanity* and a display of *ingratitude* rarely equaled in the annals of human depravity."[57]

Talley demanded: "Can the Mississippians consent that this people should be torn to pieces, Christianity banished from them, and poor and wretched, be forced into the Wilds of the West, seek a scanty subsistance on the scattered game for a few years, and then for them to die of hunger. Mississippi will be the responsible agent, and Heaven will mark and punish the horrid crime."[58]

Kingsbury called the move "wholly a most unjust & wicked proceeding." He said, "If the United States permit such a monstrous exercise of arbitrary & unjust power towards a weak & defenceless people who have placed themselves under our protection, I shall blush for my country."[59] He carried on a campaign to subvert Jackson's removal policy. He solicited testimonials from Benjamin Johnson and William Ward to prove that the Choctaws were living like their white neighbors and should not be moved. Johnson testified that "their means of living by the chase" had "much declined" and that they now lived by farming. They had also "imbibed a disposition for more regular Government" and had "discarded most of their former barbarous and cruel usages." He reported "an unusual impulse" to attend "religious exercises." Ward reported, "The Nation begin to live like white people." The Choctaws raised livestock and had largely given up drinking.[60]

Certainly some Mississippians did not accept the idea that the Choctaws were civilized. Although R. J. Nicholson objected to removal by coercion, he added: "[I] see no propriety in allowing *wandering savages* to claim a large, extensive, and fertile country which has been evidently designated by Providence to be subdued and cultivated and become the residence of civilized man. . . . The cultivation of the soil is an obligation imposed by our Creator upon the human race."[61]

Despite evidence of civilized life among the Choctaws, Mississippi's action forced the issue of removal in a most direct way. The Choctaw Nation could not continue with its leaders essentially outlawed. They responded by electing a single chief and agreeing to move, but at a stiff price.

In March, Folsom, Leflore, and Garland called a general council, attended by about eight hundred people. The Methodists were there in full force, and Byington represented the American Board. Folsom and Garland resigned their positions and acknowledged Leflore as the sole chief of the nation. Thus did the traditional tripartite division of the nation give way to ostensible unity. Folsom, the former staunch advocate of the American Board, threw his support behind Leflore, the Methodist convert.[62]

The council then drafted a treaty agreeing to cede their land in Mississippi and move west. Talley wrote it out "on 16 pages foolscap paper."[63] It provided well for its authors. The leaders of the nation implicitly accepted the principles of private property that the state was forcing on them. Leflore and Folsom would get ten sections of the ceded land and Garland five. Each Choctaw head of family would get 640 acres to be sold to pay for removal. Leflore would be chief of the nation for life, and Folsom would be judge for life, each with a salary of one thousand dollars per annum. It also acknowledged the importance of Christianity and education by providing for resettlement of the missionaries and for establishment of schools in the West, but it made no provision to compensate the American Board for its investment in mission buildings.[64]

Talley accepted the reality of removal because Leflore and Folsom accepted it. To oppose "the views of the U.S. government" and thus the views of Christian leaders would be to side with Mushulatubbee and Nitakechi, men who were "hostile to Christianity" and who represented "the old prejudices and principles of the native." A treaty would ensure that the nation was governed by "men of information and Christian principles." Talley also held on to the hope that the citizens of Mississippi might "exercise a spirit of forebearance" if they saw that the Choctaws were "endeavoring to get out of their way."[65]

Kingsbury was more circumspect in his assessment of the treaty. When Leflore asked for his advice, Kingsbury told him to "remonstrate" to the government. It would take millions of dollars to implement what the Choctaws proposed, and it was doubtful that the government would agree to it. By asking for too much, the Choctaws might get very little. Despite the advice, Leflore was "determined to remove," to preserve the nation's (and his own) autonomy.[66]

The Choctaws sent their treaty to Jackson. Although he found its terms "objectionable," he felt they could be modified to conform to the government's "humane and liberal policy" toward Indian tribes.[67] Even as the Choctaws proposed their treaty, Jackson's removal policy became law in the Indian Removal Act, passed on May 28, 1830.[68]

The act marked a political victory for Jackson, although it certainly did not represent an overwhelming mandate. The vote in its favor was only 28 to 20 in the Senate and 102 to 97 in the House. Earlier in the debates, the House had been evenly split on the bill. Congressmen were not particularly interested in Indian rights (although some were influenced by the humanitarian concerns of missionaries). The major issues came down to Jacksonian populism, the promise of readily available land, and the integrity of U.S. territory and sovereignty against the forces of eastern capitalism, the national bank, and control of private property.[69]

The Choctaw treaty would be the first major test of the new policy. It brought to the foreground a newly emergent class of propertied leaders (one cannot call them landowners, but they controlled significant resources) among the Choctaws, men who understood the value of property and were capable of bargaining for it. But their actions caused an uproar among their followers, and it precipitated a crisis of leadership. As Folsom, Leflore, and Garland espoused removal, private property, and lifetime office, Choctaws throughout the nation rose in opposition. Garland's followers among the Six Towns people were angry over his resignation at the council and his past support for missionary camp meetings, and the people around the town of Kunsha held a council and elected the full-blood Nitakechi as their leader, challenging both Garland and Leflore.[70]

Leflore sought desperately to strengthen his position by trying to persuade Mushulatubbee to support him. He argued against the traditional district system by saying that when each district had different laws, men could flee punishment in one by going to another. The draft treaty made liberal allotments of land that could be sold to pay for improvements that would be lost when the tribe moved west. Mushulatubbee was his "brother," and he asked for a "white talk," a sign of acceptance of the treaty and of his election. If Mushulatubbee would not support him, however, Leflore added a threatening note. "We will soon settle our difficulties, but not as pleasantly as I wish."[71]

Leflore and Folsom demanded too much in their treaty, as Kingsbury had predicted, and Congress rejected it as too costly. Eaton now turned to the other faction of the tribe, led by Mushulatubbee and Nitakechi, for a treaty. Their positions thus justified, the two chiefs accused "a few designing men" of attempting to "usurp the rights of the poor Indians," and they declared that "the poor as well as the rich" would receive their "just rights." They assured Eaton that Folsom had lost the confidence of the captains and warriors in both the Northeastern and Southern districts, except for a few who had "joined the missionary church" and were related to him. Even those, they reported, were now leaving Folsom, and Leflore's influence was limited to his own district.[72]

Before Eaton could arrange for negotiations with Mushulatubbee and Nitakechi, however, the situation in the Choctaw Nation approached a state of civil war. The two leaders now raised religion as an issue. Aware that Eaton was willing to treat with them, and charging that "half-breed Christian chiefs" would sell the land if Choctaws became Christians, Mushulatubbee and Nitakechi joined forces and began to threaten and harass Christian Choctaws.[73]

Opposition to preaching and camp meetings had already surfaced in some of the towns around Kunsha, inspired by Nitakechi and "young Juzan."[74] Nitakechi's supporters now threatened Christians near Chickasawhay and the Six Towns. Reports circulated that parties of armed men seized Christians and carried them off to gatherings, "where one side of the face was black and the other side painted, and then ordered [them] to get up and dance away their religion, and if they hesitated guns were fired under them to hurry them."[75] Talley reported that twelve men had been selected to assassinate Leflore and that each had drawn three charges of powder to carry out that mission.[76] Meanwhile, Mushulatubbee and Nitakechi complained to Ward that Leflore and Folsom were planning to attack them.[77]

The "Pagan" and "Christian" parties met at a council on June 14, 1830. The differences in their positions were clear and irreconcilable. The Pagan party said that no Christian should be a chief or captain. The Christian party demanded complete tolerance. The result was a stalemate, and the "Christian" party finally withdrew. Its members named David Folsom as their leader, and the party, fearing retaliation from the opposing faction, declared itself under the protection of the laws of Mississippi.[78] The move was strong evidence of the anarchy that was seizing the nation.

The conflict between the full-blood chiefs and the mixed-blood leaders came to a head in July 1830 when the Choctaws gathered for the yearly annuity payment near David Folsom's residence on the Robinson Road. Reports of the episode are confusing and conflicting. According to Folsom's account of the episode, he and Leflore arrived with some six to eight hundred men, mounted and armed with guns. They were prepared to confront Mushulatubbee, Nitakechi, and their followers, who were mainly on foot and "indifferently armed" with bows and arrows. The two forces faced each other in silence for about ten minutes. Nitakechi then advanced toward Folsom while his followers aimed their weapons. Folsom, after a hasty conference with Leflore, went to meet him. According to Folsom:

> By the time I approached within thirty steps of the chief, I resolved to offer him my hand, in evidence of my desire for a reconciliation. If accepted, I hoped a compromise might be arrived at. If refused, I knew that in five minutes both of us would die. His countenance was forbidding and scowling, his lip compressed, a dark cloud resting on his brow.
>
> I extended my hand; a smile like sunshine softened his expression, and he promptly and warmly grasped it, while each of us said Bar-ba-she-la (friends).

The two opposing sides then built a fire and held a council, and civil war within the tribe was averted.[79]

According to Ward's account, Leflore and his followers held a council and then confronted Mushulatubbee at his home. Mushulatubbee announced that he was not armed but challenged Leflore to return for a fight later. Leflore then rode away and spread the rumor that he had routed Mushulatubbee.[80] In yet another account, George Gaines, the respected trader, negotiated the conflict. Nitakechi would remain as leader of the Six Towns, and Mushulatubbee was persuaded to resign, with the understanding that his successor would be elected.[81] Mushulatubbee and Nitakechi, although temporarily stymied in their attempt to overthrow Leflore, were not themselves overthrown, and the confrontation undermined Leflore's attempt to present himself as the sole head of a unified nation.

The polarization of the nation was having a harsh effect on the work of the missions. Kingsbury decried the confrontation at the annuity payment as "a mere exercise of political sagacity and physical power." The settlement of differences between the two factions, although successful in averting overt conflict, would be "highly injurious to the cause of vital piety" if Mushulatubbee and Nitakechi retained any political power.[82] Kingsbury feared their stance both against Christianity and in favor of removal. The division of leadership along ostensibly religious lines inspired concerns not only for faith but also for the future of Choctaw lands and the investment of the missionaries thereon.

The handshake between Folsom and Mushulatubbee, if it indeed occurred, may have averted war but did not solve the problem of removal. On August 16, Mushulatubbee and Nitakechi wrote to Eaton offering to sell the Choctaw land for less than Leflore had proposed and expressing a willingness to treat with the government.[83]

Jackson's initial response was conciliatory. He sent a message to the Choctaw leaders on August 23 in which he assured them that although the treaty they had submitted had not passed, removal was in their own best interests. If they did not move, they would become subject to the laws of the state of Mississippi, a situation that neither "Your Great Father" nor Congress could prevent. They should move to a land where the government would protect them from the influences of traders, intruders, and alcohol. However, if they did not want to move, they should say so, and the subject was "no more to be talked of again."[84]

But the subject was talked of again when John Eaton and John Coffee arrived at Dancing Rabbit Creek, in the Northeastern District, on September 15, 1830. Present were the Choctaw leaders and their followers and Alexander Talley. The American Board was not represented. Although Kingsbury asked for permission for the board missionaries to be present to give the Choctaws "the advantages of religious instruction on the Sabbath," and to answer any questions about the mission stations, the request was denied. Religious instruction would take up time and cause expense, and questions about the mission buildings could be dealt with by letter. The commissioners excluded the American Board, but Talley was already present at the treaty grounds and vowed that he would not leave unless he was tied up and carried off.[85]

As the Choctaws awaited the beginnings of the negotiations, deep political divisions within the tribe became obvious in the physical layout of the treaty ground at Dancing Rabbit Creek. A branch of the creek separated Leflore and his followers from Mushulatubbee, Nitakechi, and their followers. The cultural differences were apparent in dress. Leflore wore "a suit of citizen clothes." Mushulatubbee wore a new blue military uniform, and Nitakechi was dressed in "Indian garb and seven silver gorgets."[86]

In this tense environment, Coffee and Eaton addressed the assembly, noting "with deep regret" the differences and disturbances among tribal members. Their solution to tribal division was to suggest majority rule. They also urged those present to reject the counsel of missionaries, who they asserted were attempting to influence the tribe's "general governmental relations."[87]

As the negotiations began, Leflore and Folsom spoke against the proposed cession, and the commissioners' tone grew threatening. If the Choctaws did not cede the remaining land in Mississippi, they stood to lose their land west of the Mississippi, their agent, and their annuities.[88]

After nearly two weeks of enduring threats and harangues and obstinently refusing to cede land, most of the Choctaws left the council grounds. By their action, they implicitly rejected the proposals that Coffee and Eaton put forth. But a group of about five hundred people stayed. Leflore, Mushulatubbee, and Nitakechi remained there as ostensible leaders of the nation, and on September 27, 171 Choctaw "chiefs, captains, and head men" signed the Treaty of Dancing Rabbit Creek, ceding the Choctaw homeland in Mississippi and agreeing to move west.[89]

The inevitable had come to pass, although it was formally acknowledged by only a small number of Choctaws. The forces of civilization had overtaken the nation. Debt, the value of private property, the lure of power, and the force of laws, both those preached by missionaries and those imposed by the state of Mississippi, all had conspired in the signing of the treaty.

The Choctaws signed with the government's agreement to

two guarantees. One was that George Gaines, their longtime factor and friend, would lead a party to examine the western lands to which they would move and would manage the emigration if the land was satisfactory. The other guarantee, suggested by Leflore and embodied in the fourteenth article of the Treaty, was that those who wished to remain in Mississippi could apply to the agent for 640 acres of land for themselves and additional land for their children.[90]

The Treaty of Dancing Rabbit Creek epitomizes the changing nature of tribal identity and individual political power in the Choctaw Nation. The government had gotten its first major cession (Doak's Stand) by exploiting the division in the tribe between the hunters who constituted a virtually separate nation west of the Mississippi and those who remained in Mississippi and were becoming settled farmers. By 1830, the tribe was arbitrarily stripped of its political autonomy in Mississippi, and the division the government could exploit was no longer based on geography but on the disputes over leadership and who would profit most from the inevitable removal.

Mushulatubbee and Nitakechi represented the traditional way of life, even if they no longer lived it. They came from full-blood lineages, the source of leaders before them. Their followers drank and played ball and held their cries and dances. They presumed to protect the interests of the "poor Indians." What they really had to protect was not the welfare of "savage" hunters over "civilized" farmers but the control of economic resources that would come from the sale of Choctaw lands east of the Mississippi.

Leflore and Folsom represented the forces of change—white settlement, trade, cattle raising, private landownership, and Christianity. They stood for constitutional government and codified laws. They spoke publicly against removal because of their elected positions, but they favored it privately in order to consolidate their political positions.

Ultimately, however, they all signed the treaty, both full-bloods and mixed-bloods—Mushulatubbee, Nitakechi, David

Folsom, Greenwood Leflore, and John Garland—and each received four sections of land. The treaty guaranteed the Choctaws political autonomy in their western lands. They would have jurisdiction over all people and property in their territory. "No territory or state shall ever have a right to pass laws for the government of the Choctaw Nation of Red People and their descendants; and . . . no part of the land granted them shall ever be embraced in any Territory or State."[91] The promises are ironic, however, in the light of history: the governments of the Five Civilized Tribes in Indian Territory were dissolved to allow for the establishment of the state of Oklahoma in 1907.

The treaty provided for the trappings of civilization in the form of three blacksmith shops, one thousand axes, ploughs, hoes, spinning wheels and cards, and four hundred looms. Each district would receive one ton of iron and two hundred weight of steel annually for sixteen years. A central council house would be built, as well as a chief's house and a church in each district. The churches would serve also as schoolhouses, and teachers' salaries would be paid. Forty Choctaw youths a year were to be educated for a period of twenty years. The chiefs, their captains, and their speakers were to get salaries, and the captains were also to get "a good suit of clothes and a broad sword."[92] From a black silk handkerchief in 1816 to full suits and swords in 1830, so had the Choctaws progressed in civilization.

Any fiction of political unity in the Treaty of Dancing Rabbit Creek was lost in the reality of the virtual anarchy within the nation following its passage. In Leflore's district, many of his followers revolted and elected his nephew George Washington Harkins (who was also Folsom's son-in-law) as chief.[93] A faction of the Six Towns leaders elected Joel Nail as their chief and threatened the leaders of the faction that remained loyal to Nitakechi.[94]

The treaty was also a major blow to the American Board. Kingsbury despaired, "The instability (some say 'duplicity') of Leflore and Folsom have sunk all my hopes."[95] He urged the board to oppose the treaty. He asked David Folsom to persuade

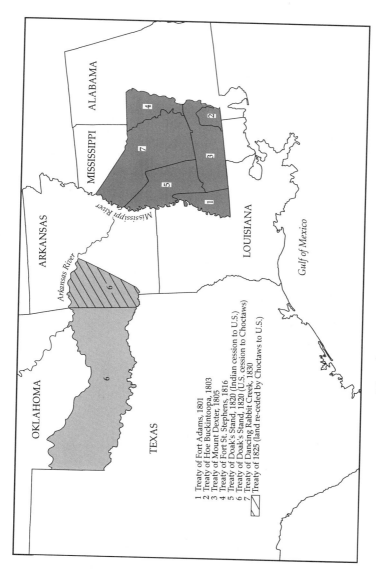

The Status of Choctaw Lands by 1830

1 Treaty of Fort Adams, 1801
2 Treaty of Hoe Buckintoopa, 1803
3 Treaty of Mount Dexter, 1805
4 Treaty of Fort St. Stephens, 1816
5 Treaty of Doak's Stand, 1820 (Indian cession to U.S.)
6 Treaty of Doak's Stand, 1820 (U.S. cession to Choctaws)
7 Treaty of Dancing Rabbit Creek, 1830
  Treaty of 1825 (land re-ceded by Choctaws to U.S.)

the National Council to send a memorial to Congress opposing the treaty, but Folsom refused, saying that the missionaries should pray for themselves. It was fully apparent that the Christian party had only political interests at heart.[96]

Helpless before the force of the removal policy, Kingsbury and the American Board had to decide whether to continue their work among the Choctaws. The missions represented a significant financial investment of $147,920.71, of which $61,981.79 had come from the board through charitable donations, $64,000 from the Choctaw annuities, $1,697.26 from donations from individuals in the Choctaw Nation, and $20,241.66 from the Treasury of the United States.[97]

What was the overall impact of the American Board schools and missions on the Choctaws in terms of civilization? Numerically, it was small. The missionaries established schools at thirteen locations between 1819 and 1830 and served approximately 1,500 students, although the actual number of children educated in mission schools is difficult to estimate because it is hard to tell how many of the count for each year were returning students.[98] Most of the schools were associated with mixed-blood communities—Bethel with Louis Leflore, Emmaus with Joel Nail, and Juzan's school with Charles Juzan, a Frenchman.[99] The schools at Aikhunnah (1825), Yoknokchaya (1829), and Hikashubaha (1830) served Choctaw communities that had coalesced around David Folsom and his brother Robert because of their political influence. These three schools began relatively late in the American Board's efforts. The number of students was small (36 at Aikhunnah and 25 to 30 at Yoknokchaya).[100]

The effort to establish schools at the homes of Choctaw leaders largely failed. The school at Mushulatubbee's was problematic from the start and lasted only two years before it closed. The school near Robert Cole's home merited recognition only in the amount of money that had been spent before Wiley Ledbetter took it over.

At the time of the Treaty of Dancing Rabbit Creek, American Board missionaries taught 528 students (including 67 new students), 278 at the schools associated with mission stations and 250 in Choctaw villages. Of that number, 299 were full-blood Choctaws, and 229 were mixed-bloods.[101] An average of 176 children boarded with the mission families, and the average school attendance was 194.[102] These numbers constitute a small percentage of the population, which numbered 19,554. Of that number, the potential school-age population was comprised of 6,375 children under the age of ten. An additional 4,630 males over sixteen were counted, although the missionaries generally discouraged parents from sending older boys, who caused the greatest problems and complained the most. The ages of the students in the American Board schools were not generally recorded; however, the 528 people educated by the board, whether children and possibly adults who lived in the villages or younger children who generally boarded with mission families and attended schools at mission stations, comprised only 2.7 percent of the population. Even counting only children under ten and males over sixteen as potential students, the school population in 1830 rises to only 4.8 percent of the total.[103]

For their educational achievements, 36 were learning to spell in English, 36 were studying English reading lessons, 63 read in the English Bible, 58 read in the English reader, and 57 could write in English; 126 read in Choctaw and English, 90 spelled and 245 read in Choctaw only, 12 composed in Choctaw only, 11 wrote in both Choctaw and English, and 137 could write in Choctaw. In addition, 51 studied arithmetic, 64 geography, and 22 grammar.[104]

The number of conversions reported by the board was also miniscule compared with the total population. Churches were organized at Elliot, Mayhew, Bethel, Goshen, and Emmaus. At Mayhew and its outlying stations, Aikhunnah and Yoknokchaya, 284 persons had become members—8 blacks, 20 whites, and 256 Choctaws. About 50 had become members at Goshen and about 40 at Emmaus. About 360 people belonged to the churches in the Choctaw Nation by the end of 1831, and the number of children baptized was 244.[105]

The missionaries of the American Board entered the Choctaw Nation with faith in the power of preaching and education to change the life-styles and lead to the salvation of the natives, but they made several crucial mistakes. They allied themselves primarily with the mixed-blood element of the tribe and alienated at least two full-blood leaders who might have given them access to native communities. They subjected their pupils to physical discipline and labor that was at odds with traditional Choctaw child-rearing practices, thus stirring up discontent. Their schools became pawns in power struggles among political leaders. They remained underfunded by the government and the board, and they never could muster the personnel and financial support to extend their efforts throughout the Choctaw Nation. The board's assessment of its schools west of the Mississippi after 1830 could well be applied to those in Mississippi between 1818 and 1830. The conflicting motives of Indians, missionaries, and enlightened Americans were clear. "The object, with most of the parents, was not the spiritual good of their children, but their social and material elevation; . . . the patrons of the missions were impatient for the civilization of the Indians, and would not give them time."[106]

He Who Puts Out and Kills, Chief of the Tribe, painted by George Catlin, 1834. Courtesy of National Museum of American Art, Smithsonian Institution, gift of Mrs. Joseph Harrison, Jr.

Allen Wright, American Board missionary and translator, photographed by W. H. Jackson, 1869–1873. Photograph courtesy of National Museum of the American Indian, Smithsonian Institution.

Man in costume with ball sticks. Photograph courtesy of National Museum of the American Indian, Smithsonian Institution.

Portrait of Cyrus Byington. Courtesy of the Houghton Library, Harvard University.

Israel Folsom was educated at the American Board for Foreign Missions school in Cornwall, Connecticut, early nineteenth century. Photographed by W. H. Jackson, 1869–1873. Photograph courtesy of National Museum of the American Indian, Smithsonian Institution.

Peter Folsom, Baptist missionary to the Choctaws in the late nineteenth century. Photograph courtesy of National Museum of the
American Indian, Smithsonian Institution.

Drinks the Juice of the Stone, in Ball-Player's Dress, by George Catlin, 1834. Courtesy of National Museum of American Art, Smithsonian Institution, gift of Mrs. Joseph Harrison, Jr.

Mississippi Choctaw group, photographed by M. R. Harrington, 1908. Photograph courtesy of National Museum of the American Indian, Smithsonian Institution.

Pushmataha, Chief of the Southern District. He is buried in the Congressional Cemetery in Washington, D.C. Photograph courtesy of National Museum of the American Indian, Smithsonian Institution.

Fat Tom in costume with ball sticks, in Mississippi, photographed by M. R. Harrington in 1908. Photograph courtesy of National Museum of the American Indian, Smithsonian Institution.

Gilbert Webster Thompson, his wife, Isabelle, and his family, including the author's grandmother, Susie, on their farm in Oklahoma about 1900. This Choctaw family was representative of life in Indian Territory at the turn of the century. Photograph courtesy of author's family.

William Ketcham and Victor Locke, a Choctaw chief, at Antlers, Indian Territory. Photograph courtesy of Marquette University Memorial Library, Milwaukee, Wisconsin.

8 / The Choctaws in Mississippi after 1830

At the end of the year 1831 I was on the left bank of the Mississippi, at the place the Europeans call Memphis. While I was there a numerous band of Choctaws . . . arrived; these savages were leaving their country and seeking to pass over to the right bank of the Mississippi, where they hoped to find an asylum promised to them by the American government. It was then the depths of winter, and that year the cold was exceptionally severe; the snow was hard on the ground, and huge masses of ice drifted on the river. The Indians brought their families with them; there were among them the wounded, the sick, newborn babies, and old men on the point of death. They had neither tents nor wagons, but only some provisions and weapons. I saw them embark to cross the great river, and the sight will never fade from my memory. Neither sob nor complaint rose from that silent assembly. Their afflictions were of long standing, and they felt them to be irremediable. All the Indians had already got into the boat that was to carry them across; their dogs were still on the bank; as soon as the animals finally realized that they were being left behind forever, they all together raised a terrible howl and plunged into the icy waters of the Mississippi to swim after their masters.

—Alexis de Toqueville

ALEXIS DE TOQUEVILLE, ELOQUENT OBSERVER OF AMERICAN LIFE, watched a group of Choctaws on their way west and captured their despair.[1] Beginning in the fall of 1830, parties of Choctaws began the trek to the western lands. A small group set out almost immediately after the signing of the treaty, and larger groups went during the winter of 1831–32 and during 1833.[2] The missionaries of the American Board had to decide whether they would follow. To go was to risk the continuing opposition from Mushulatubbee and the lack of interest of large numbers of the Choctaws. Not to go was to give up whatever gains they had made.

Mushulatubbee objected strongly to the possibility that the missionaries would move west. He complained to Andrew Jackson that although the Choctaws had paid "those Yankee Missionarys" for twelve years, the tribe had "never Recd. a Scholar out of their Schools that was able to keep a grog shop Book."[3] Cyrus Kingsbury was thoroughly disillusioned by the events of treaty making and political turmoil in the Choctaw Nation and advised "very serious deliberation" about whether the board had any duty to establish boarding schools in the new country. If the board would release him from the mission, Kingsbury was more than willing not "to have any thing more to do with Choctaw funds."[4]

The board was not the only arbiter. Kingsbury and his fellow missionaries received a request from fifteen of their converts asking that they accompany the Choctaws west of the Mississippi, and the treaty had promised support for schools and teachers' salaries in the new territory.[5] Although the board could no longer count on appropriations from the Civilization Fund, which Jackson proposed to turn over to Isaac McCoy, the Baptist missionary who had worked so diligently to move Indians to the West, it decided to go with the tribe. Kingsbury, Loring Williams and his wife, and Cyrus Byington, who had pioneered the Choctaw territory for Christianity, went west, where they would establish churches and boarding schools. In Mississippi, Bethany and Elliot stood vacant by 1832. Byington, Kingsbury, and the missionaries at Mayhew did not leave the Choctaw country until 1835, but their labors effectively ended in 1831.[6]

Civilization in the West was as problematic for the missionaries as it had been in Mississippi. The nation, approximately 15,000 people, was confronted with the prospect of rebuilding its villages and its government. It fostered the board's schools and missions as instruments of adaptation in a new environment, although the number of converts remained a small percentage of the nation. In 1848, the American Board had six churches with a membership of 536 (including 64 slaves). By 1855 there were eleven churches with a membership of 1,094, and in 1860, the board reported twelve Choctaw churches with a membership of 1,362.[7]

Other missionary groups had entered the field, and there were several large boarding schools. Spencer Academy was supervised by the Presbyterian Church, Armstrong Academy by the Baptist Church, and Fort Coffee and New Hope by the Methodist Episcopal Church South. The Choctaw Nation had assumed control of the school system in 1842, and missions operated schools on a contract basis with tribal support, although the imposition of a secular government caused some problems. The Choctaw Academy in Kentucky was largely repudiated by the National Council after 1842 and finally closed entirely in 1845.[8]

The issue of slavery, only temporarily resolved in Mississippi, continued in Indian Territory. Choctaw slaveholders took their slaves west, and the institution became firmly entrenched. Missionaries could not risk undermining their own efforts by promoting abolition, and Kingsbury continued to justify the use of slaves as a matter of Christian concern for their souls and the role that their labor played in sustaining the missions. Even Byington, who had been so outspoken against the institution in 1824, wrote to the American Board in 1848 that slaves had greater protection as property than they would as free men under U.S. laws.[9]

The American Board came under increasing attack from antislavery forces. It took a stronger antislavery position in 1845 and pressured the missionaries to adopt a policy forbidding admission of slaveholders to their churches. They refused, and in 1859 the board finally withdrew its support from the Choctaw missions. Kingsbury appealed to the Presbyterian Church, which took the missionaries under its auspices, thus ending the long association of the American Board and the Choctaws.[10]

By 1860, Kingsbury could declare that the Choctaws were to all intents and purposes a Christian nation. Council meetings were opened and closed with prayer. Business was not conducted on the Sabbath. And no one who denied the existence of God or "a future state of rewards and punishments" could testify in court or hold civil office.[11] Although the Choctaws kept the tripartite division of the nation in three districts—Mushulatubbee's, Puckshanubbee's, and Pushmataha's, each with its district chief—they finally adopted the convention of a principal chief in 1857.[12]

A school system, a formal government and laws, and a declaration of Christianity did not, however, mean that the Choctaws were becoming like other Americans. Their legislature promulgated and printed laws in the Choctaw language, and missionaries taught the gospel in Choctaw.[13] And although it appeared that "antiquated rites and pagan ceremonies were almost wholly discarded," some still practiced "ancient Indian funeral rites." Ball games remained important social activities. Choctaw culture was changing, but not disappearing.[14]

They had also, perhaps, learned a lesson from the experience of their forebears in Mississippi, where white men had married into the tribe. They "amalgamated less" with whites, discouraged strangers, and retained a strongly matrilineal sense of property and descent that excluded non-Indians. If a Choctaw woman married a man from outside the tribe, her children took her name, and the husband did not automatically become a tribal member.[15]

Although political autonomy allowed the western Choctaws to adapt American culture and Christian religion on their own terms, and the white man's institutions took on a peculiarly Choctaw character, the Choctaws in Mississippi lost all political autonomy. Without federal recognition or a land base, they underwent a process of enclavement, surrounded by black and white communities but part of neither. With the departure of some fifteen thousand of their kinsmen from the state, they largely disappeared from the history of the Southeast, but they persisted culturally in their enclaves, as did the descendents of tribal cultures that seemed to be extinct—Lumbees, Powhatans, and Creeks and Cherokees who, like the Mississipi Choctaws, had consciously decided to remain on their lands.[16]

Despite the loss of land and status entailed by the Treaty of Dancing Rabbit Creek, the Choctaws marked themselves by language, kinship groups, ball games, and a strong sense of community. Throughout the nineteenth century, traditional funeral "cries" took place around graves marked with poles, followed by feasting and all-night dancing.[17]

The position of Indians in the South was anomalous—they were neither white nor black. The Choctaws were free, but for the most part, despite guarantees of land in the Treaty of Dancing Rabbit Creek, they were not landowners. They remained separate from southern society, constrained subjectively by their fear and suspicion of white men, a legacy of numerous instances of forced dispossession, and objectively by the racial stratification of the antebellum South. They moved within a very fluid economic situation of subsistence farming, hunting, wage labor, and minor entrepreneurship, selling baskets and firewood in Mobile and New Orleans. Men hunted, sometimes ranging west of the Mississippi in the fall after the harvest season. Family groups sometimes traveled to pick cotton in the Delta region and along the Yazoo River.[18]

An important marker of their identity was the persistence of a strongly matrilineal kinship system. Women often farmed, and men often followed their wives to live near their mothers-in-law. Kinship terminology in Mississippi retained its matrilineal pattern, whereas that in Indian Territory shifted significantly to a male-oriented one during the 1840s and 1850s. In Mississippi, in the 1840s, terminology named the father's sisters and their female offspring as aunts, or "aunts in a row," thus emphasizing female descent. In Indian Territory, by 1859, the father's sisters' sons were classified together as fathers, an emphasis on male lineage that cut across and diminished female matrilineages.[19]

Reciprocity and sharing were strong cultural values. Family groups who were related by blood or marriage would grow crops on individual plots of land but "under a common fence" and would cook together and share food from a common cooking pot, a sign of family identity.[20]

The federal policy of civilization through Christianity had had little impact on the lives of the Choctaws who remained in

Mississippi. Toblachubbee had a Methodist congregation on the Leaf River in the old Southern District in 1830. After the Treaty of Dancing Rabbit Creek, he explained to his followers how to follow the requirements of the Treaty of Dancing Rabbit Creek if they wished to stay on their lands.[21]

Choctaw communities in 1830 clustered around local head-men—Samuel Cobb, James Pickens, Captain Weshockshehoca, Anthony Turnbull, and Captain Chishehoma.[22] By midcentury, driven off their lands by white men, they were identified for government purposes as clans associated with specific locations—the Six Towns, Chunky, Moglusha, Yoknuckne, Pearl River, Bok Chito, Halunlawi, Sukanache, Tallachulak, Tushkalameta, and Lobutcha.[23] They were not recognized by the white population of Mississippi in any way except for their racial, linguistic, and cultural differences. They had none of the formal structures identifiable by white society in the South after 1830. There were no missionaries to advocate for them. They had no political base from which to make demands on missionaries, the federal government, or the state of Mississippi.

What the Choctaws did have in the eyes of white society after 1831 were their claims to land under the fourteenth article of the Treaty of Dancing Rabbit Creek. The fourteenth article embodied both the humanitarian aim of federal policy to make Indians into settled farmers who would assimilate peacefully with their white neighbors and the political ploy of Greenwood Leflore to make the Treaty of Dancing Rabbit Creek palatable to the Choctaw leadership.

Although the fourteenth article may have played some role in persuading the Choctaws at Dancing Rabbit Creek to sign the treaty, it failed almost completely to ensure that those who remained in Mississippi would have their land. The land hunger of settlers and speculators was far greater than the power of treaty rights, and the Mississippi Choctaws were dispossessed of the very lands that were supposed to integrate them into the citizenry of the state and into white society. What Christianity did not accomplish, land did not accomplish either.

The fourteenth article guaranteed that individual Choctaws who remained in Mississippi could take allotments of 640 acres for themselves, 320 acres for each child under ten, and 160 acres for dependent children over the age of ten. Claimants had a period of six months from the ratification of the treaty to register their intent to stay in Mississippi, and they had to reside on the land for five years before they could receive clear title to it.[24]

These rights of individual Choctaws vastly complicated the status of public lands in the state during a period when the "Cotton Kingdom" was rapidly emerging and with it a clamor for land. The previous Choctaw cessions of rich Delta lands had spurred the development of the cotton industry, and by 1830, there were reports that planters were clearing as much as fifty thousand dollars from a single cotton crop. With such incentives, people were eager to exploit the vast tracts of the Choctaw and Chickasaw cessions of that year.[25]

Government bureaucracy also complicated the matter of claims. Although William Ward was charged with the task of registering the intent of individual Choctaws to take claims, he was not notified of his responsibility until May 1831, three months after the ratification of the treaty. That left only half of the six-month time period for him to receive registrations, and when he completed his list of fourteenth article claims to Congress on August 24, 1831, it included only sixty-nine heads of families. Of those, fifteen were white men with Choctaw wives, and an additional twenty-four were mixed-bloods.[26] George Martin, the agent assigned by the government to survey Choctaw claims, did not have access to the plat maps of the Choctaw cession and in many cases had to rely on verbal descriptions of land.[27]

Nevertheless, Jacksonian politics and the growth of the Cotton Kingdom created intense pressure for sale of the Choctaw cession. Potential buyers were poised to enter newly opened lands, and the revenue from land sales was a major source of income for the financially hard-pressed U.S. government. Jackson rushed to fulfill the promise of Indian removal by pressuring the Surveyor General's Office to complete the survey and put the land on the market. Public sales of the Choctaw cession began at the land offices at Columbus and Mt. Salus in October 1833, despite the fact that Martin had not completed his survey of the Choctaw claims. As a result, many plots were sold out from under their claimants, and many Choctaws were unable to remain on their lands for the five years stipulated by the treaty because white buyers drove them off the land.[28] Many Choctaws were dispossessed even before the sales. Ishtahona was told by a white man about a year after the treaty to leave her land because he wanted to plant corn, even though she had asked one of her neighbors to register her claim for her.[29]

As Martin traveled through the Choctaw cession marking claims, he also heard many complaints that Ward had turned away claimants or that he had not recorded them on his register. Martin suspected that white speculators were encouraging Indians to put forth fraudulent claims, but Secretary of War Lewis Cass instructed him to post notices and hold formal hearings, and by December 1835 he presented a list of over fifteen hundred names of family heads and their dependents who had not been registered.[30]

Choctaws thus joined both settlers and speculators in the contest for land. Whites who had already settled in the Choctaw cession, hoping to take advantage of preemption laws, petitioned Congress to dismiss most of the Choctaw claims as the work of "vicious speculators" who had fraudulently acquired millions of acres for themselves, whereas another petition defended white men representing Indian claimants as "of irreproachable character" and called for a hearing on the matter. A group of Choctaw headmen petitioned Congress to set aside sufficient land in the ceded territory to satisfy all Choctaw claims.[31]

In 1837, the economy of Mississippi collapsed, together with that of the United States. Speculation in public lands was a major factor. Just as the Choctaw land sales had propelled Mississippi's flush times of 1833–37, now the burden of debt assumed by land speculators and the inflation of prices, together with the specie circular of 1837, led to financial catastrophe.[32]

In the face of charges and countercharges concerning speculation, and under the cloud that competing claims cast on land titles, Congress appointed a commission to investigate Choctaw claims and recommend action on individual cases.[33] Publius Pray, P. D. Vroom, former governor of New Jersey, and James R. Murray were appointed as commissioners, and they began hearings on November 22, 1837.[34]

The story that emerged was one of bureaucratic incompetence and the often violent dispossession of Choctaws from their homes. Ward was accused of drunkenness, sloppy record keeping (one witness reported his using a page from the register book to strop his razor), and statements and acts deliberately discouraging individual Choctaws from registering claims. Ward was blatantly insensitive to Choctaw customs. He refused to recognize the role of headmen in representing their communities. He would not accept the bundles of sticks that headmen presented to count the members of extended family groups but insisted that each individual come forward to register in person.

Ward, overwhelmed by claimants and his own inability to deal with them, did indeed discourage people from registering for land. He admitted to his actions but defended himself by saying that he suspected that many claims were inspired by land speculators. He felt that he was carrying out federal policy by discouraging claimants because there were far too many of them. In a perverse way, Ward seems to have taken it upon himself personally to enforce the government's removal policy.[35]

While controversy over their claims raged around them, the Choctaws went on with their lives—hunting, farming, and earning wages by picking cotton. They ignored the agents' calls to councils to discuss removal.[36] Jeremiah Burns, a missionary from the American Baptist Home Mission Society of Mississippi, preached to them in 1834, but since the government was actively encouraging them to move west, he accomplished little.[37]

The commission hearings dragged on through May 1838 and

became for a while a part of Choctaw social life. The government provided rations for those who came to testify, and encampments of Indians lingered at commission hearings for extended periods. The commissioners, to their dismay, found themselves inadvertently encouraging such traditional activities as ball games.[38]

The outcome of the hearings was not promising. The commissioners had 1,349 names on their list of claimants, but they acted on only 261 cases, of which they approved 165, rejected 65, recommended 26 for favorable action by Congress, and left 5 unfinished.[39] The large number of outstanding claims led to the appointment of a second commission in 1842. Its members were J. F. H. Claiborne, congressman from Mississippi, and Ralph Graves. Its docket ultimately contained 1,093 claims, virtually all of which were represented by white lawyers and most of which proved to be covered by contingency contracts promising their representatives half the land obtained if the claim was successful. Revelation of this fact led Claiborne to resign from the commission and call for the dismissal of all Choctaw claims.[40]

Claiborne's outrage against Indian heathenism covered his own interests. He himself was a speculator in Choctaw lands, a silent partner with William Gwin. His public attacks were an attempt to discredit some of the more highly visible speculators in the state, one of whom, Sargent Prentiss, challenged him to a duel. Claiborne agreed to meet him with "tea and pistols." Claiborne was sincere in his desire to clear the state of Indians so that their lands would be available for sale.[41]

Despite Claiborne's vehemence, the commission continued. George Gaines and Samuel Rush were appointed, and the process dragged on until 1846, when John Tyler signed the final documents that gave land patents to 143 Choctaw claimants.[42]

By that time, most of the Choctaws had been driven off their land, and some had congregated around the homes of a few successful claimants (James Shote and Samuel Cobb were two). Out of the 1,349 persons listed by the original Choctaw commission in 1837, only 143 had received patents for land, and most of those had assigned their claims to white buyers. The land of the rest of the Choctaws whose claims had been validated, 1,009 individuals, had been sold before the final decision was made. For them, Congress provided scrip that would allow them to claim any available public land in Mississippi, Alabama, or Louisiana. Claimants could receive only half of it in Mississippi, however. They could collect the other half only by going to Indian Territory in the West.[43] Congress obviously did not intend for them to settle east of the Mississippi River. Scrip was only a payment, not an assurance of a home in Mississippi. Its use was an obvious ploy to get the Choctaws out of Mississippi.

The strategy often worked. The federal government continued an active effort to move the Choctaws, and throughout the 1840s, groups of them continued to go west. John McRae, the Choctaw agent, had five thousand dollars available to provide subsistence payments for those who would move. The enticement of scrip for land drew some, and others went to join relatives.[44] By 1855, the Choctaw population had dropped from approximately 5,000 to 2,261. The largest single group was the Six Towns "clan," centered primarily in St. Tammany Parish, New Orleans, and Mobile and in Jasper and Newton counties in Mississippi. The next largest was the Bok Chito, in Neshoba County. Other clan groups were scattered throughout Neshoba, Leake, Kemper, and Scott counties.[45]

Not all the Choctaws who left their homes went west. The Bay Indians, about two hundred people, had fled en masse from their homes on Sukanachee Creek in Kemper County on hearing a rumor that white men were going to drive them from their lands. They settled in Hancock County on the Gulf Coast, where they built homes on the land of a Catholic man, whose daughter set up a school for them.[46]

The Six Towns group in Louisiana came under the influence of the Catholic Church through the efforts of a French Catholic priest, Father Adrien Rouquette. He settled and worked among the Choctaw colony on Bayou Lacombe in St. Tammany Parish in Louisiana during the 1850s and 1860s, where he learned and preached in the Choctaw language. He maintained his post during the turmoil of the Civil War and carried supplies through Union lines to his parishioners, whose villages suffered attacks by both Union and Confederate forces.[47]

Rouquette and his church provided a central point for Choctaw community life in Louisiana. There, in a life-style very similar to that in Mississippi, the Indians lived off the land. They still gathered wild plants and hunted, but they also raised cabbages and tended flocks of chickens and hogs that ran on open land. They earned cash by selling baskets and filé powder and working for wages in timber camps. During the winter they lived on high ground in the swamps, and in the summer they migrated to areas on the edges of the swamps where they could plant their crops.[48]

In the turmoil of the Civil War, as the Confederacy grew increasingly desperate for manpower, the Choctaws gained the attention of the Confederate army. The Mississippi militia had not chosen to use them, but General Arnold Spann organized the First Battalion of Choctaw Indians for the Confederacy in February 1863.[49] A number of Choctaw soldiers were captured in a battle near Ponchatoula, Louisiana, and several died in a Union prison hospital in New York.[50]

In an act of heroism in Mississippi, Choctaws rescued twenty-three survivors and retrieved ninety bodies when a Confederate troop train plunged off a bridge and fell into the Chunky River.[51] After this brief moment of glory in the history of the state, the Choctaws again faded from view. They disappeared into the landscape of Reconstruction, and their social and economic status became very similar to that of the newly freed slaves. Many of those who had been living on the remains of the Choctaw cession became sharecroppers for white farmers. They continued in the wage labor market as seasonal farmhands and peddlers in and around Mobile and New Orleans. They were largely ignored by the white population of the state. There were no large or obvious Choctaw communities to attract attention, and the turmoil of Reconstruction focused attention on the black population of Mississippi. The Choctaws lived in relative obscurity, a fact that perhaps explains why they maintained their identity and their language. They had long since ceased to be subject to pressures to become civilized. In the segregated South, they could not, in fact, expect to assimilate into white society. They could simply be Choctaws.[52]

At this point they might have disappeared entirely from the history books, if not for the fact that their legal identity was still connected, albeit tenuously, to the Choctaw Nation in Indian Territory. As individuals, they went about their daily business as sharecroppers or farm workers. But the language of the fourteenth article of the Treaty of Dancing Rabbit Creek stipulated that the Choctaws who remained in Mississippi to take land would "not lose the privilege of a Choctaw citizen" so long as they did not receive money from annuities under earlier treaties. The question was, did that right of Choctaw citizenship extend to claims on the property of the Choctaw Nation in Indian Territory?[53]

The troublesome fourteenth article would not go away. It had created a morass of conflicting and unsettled claims, and the nineteenth article proved equally troublesome in that many Choctaws had not been paid for land and property that they had left behind when they went west. The Choctaw Nation in the West was increasingly anxious to settle the claims.

Although the fourteenth article had ostensibly guaranteed the rights of Choctaw individuals, the vast majority of the Choctaws who remained in Mississippi had lost their land soon after the treaty. The fate of their claims ultimately rested not with them as individuals but with the Choctaw Nation. The legislation awarding scrip to Mississippi Choctaw claimants in 1842 was part of an attempt to make a final settlement of various tribal claims under the Treaty of Dancing Rabbit Creek.[54] On June 16, 1845, the Board of Choctaw Commissioners recommended approval of patents of land for 143 Choctaws and scrip for 1,023 Choctaws and their 2,683 children.[55] Half the scrip was placed in the hands of the Choctaw agent in the West, a measure that both gave the Mississippi Choctaws an incentive to move and gave the Choctaw Nation the standing, through its agent, to control the fate of its eastern kinsmen.

The legal fate of the Choctaws was now in the hands of the U.S. government. The recommendations of the Choctaw commission led to a final government effort to move the remaining Choctaws from Mississippi. Congress "funded" the scrip in 1845, providing a cash payment of $1.25 an acre for outstanding scrip and placing the amount in a fund to bear 5 percent interest and to be paid out to claimants on an annual basis.[56] Contracts were awarded beginning in 1844 to move the remaining Choctaws out of Mississippi, and throughout the late 1840s, groups moved west periodically.[57] By November 30, 1846, the commissioner of Indian affairs could report that 1,786 Choctaws had emigrated.[58]

Under the pressure of government policy, and in many cases influenced by the fact that they had relatives in the West, Choctaws moved west. Their migration had significant consequences both east and west. For the Choctaw Nation, the influx represented a minor population boom that put some strain on resources.[59] The gain of about seventeen hundred people to a population that numbered approximately twenty thousand was about 8.5 percent. But much more significant was the loss to the Mississippi Choctaws of about one-third of their population. The roll of Douglas Cooper, U.S. agent in Indian Territory, is mute evidence of the effects of government policy and the stubbornness of the Choctaws who remained in Mississippi and Louisiana.

The Choctaw Nation moved ahead with its attempts to settle its claims. It agreed in 1852 to accept $872,000 in final settlement of fourteenth article claims, thus preempting the rights of individual Mississippi Choctaws to their entitlements.[60] The push toward a final and complete settlement of the nation's claims came in 1853, when the Choctaw Nation appointed Peter Pitchlynn, Dickson W. Lewis, Israel Folsom, and Samuel Garland as a commission to settle all claims.[61]

The move led to the last census of the Mississippi Choctaws reported by Cooper in 1855, a census on which the final distribution of their remaining claims could be made.[62] The final dispossession of the Mississippi Choctaws created a kind of domino effect for the Choctaw Nation in the West. It was suddenly faced with a population boom and with the growing discontent of the Chickasaws, who had been pushed into the Choctaw lands by their own removal treaty in 1832 and a subsequent treaty in 1837 that gave them a share of the Choctaw lands in the West.[63] In 1855 the Choctaws and Chickasaws, plagued by "unhappy and injurious dissensions and controversies" concerning the government of their territory, signed a treaty with the United States that finally settled the poorly defined western boundary of the Choctaw lands, created a district that the Choctaws would lease to the United States for the settlement of the Wichitas and other western tribes, and established a specific territory for the Chickasaws.[64]

The uneasy relationship between the Choctaws and the Chickasaws had to be resolved. That relationship could be traced far back into oral traditions and historical circumstance, but by the 1850s it devolved into a written agreement defining territory. The 1855 treaty settled certain political disputes. It also settled, in a very legal way, the long-standing dispute between Choctaws and Chickasaws and mediated their separation.

The Choctaws, having established their own rights, now had a discrete territory as their private property, and property rights both east and west had to be settled. The delegation that had gone to Washington in 1853 continued its work. The prime mover of the effort was Peter Pitchlynn. Although he was never an elected chief in the Choctaw Nation, he was a major spokesman. He was committed to asserting the nation's legal rights, even though there is ample evidence to suggest that he also stood to profit financially by arrangements with the lawyers who represented the nation's claims.[65] The Choctaws pressed their rights in the Treaty of 1855. Their claims to the net proceeds of the sale of Choctaw lands under the Treaty of Dancing Rabbit Creek were submitted to the U.S. Senate for final resolution.[66] Those rights drew the Mississippi Choctaws into a complicated tangle of legal disputes and conflicting claims between the federal government and the Choctaw Nation.

After the Treaty of 1855 was ratified, the Senate, on March 9, 1859, acted to allow the Choctaws the proceeds of the sale of lands in the Choctaw cession, deducting the costs of the survey and sale of the land. The secretary of the interior reported proceeds of $8,078,614.80 from the sale, $5,097,367.50 paid to the nation and a balance due, the net proceeds, of $2,981,247.30. Encompassed in those amounts were the cash payments that were supposed to be made to Mississippi Choctaw claimants. With that act, the government finally settled whatever legal rights to land the Mississippi Choctaws might have had under the Treaty of Dancing Rabbit Creek. In 1861, Congress appropriated $500,000 toward the payment, $250,000 in cash and $250,000 in bonds to be issued by the government.[67]

The outbreak of the Civil War abruptly ended bond payments, especially since the Choctaw Nation allied itself with the Confederacy. In Mississippi and Indian Territory, Choctaws fought on the losing side. After the war, the tribes in Indian Territory, by now designated as the Five Civilized Tribes because of their adoption of white systems of government, were forced, as part of a defeated Confederacy, to sign treaties with the federal government giving up significant amounts of their land. The Choctaws signed a treaty in 1866. The treaty not only ceded land but also, following precedents long established in federal policy, called for the allotment of the remainder among individual tribal members.[68]

The Choctaws voted down the treaty's allotment provision in a tribal election. Although they had adopted the conventions of constitutional government, ownership of slaves, and Christianity in significant measure, they were not ready to embrace the idea of private ownership of land. They might be civilized by many measures of white society, but their identity was still based in tribal land, which belonged to them all.

The Treaty of 1866 nevertheless opened a Pandora's box of questions about tribal identity and legal rights to land. If lands were to be divided among tribal members, who were those members? The fact that tribal lands might be divided brought forth a number of people who claimed to be Choctaws. Most had little or no idea about Choctaw customs or culture. Since the tribe had abrogated the provision of the 1866 treaty that called for individual allotments, the question of the rights of the Mississippi Choctaws to a share of the tribal estate was moot. It was not, however, resolved, and it would rise again.

The Choctaws in the East and the Choctaws in the West, despite their common origin, were undergoing quite different forms of change. The Mississippi Choctaws maintained their language and identity in an environment that insisted on racial separation. The Choctaw Nation confronted the issue of its slave population and accepted the status of its freedmen as members of the tribe.

And the still unresolved rights of the Choctaw Nation under the Treaty of Dancing Rabbit Creek also surfaced. If the Choctaws were a defeated people, and were forced to cede land in Indian Territory, they should receive just compensation for the lands that they had given up to the United States in 1830. Peter Pitchlynn was bent on obtaining for the nation the proceeds of the sale of Choctaw land under the Treaty of Dancing Rabbit Creek. In 1872, he published a document setting forth the claims of the nation.[69] When the situation had not been resolved by 1884, Pitchlynn and the Choctaw Nation filed a major claim with the U.S. Court of Claims. The *Net Proceeds* case thus kept the claims of the Mississippi Choctaws alive in the politics of the Choctaw Nation in the West.

9 / Religion, Racism, and Identity

THE CHOCTAWS IN MISSISSIPPI AFTER 1830 LARGELY DISAPPEARED from the history of the South. They no longer had land or legal identity, but they still had their language and customs. Men still hunted, and women farmed, even as they adapted to a new southern economy as wage workers. Even without a land base, they held on to the language, customs, and race that set them apart in antebellum Mississippi society. They were largely ignored by white society, and they deliberately distanced themselves from it. Given that the removal of their kinsmen had been so involved with Christianity, it is ironic that they finally achieved legal recognition of their status as Indians largely through the agency of Christian missions.

Missionary churches were an important part of Mississippi history after 1830 for both white and Indian populations. The rapid influx of whites into the state and especially into the Choctaw cession created a new frontier, with the attendant evils of alcohol, gambling, and dancing. Vices of "intemperance, skepticism, profaneness, gambling"—decried by American Board missionaries among the Choctaws before removal—were now widespread in the state.[1]

In the religious fervor of post–Civil War Mississippi, where blacks and whites sought the solace of religion in troubled times, Christianity came to play an important social role for the general population. The Baptist Church was the most rapidly growing denomination in the state, but Mississippi Baptists were not interested in the Choctaws. The major initiative came from the national level when the American Baptist Home Mission Society authorized Sidney Dyer to work with them in the 1840s. Given that the federal government was still trying to move all the Choctaws from Mississippi, Dyer had little success.[2]

Indian "heathenness" remained of particular concern to missionaries. By 1846 the Baptist Church was actively missionizing among blacks and Indians and in New Orleans, which was evidently considered a hotbed of depravity. The Mt. Pisgah Baptist Association estimated that about three thousand Choctaws were "perishing for the bread of life" and resolved to seek an "energetic" missionary to serve them.[3]

A Methodist minister asked: "Is it possible that we have and will continue here in the very heart of Christendom and the blazing light of the nineteenth century, to allow them to sit in darkness and heathen superstition and die without God and without hope in the world or the world to come? *No! no! no!* Let us say with our dollars, No! and may God help us to say, No!"[4] Cornelius Janssens, Catholic bishop of Natchez, sympathized with the poverty of Choctaw sharecropper families even as he condemned their "moral failing" of polygamy, and he recruited a priest to establish a mission in 1883.[5]

By the late nineteenth century, Christianity was no longer an agent of civilization and assimilation but was, in the racially segregated South, an agent of separation. The secretary of the Methodist Mission Conference declared, "It is not in the best interests of either the Choctaws or the whites for the Choctaws to attend white churches." And among the virtues the Methodist missionary ascribed to them—"truthful," "honest," and "virtuous"—was the fact that they refused to "amalgamate with other races," something in which they appeared to be "superior to our own race."[6]

For their part, the Choctaws were justifiably suspicious of the motives of whites, and they deliberately chose to remain apart from white society. The Bok Chitos were particular fearful.

Long time ago, after the wars with Indians, they commenced having preaching for Indians, and got them together, and then carried them off West and deceived us. Several years after this they had preaching again, and got Indians together, and told us there was money for us off yonder somewhere, and if we would sign a paper or go, we could get it. Some went; some sign paper; some get money, and some get none. We were deceived the second time, and we will never forget it.[7]

The Bok Chitos were one of the most coherent and thus most culturally intact of the Choctaw communities in Mississippi. As a result, the Methodist missionary William Carmack considered them "the worst Indians . . . least disposed to be religious" and thus most in need of the gospel. Henry Halbert, teacher of the Catholic school at Holy Rosary mission, called them "the most barbarous and non-progressive of all our Choctaws" after hearing about their fear of losing their land.[8]

Although the Bok Chitos resisted, other groups found that Christian churches could be hospitable places. Mission churches provided what had been lost as a result of the historic effort to civilize the Choctaws—land. The Catholic mission in the community of Tucker acquired 1,480 acres. By 1888, several Indian families occupied fifteen-acre tracts around Holy Rosary mission, and by 1899, when a new group of Carmelites arrived, the church owned 2,000 acres.[9]

Carmack, in an attempt to protect the Choctaws from exploitation by "avaricious white men," bought 160 acres of land, where they could be settled and "taught agricultural and mechanical arts." Although he appealed for money for more land, donations from readers of the *Christian Advocate* were not forthcoming, and even his 160 acres were never fully paid for.[10]

The national Baptist Missionary Board, concerned about the influence of white immorality on Indians, went so far as to urge the federal government to create a territory for them in Mississippi, similar to Indian Territory in the West. The idea died quietly. The Baptist Church never acquired land, but a Baptist missionary preached to Choctaws regularly during the 1870s.[11]

Despite their sense of separateness, some Choctaws began to attend services at a Baptist church organized by blacks near Carthage around 1878. Cultural differences blurred when Choctaws and blacks worked together as wage laborers or tenant farmers.[12] The Mt. Pisgah Association initiated a request for a missionary to the Choctaws that led to the Choctaw and Chickasaw Baptist Convention in Oklahoma. Peter Folsom, whose ancestors Israel and McKee had preached to the Choctaws in the 1820s, answered the call. Although his own health was failing, he went to Mississippi, and in the eight months before he died, he baptized forty persons, established a church, and ordained one Choctaw minister.[13]

Baptist missions proliferated rapidly. They flourished because they were highly democratic and virtually autonomous. They were run by Choctaw preachers, and they provided a place where people could come together. By 1888 the Choctaw Baptist Association had been formed, and church membership stood at about three hundred. By 1891, there were nine churches and eight ordained ministers, and by 1894 the Baptists "claimed that some 400 in the country had been immersed."[14]

In 1891, the Methodist Church in Mississippi had appointed Carmack as missionary to the Choctaws. Beginning in Union, he quickly established an extensive circuit, preaching to the Tonuby Indians four miles north of Union, to the Philips Indians (whose children attended the Catholic school), to the Tallachulok Indians in Kemper County, and to the Beesher Indians west of Philadelphia, where except for Carmack's sermon, the service was conducted in Choctaw, and about fifteen people attended. Ben Williamson, the Baptist preacher, joined him in preaching at one Indian community that he visited.[15]

By the end of 1892, Carmack's efforts had netted nineteen Choctaw Methodist converts, and two brush arbors that had served as churches were becoming frame buildings, one in Winston County and one in Kemper County. Two Sunday schools had been organized. By 1896, the mission comprised one "nice small church," two mission stations, two Sunday schools, and two "literary schools." About 50 people had joined the church, and one native preacher, Jim Johnston, had been licensed. In Cushtusa (about fourteen miles west of Tallachulok) were 6 members and 12 "earnest seekers." Between 1898 and 1903, the church at Tallachulok grew from 56 members to 157, and Methodists were preaching at twelve locations.[16]

By the early 1890s, the old Choctaw homeland in central Mississippi was dotted with churches and schools. They flourished because they used the Choctaw language and because they provided a new voice for Choctaw leadership. Language was both a barrier against ready communication with the English-speaking population of Mississippi and a protection against intrusions. In an ironic turn of history, the efforts of Cyrus Byington and Alfred Wright in the 1820s to convert Choctaws produced materials that would serve to promote Choctaw communities and cultural identity in the 1880s and 1890s.

In the Catholic mission school at Tucker, Henry Halbert, one of the few white men in Mississippi who mastered the Choctaw language, taught in Choctaw and English. He observed, "Our Mississippi Choctaws are strongly attached to their native tongue." Many children knew no English at all. In the two Baptist churches in Newton County, young men learned to read and write Choctaw from a literate Choctaw missionary. At the Methodist school at Tallachulok in 1893, fourteen students learned to read, spell, write their letters and numbers, and recite the Lord's Prayer. Carmack, the teacher, could not speak Choctaw, but he used Choctaw testaments, bibles, hymnbooks, and spellers in his services and schools.[17]

Choctaw hymns and traditional songs were an important part of church services. In the Baptist churches, songs of rejoicing, of victory, of sadness, of the deaths of children, and of the loss of a blanket or a gun mingled with Christian hymns sung in Choctaw.[18]

Choctaws could come together at churches in ways that were familiar. One Baptist service was attended by about one hundred Choctaws, who arrived with their children and dogs; some were on foot, some on horseback, and some in ox-drawn wagons, "much as they had done when they attended the ballplays, and at their cries, to mourn for their dead." Men and women sat on opposite sides of the church. Men passed around their pipes of tobacco. After services they adjourned to the church lawn for a meal, during which men and women either ate separately or sat on opposite sides of the long tables that were set up. Sometimes ball games would be held in the afternoon.[19]

Catholic Choctaws had to be enticed by gifts of tobacco, cloth, beads, and medals to come to mass on Sundays, but they did arrive in wagons on Saturday evenings, went to confession, and then camped in the woods near the church. After mass, they visited, danced, and played ball in the churchyard.[20]

Churches provided places for social gathering, but they also created social disruption. Choctaw Baptists began to frown on the traditional activities of dances and stickball games (with the drinking and gambling that usually accompanied them). Non-Indian Baptists certainly did. The Mt. Pisgah Association complained that Choctaws still played ball and held cries for the dead, and it resolved that the Patrons' Union not encourage ball playing because the practice was "demoralizing" to the work of trying to "Christianize them with the Gospel." Halbert considered ball games, "to put it mildly . . . the most demoralizing institution in Mississippi."[21]

Ball games were evidence of demoralization among the Choctaws, accompanied as they often were with drinking and gambling, but they also reflected the demoralization of missionaries who could not wipe out persistent cultural practices. Church grounds now became venues for ball games, and despite their ostensible adherence to Christianity, the Choctaws were not giving up their customs. Church became a new place where they could congregate and socialize in ways that reinforced their cultural identity.

Churches also provided a new visibility for families that had been largely invisible. Native missionaries began to play leadership roles in newly revitalized communities. Ben Williamson (Nenacintucubby) preached in the Baptist church near Conehatta. Isham (Johnston) preached in the church near Talasha Creek in Newton County. Carmack trained Simpson Tubby as a preacher and enlisted a number of Choctaw men as "exhorters" in the service of his schools. The Catholic priests at Tucker mission trained native catechists.[22]

When the Methodist mission and the small number of Choctaw converts were threatened by demands from the creditor of

Carmack's 160-acre land purchase, Simpson Tubby wrote a frantic plea to the editor of the *Christian Advocate.* "Don't, don't let us poor red men and our families go." He said, "I am doing all I can to get my people to quit dancing and playing ball, and quit everything that is unclean; and my wife has quit using snuff."[23] His plea, and Mrs. Tubby's gesture, saved the mission. The Methodists considered the Choctaws "ignorant and superstitious." They still drank whiskey and gambled, but they were "not idolaters," and their moral standard was "high." They could not be abandoned.[24]

The Catholic mission, Holy Rosary, did not reach out as did the Baptists and Methodists. With the luxury of land, it could keep its parishioners nearby, although Choctaws within about a ten-mile radius would come to mass.[25] The Catholic influence on the Choctaws may have been more limited than that of Methodists and Baptists during the late nineteenth century, but its ultimate importance came in a different arena in the early twentieth century.

Mission churches fostered schools, which provided additional institutional recognition for Choctaw communities. Although there was little to inspire Choctaw faith in education, Father Bartholomew J. Bekkers established a school at the Catholic mission at Tucker. The Choctaws would rather play ball than go to school, and the opening was delayed a day by a ball game, but instruction began on September 18, 1884, with Henry S. Halbert as teacher. The school survived the uncertain start, and in 1887, three Sisters of Mercy arrived to take charge.[26]

The state of Mississippi had already passed a law in 1882 providing for the establishment of separate Indian schools. In 1888, faced with the prospect of numbers of Choctaw children to educate, the state called on the Bureau of Indian Affairs for financial support and appointed Halbert as state superintendent for Indian education.[27] His reports between 1891 and 1899 covered seven public and private Indian schools. Teachers praised the intelligence and quickness of their pupils.[28]

By 1897 Carmack was teaching two "literary schools," in

which eighteen children were learning a curriculum that included U.S. history, grammar, physiology, history of Mississippi,
civil government, and geography.[29]

Education did nothing to relieve the grinding poverty of
Choctaw life. School attendance at Tucker suffered because parents often needed their children as farm or wage laborers. The
children who did attend the schools often did not have adequate
clothing.[30] A Choctaw sharecropper in 1902 might expect to
support himself, his wife, and four children on $150 a year, with
luck.[31] Schools were important not because they provided economic opportunities but because they gave Choctaw families the
formal structures of community life that made them more visible
in white society. The churches provided gathering places, and
the Methodist and Catholic missions provided land for some
families and with it some security from the vagaries of wage
labor.

Missions in Mississippi once again brought to the fore the
irony of the way in which Choctaws appropriated Christian efforts for their own ends. The Choctaws took advantage of mission churches as places where they could congregate and be
themselves, where they could speak their own language and visit
and play stickball, with its attendant gambling and drinking.
Missionaries wanted to change the Choctaws' life-style, to get
them to give up stickball and polygamy and gambling and drinking, but the missionaries' efforts to bring about that change were
often futile. Although the Choctaws had no political autonomy
or governmental recognition, they remained stubbornly, culturally Choctaws. That fact carried with it certain legal ramifica-
tions in a political arena far removed from their communities in
Mississippi.

10 / The Second Removal

LAND RIGHTS AND REMOVAL BECAME ISSUES ONCE AGAIN FOR THE Choctaws in the early twentieth century. The failure of education and Christianity to amalgamate American Indians into American society as self-sufficient landowners led Congress to a new policy of assimilation in 1887. Embodied in the General Allotment Act of 1887, it called for the allotment of tribal lands to individuals and conferred the benefits of American citizenship on Indians who voluntarily took up residence "separate and apart from any tribe of Indians therein" and "adopted the habits of civilized life." Theodore Roosevelt described the act as "a mighty pulverizing engine to break up the tribal mass." If religion and education had failed, private property would now be the means of melding Indians into the agrarian ideal of American society.[1]

Landownership as forced assimilation was certainly nothing new in the Choctaw experience. The fourteenth article of the Treaty of Dancing Rabbit Creek of 1830 embodied it as government policy. In 1887, the Choctaws and a number of other tribes in Indian Territory were specifically exempted from the provisions of the General Allotment Act, but in 1898 the Curtis Act extended the allotment process to the Five Civilized Tribes—the Cherokees, Choctaws, Chickasaws, Creeks, and Seminoles—and provided for the dissolution of their tribal governments. The Dawes Commission, established in 1893 to negotiate an allotment agreement with the Five Civilized Tribes, continued the work it had begun in 1896 of enrolling tribal members to establish their rights to individual allotments and to oversee the distribution of the tribal estate.[2] Its work was to have a significant impact on the Choctaw communities in Mississippi, and the Bok Chitos' suspicion of government actions turned out to be justified for the Mississippi Choctaws as a whole. The process of allotment and the resulting Mississippi Choctaw claims created a situation remarkably similar to that in the 1830s.

The General Allotment Act, in its stress on individual citizenship, ultimately placed a premium on tribal citizenship. To gain land, one must prove oneself a member of the tribe. The Five Civilized Tribes had clung tenaciously to their powers to confer citizenship, and the Choctaws established a Citizenship Comittee and passed a series of regulations concerning citizenship claims.[3] The Curtis Act drew specific attention to the Mississippi Choctaws by asking whether they were entitled to allotments in Indian Territory. The fourteenth article of the Treaty of Dancing Rabbit Creek had provided, "Persons who claim under this article shall not lose the privilege of a Choctaw citizen."[4] Choctaw citizens could now take land in the Indian Territory, which raised the possibility that the Mississippi Choctaws could be encouraged to leave the state en masse to take up residence in Indian Territory.

Some Choctaws had already gone west. There were still close ties and a good deal of visiting between the Mississippi Choctaws and their friends and relatives in Indian Territory. The Council of the Choctaw Nation had gone so far as to ask Congress for money to move the Mississippi Choctaws to Indian Territory in order to secure their rights, and it readily passed acts granting citizenship to those who came. When Congress would not give money, the council appropriated $1,792.50 in 1891 to pay the expenses of removal and appointed two commissioners to go to Mississippi to escort the Choctaws to Indian Territory.[5] In 1898 the Dawes Commission decided that the Mississippi Choctaws were eligible for individual claims as Choctaw citizens, if they moved to Indian Territory and remained three years.[6]

The prospect of Mississippi Choctaw land claims in Indian Territory attracted the attention of two lawyers, Robert Owen and Charles F. Winton. In a situation reminiscent of the 1830s, Winton went to Mississippi and made contracts with approximately one thousand Choctaws to represent their claims in exchange for 50 percent of whatever they were awarded. Owen,

Winton, and John Sharp Williams, representative from Mississippi, then memorialized Congress on the claims and rights of the Mississippi Choctaws to share in the tribal estate.[7]

Catholic Choctaws signed contracts with the firm of Winton and Owen for the move. Methodist and Baptist preachers were accused of "selling their Indians" to cattlemen in Texas who had interests in Indian Territory and who would represent Indian claims in exchange for part of the land.[8] Eugene Easton, an agent in Antlers, Indian Territory, tried to make a contract with the government to provide subsistence for their move. Such contracts generally benefited the contractors because they provided a flat fee for each person who moved, and a clever man could make a good profit per head by cutting his expenses.[9]

A lawyer representing Logan, Demond and Hartig, a firm in Philadelphia, Mississippi, approached Father Augustine Breek at Holy Rosary mission seeking to represent Indian claims "in exchange for a percentage of the rents and profits of their lands." When Breek questioned his motives, he appealed to officials of the Board of Catholic Indian Missions in Washington to advise the Choctaws to move to Indian Territory.[10]

The Catholic Church became a player in the fate of the Choctaws at this point. William Ketcham, director of the board, had a special interest in the Choctaws because he had worked with them as a priest in Indian Territory and he knew that the land of the Oklahoma Choctaws was "not nearly as good as in Mississippi, the Indians not so industrious, and the climate colder and more disagreeable."[11] But the Bureau of Catholic Indian Missions was cutting back on its support to the diocese of Natchez, and Holy Rosary mission was feeling the financial strain. In the face of financial exigency, removal was an expedient for the church. Breek would support the move, provided that the Mississippi Choctaws could be settled together near the Catholic mission at Antlers, and Winton, eager to collect his fees for representing Choctaw claims, promised Breek that he would support this plan.[12]

Ketcham's reasons to support a move were based on more

than finances. He recognized the strength of the Choctaws' desire to remain separate, and he feared that their communities were so small that they would have to intermarry among themselves to maintain their distinctiveness. Although he thought that they might be able to intermarry with "a good class of whites," he felt that it would be better if they could go to Indian Territory as a group, with the priests and teachers to accompany them and teach them the Baltimore Catechism, which Ketcham was translating into Choctaw.[13]

The Carmelite fathers at Tucker did not feel that removal posed a strong threat to any religious gains among the Choctaws because they had gained little. Although each family could have "from 15 to 40 acres of land free," the Choctaws preferred to work for wages rather than take land. They were also hard to teach, and Father Breek requested a catechism printed in both Choctaw and English so that he could teach religion more easily.[14]

The Dawes Commission had enrolled 2,240 Choctaws in Mississippi during the winter of 1899 (1,961 full-bloods and 279 half-bloods). The roll was incomplete, however, because the more remote communities were not included, and the weather was too cold for Choctaws to reach the commission. The Bok Chitos, suspicious as always, simply refused to appear, and an estimated 500 Choctaws were not enrolled.[15]

Removal became a reality for the Choctaws in 1903. Congress appropriated money and appointed an agent in Mississippi to encourage them to move and assist them in the process. On August 12, 1903, a train at Meridian bound for Indian Territory carried 259 Choctaws. In October, 26 additional full-bloods were removed to Fort Towson, Indian Territory.[16] Altogether, 420 Choctaws were moved by the government, and others were moved by land speculators who packed them into boxcars and delivered them to Ardmore, Indian Territory, where they were housed in barracks and allotted lands in the area. Congress thwarted the ends of attorneys and land speculators by amending the Dawes Act so that Choctaw claimants could not alienate their land.[17]

This second removal had a devastating effect on the Missis-sippi Choctaws. Of the approximately 2,700 reported by the Dawes Commission early in 1903, about 10 percent left the state by October of that year.[18] By 1910, the federal census showed a Mississippi Choctaw population of 1,253, a figure that, if correct, represented at least a 50 percent loss of population between 1903 and 1910. A population decline of that magnitude would have had a significant influence on community stability.[19] It certainly disrupted the schools and missions that had become part of Choctaw life. The state of Mississippi had abandoned the Indian schools in 1900, in expectation of removal, and Henry Halbert filed his last report in the biennial school report of the state in 1899–1900.

The Methodist missions, struggling constantly against financial adversity, had dwindled away even before the removal, leaving Simpson Tubby to lament that where the Methodists "once had large congregations of happy Choctaws on their way to heaven," there were "now, oh! so few," and those were "greatly discouraged and confused." Only one Methodist church remained in 1903. By October of that year all the Catholic Choctaws at Tucker, with one exception, had gone to Indian Territory, where the majority were settled near Antlers with their Carmelite priests.[20] Baptist churches had been moving rather steadily to the West even before the 1903 removal, and the last two missionaries left for Indian Territory during the year.[21]

But not all the Choctaws went west. The persistent core of Choctaw language and customs remained with those who stayed in Mississippi, and although the population declined precipi-tously, communities regrouped with remarkable resilience. Their life-style was like that of many of their black and white neigh-bors. They were absorbed into the economic system of the state primarily as wage laborers and secondarily as sharecroppers. Women, though, often supplemented family income by making and selling baskets, something that they had done in the 1830s and that they still do in the 1990s. They maintained their sep-aration from both whites and blacks.[22]

And they still had their churches. The survival of these efforts bespeaks both the tenacity of missionaries and the importance they had for isolated communities. The Methodist Indian church at Tallachulok persisted on its 160 acres.[23] A Catholic Choctaw community remained in Scott County, surviving despite its distance from Tucker (thirty-six miles) and its isolation due to impassable roads for a good part of the year. Clustered around the home of John Wesley, one of a very few Choctaws who owned his own land, were 174 people. The mission house and equipment remained at Tucker, and by 1907 there were 52 Catholic Choctaws there.[24]

The Tucker mission still had over one thousand acres of land, and the Bureau of Catholic Indian Missions and the diocese of Natchez maintained two churches, served by Father Joseph Enis, a layperson, and two Indian catechists. In 1907, three adults and twelve children were baptized, 115 communions were held, one couple was married, eight people were buried, and seventeen people were under instruction for first communion. There were also two schools, one at Tucker with an enrollment of sixteen and one at Forest in Scott County with fifteen children.[25] Although the school at Forest burned sometime around 1912, and Father Enis left the mission in 1913, Father P. J. Ahern was appointed as missionary in 1916 and established new outposts in the town of Stratton and at Wesley Johnson's home in Leake County. He also established a school at Stratton, where thirty-five students studied spelling, reading, writing, and arithmetic in English, and a day school at Tucker in 1917 to provide religious instruction and the rudiments of formal education and industrial training.[26]

A number of Choctaw Baptists remained, and by 1904 the Reverend Scott York was recruited to work with the several hundred who still lived in the southeastern part of the state, particularly around Conehatta, Tuscalameta, and Trapp, although York preached at some twenty places to reach the scattered Choctaw population.[27]

Choctaw was still the primary language of the communities

and the churches. One of Ahern's first requests was for cate-chisms in the Choctaw language, and Ketcham assured him that the Choctaws would "only fully appreciate their religion" when it was "imparted to them in their own language." At Tucker a choir was formed and on the second and fourth Sundays the mass, benediction, all announcements, and prayers after mass were in Choctaw. The *Indian Sentinal* proclaimed, "The key to an Indian's heart is his mother tongue." The newspaper main-tained that Indians underwent a change after hearing confes-sions in their own language for the first time. Ahern indeed concluded, "Everything done for them in their own tongue has a telling and lasting effect."[28]

Despite such protestations about the religious effects of spo-ken Choctaw, it was obvious that cultural change was not as noticeable. Ahern complained: "It is always patience with the Indians. Today you think you have them all and under your control. Tomorrow they will attend a dance and forget to go to Mass."[29]

Choctaw Baptist missionaries were so active that by 1911, the Choctaws formed their own group at Hopewell, and in the pe-riod between 1911 and 1918, the Choctaw Baptist Association comprised seven churches. In 1914 church membership stood at 144, and there were six Sunday schools with 85 pupils.[30]

The Choctaws might well have remained a largely invisible population had it not been for the potential value of land, to which many probably did not even realize that they had claim. Many others were willing to come forward, however. The attrac-tion of land or its money equivalent drew claimants from as far away as Shreveport and Mobile. Between December 1900 and October 1901, agents of the Dawes Commission heard testimony involving approximately 1,800 claims for enrollment as Missis-sippi Choctaws. The commission doubted the heritage of many of the claimants, many of whom were represented by white law-yers who had contracted for part of the proceeds if the claimants were successful in securing land.[31]

By the time the citizenship rolls in Indian Territory closed in

1907, the Dawes Commission had examined applications from 24,634 alleged Mississippi Choctaws but approved only 1,640 for enrollment. Disappointed applicants appealed to the commissioner to the Five Civilized Tribes, the Department of the Interior, federal courts, and Congress.[32] Their stakes were high. By 1912 the Choctaws and Chickasaws in Oklahoma had a cash balance of over $5.5 million dollars, deferred income of $5.25 million from land sales, and $19.5 million worth of property. As long as this estate remained undivided, there would be claimants, legitimate or not, to a share. The only way to legitimate a claim was to be placed on the Dawes rolls.[33]

Once again the infamous fourteenth article reared up to complicate the lives of the Mississippi Choctaws. An organization called the Society of the Mississippi Choctaw was organized in Gulfport, Mississippi, in 1912, its stated purpose being to secure the rights to which the Choctaws were "justly entitled in law and in equity under the 14th Article of the Treaty of 1830." One of the society's most active members, Luke Ward Conerly, was later revealed as an agent of the St. Louis law firm of Crews and Cantwell, which sought to profit by representing Choctaw claims.[34]

H. J. Cantwell persuaded Representative Pat Harrison of Mississippi to investigate the situation, and under pressure also from constituents, Harrison introduced a bill in Congress on February 1, 1912, calling for the reopening of the Dawes rolls and invoking the Fourteenth Amendment rights of Mississippi Choctaws. Cantwell's interest in the matter was protected by a provision that Choctaw claimants could be represented by lawyers of their choosing. If the claimants could not be given land, they were to receive cash payments.[35]

The situation was remarkably similar to that in the 1830s. And once more, a congressional investigation produced evidence of large-scale speculation and legal chicanery. James McLaughlin, a federal inspector, discovered a number of law firms, including Crews and Cantwell, advertising their services to prospective Choctaw claimants in several states for contingency fees of 20 to 35 percent of successful claims. The Texas-Oklahoma Investment Co. had been chartered in Arizona in 1911 to capitalize on the effort to consolidate profits from Choctaw claims.[36]

In the meantime, the Choctaw Nation in Oklahoma was adamantly opposed to reopening the rolls. The commission had done its work, and any Mississippi Choctaws with legitimate claims could simply be added by administrative fiat. The nation certainly had a stake in limiting the number of tribal members among whom its funds would ultimately be distributed.

In Mississippi, some leaders of the Choctaw communities were inspired by J. E. Arnold, an erstwhile Baptist minister, to put forth their own proposal for a financial settlement of their claims. At a public meeting at the Carthage courthouse on April 21, 1913, a group of Choctaws initiated a memorial to Congress asking that each Mississippi Choctaw receive "an equal part in money" to the value of land given to those who removed to Oklahoma. The final draft of the memorial was approved at a second meeting, which Arnold opened with a prayer and which Simpson Tubby chaired, in the parlors of the Great Southern Hotel of Meridian on May 10, 1913. It called for cash payments to Mississippi Choctaw claimants, an agent to oversee the money appropriated to individuals, money to purchase lands and other necessities, a school at Carthage, and attorney's fees for those who had prosecuted their claims.[37]

Arnold claimed that he had represented the Mississippi Choctaws for a number of years and had moved several hundred of them to Oklahoma, where he had secured rights for them.[38] He also claimed to be part Choctaw, but Ketcham knew that the Oklahoma Choctaws did not recognize him. Ketcham had come to regret his own support of the 1903 removal because he saw that land claims cases generated sizable lawyers' fees, and he suspected Arnold of seeking to profit from this latest situation. Patrick Hurley, attorney for the tribe in the Choctaw Nation, bluntly characterized Arnold's efforts as "simply in the interest of graft."[39]

If Arnold stood to profit personally from his efforts to organize the Choctaws, he also brought forth a newly visible leadership among them. The meeting in Meridian resulted in the formation of an organization of full-blood Choctaws, the Mississippi, Alabama, and Louisiana Choctaw Council. Its leadership was composed of the Christian element of the Choctaw communities in Mississippi. Wesley Johnson of Leake County was chief. Peter Ben was elected assistant chief. William Morris was secretary. Simpson Tubby, long affiliated with the Methodist Church, was assistant secretary and treasurer.[40]

Their memorial did not sway Congress, but Mississippi politics kept the issue alive. Pat Harrison, undaunted by the initial failure of his bill to reopen the Dawes rolls, reintroduced the measure in succeeding sessions through 1915, and with the assistance of John Sharp Williams and James Kimble Vardeman, senators from Mississippi, he succeeded in blocking per capita payments of one hundred dollars to Oklahoma Choctaws unless the Mississippi Choctaws were included. There were two factors at work. Harrison feared that per capita payments would deplete the Choctaw estate to the point that there would be nothing left for the Mississippi group. Vardeman and Williams saw that their state would benefit by the influx of money that a payment to the Mississippi Choctaws would bring.[41] Harrison's efforts to hold the Choctaw and Chickasaw per capita payment hostage to the cause of Mississippi Choctaw claimants ultimately failed in 1917, but they focused congressional attention for long enough to inspire action. Congress appropriated one thousand dollars in 1916 for an investigation into the situation.[42]

This investigation revealed the social isolation and economic poverty of the Mississippi Choctaws and the failure of the promises that individual citizenship and landownership had held out in 1830. Indian children were not allowed to attend white schools, and their own beliefs kept them from attending schools for black children. Neshoba and Leake counties funded Indian schools, but in Leake County, only 45 of 95 Indian children of school age were enrolled, and in Neshoba County, only 40 of the 254 children were enrolled. The schools were "of the most elementary character" and in session only four or five months a year. Forty-one Choctaws owned land, but most of the farms were eighty acres or less, heavily mortgaged, and "of the most inferior quality." A severe storm in 1915 had destroyed much of the corn and cotton crops. The major source of income was wage labor, usually picking cotton or cutting cordwood. The Choctaws owned virtually nothing and were practically destitute, living in decrepit shacks and often on the verge of starvation.[43]

A congressional commission headed by Vardeman heard testimony from Choctaws around the town of Union in 1917. They learned that cornbread was the primary staple of the Choctaw diet and that fishing in the Pearl River had replaced deer hunting. Tuberculosis was prevalent, and people lived in poorly ventilated shacks. Men worked splitting rails or at public jobs, and some women were laundresses. Some could read Choctaw, and Olmun Cumby said that he could write it, although he had never been to school. Scott York, a Baptist preacher, conducted a Sunday school. But despite the long influence of Christian churches and schools in Choctaw life, Simpson Tubby reported, "All the older people as a rule believe in the old way of worshiping."[44]

The Reeves report of 1916 and the Vardeman commission in 1917 gave Ketcham an opportunity to advocate for the Mississippi Choctaws and the Catholic missions. As a member of the Board of Indian Commissioners in Washington, he had worked to reverse the anti-Catholic bias in the federal administration of Indian education. Ketcham's command of their language earned the trust of the Mississippi Choctaws and allowed him to understand their concerns. He toured the Choctaw communities in Mississippi in October 1917 to see conditions for himself.[45]

He attended a meeting organized by two Choctaw catechists which began with speeches to "root out all feuds and misunderstandings" before dinner so that all could enjoy the meal "in perfect amity and peace." At the dance held in the evening, it was announced that if anyone was drinking whiskey, the dance would be stopped. Two white bootleggers got on their horses and rode off. After dancing all night, the Choctaws asked Ketcham to say mass. Although what he saw was an overlay of Catholic ceremonialism on traditional Choctaw customs of speechmaking, feasting, and dancing, he returned from his trip "edified" by the behavior of the Choctaws. He proclaimed them "far more Christian than any of the white nations of the present day" and was committed to improving their conditions.[46]

The prospect of help for the Choctaws galvanized J. E. Arnold once more. He organized a Baptist church and school at Union in 1917, although it was not affiliated with the Choctaw Baptist Association. He placed himself squarely in competition with the Catholic Church for Choctaw converts, and he told the Choctaws that their children must attend the school before the government would give them land and horses. Arnold also represented himself as a government agent, although Ketcham assured them that he was not.[47]

The failure of Harrison's bills concerning the reopening of the Choctaw rolls had finally convinced Ketcham that the Mississippi Choctaws would never obtain any claims in the estate of the Oklahoma Choctaws. Unless they received aid directly from the government, "the present Indian population of Mississippi" would "perish for want." He appealed to Senators Vardeman and William Webb Venables of Mississippi for their support of an appropriation of $150,000 for Choctaw land and schools.[48] They saw the chance to gain the financial advantage for Mississippi that they had failed to achieve through Harrison's efforts. Although their proposal for $150,000 in the Indian Appropriation Bill of 1918 was initially rejected by the House, they kept it alive in the Senate, and after some delay, the bill passed with $75,000 for the Mississippi Choctaws.[49]

At long last, the Mississippi Choctaws' identity as an Indian tribe had been recognized by the federal government. Ketcham had not been able to lobby openly for the Choctaw appropriation because of his position with the church, but his covert influence, his contacts with congressmen, and his position as a member of the Board of Commissioners had all served to obtain the appropriation.[50]

In a final burst of interdenominational pique, J. E. Arnold and his wife charged that the money for the Mississippi Choctaws would be controlled by the Catholics, but they were not able to gain a hand in its distribution.[51]

The year 1918 was a momentous one for the Choctaws. They gained recognition, but they also confronted two major threats to the stability of their communities. The first was World War I and the draft, which called into question the patriotism of men, some of whose ancestors, most notably Pushmataha, had fought so valiantly in previous U.S. wars.[52] J. A. Charley said: "We Choctaws do not want to go to war. All we want is to stay here and learn how to pray and sing." Culberson Davis, a Choctaw convert, also wrote that the Choctaws did not want to go to war. "All we know how to do is work and play ball."[53]

The year also brought the great influenza epidemic of 1918–19. Many Choctaws suffered and died. A proposal to move all the Catholic Indians to Tucker failed because those at Union were reluctant to abandon the sizable graveyard of flu victims for fear the whites would plow it up.[54] Between 1910 and 1920, the Choctaw population declined from 1,253 to 1,105, a 12 percent decrease.[55]

Such a significant loss of life was a major blow to the Choctaw communities. But they survived, as they had survived previous attempts at removal and as they had survived the disruption caused by the loss of their lands. After the major effects of the epidemic passed, many of them slowly began to establish themselves as farmers on land purchased by the U.S. government.[56]

Ketcham's efforts had given the Mississippi Choctaws the stability of federal recognition and the money to support the schools that were to become the focal points for the future development of their communities. With the establishment of an agency, they began to receive services from the federal government, and a very small part of the land base that they had

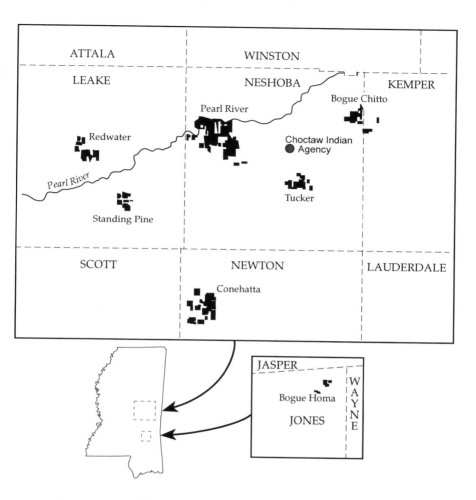

Contemporary Choctaw Reservation Communities in Mississippi

lost in the Treaty of Dancing Rabbit Creek was gradually restored. When Commissioner of Indian Affairs Cato Sells visited Tucker in November 1918, he watched the Choctaws play stickball, and he attended a religious service conducted in Choctaw. Churches were places where Choctaws could gather to sing and pray in their own language and maintain their sense of community.[57]

Epilogue

WRITING HISTORY CAN BE AN EXERCISE IN IRONY—AN EXAMINA-tion of what people intended by their actions and what actually happened. The history of relations between American Indians and missionaries is a particular source of irony because the relationship is based so strongly in cultural beliefs and so clearly shows the disjunction of intent and outcome.

The federal government intended Christian missionaries to be agents of cultural change and adaptation to American society so that the Choctaws would settle as farmers and cede their hunting lands. The Choctaws intended missionaries to be educators who would teach them the skills necessary to cope with an encroaching white society so that they could remain on their lands, and they appropriated the message of Christianity and mission schools to their own understandings and ends. The missionaries considered themselves agents of Christian civilization who would bring the Choctaws to salvation.

The seven Choctaw communities in Mississippi today deny that history can entirely eradicate a people's identity. Christian churches are important, and the Choctaws are a federally recognized reservation in large part because of the efforts of William Ketcham, a Catholic priest, but they maintain a strong sense of cultural identity. Choctaw is the working language of daily life and Choctaw and English are used together in tribal council meetings. Choctaw Fair in July brings people together from all parts of the reservation. The Catholic mass is said in Choctaw at least once a month at Holy Rosary Church in Tucker. Baptist and Methodist services include hymn singing in Choctaw. When Cyrus Byington and Alfred Wright learned Choctaw from David Folsom and taught students in their schools to read and write the language, and translated New Testament texts into Choctaw, they could not foresee the role that the language would play in drawing Choctaws in Mississippi to mission churches, which became community centers. Folsom only wanted the young men in his neighborhood to learn to read and write so that they could adopt written codes of laws, a sign of incipient civilization.

The Choctaws in Mississippi remain because the best intentions of Choctaws, federal agents, and missionaries were thwarted by conflicting aims. The government never funded the American Board missionaries to the extent needed to maintain the elaborate physical establishments they had built and within which they separated themselves from the Choctaws. The Choctaws devoted a substantial amount of their annuity income to education, but Mushulatubbee bemoaned the fact that the American Board schools had not produced a scholar able to keep a grog-shop book (evidence perhaps of his own predilection for drinking but also of his awareness of his indebtedness at the American trading factory and his hope that if Choctaws kept the book, things would be different).

The result of conflicting expectations was the failure of all. The Choctaws as a nation would not be civilized, government agents abandoned the policy, and Choctaw leaders were divided. The Treaty of Dancing Rabbit Creek was the great watershed for the Choctaw Nation. Those who went west took up farming and trade in a new country, and Christianity became part of their changing culture.

Choctaws could understand Christian beliefs in their own terms, but it was impossible to offset a complete replacement. Federal policy and missionary efforts were aimed at erasing Choctaw identity completely. Federal bureaucrats and missionaries did not see fully the complexities of cultural change and adaptation that were taking place within the nation, but the missionaries found themselves caught up in that change. Their own interests in their converts and their investments in the missions led them to resist the government's efforts to move the Choctaws, as Choctaw leaders (by the late 1820s, mainly mixed-bloods) were concerned with preserving their nation.

Those who remained in Mississippi lost the lands that they

claimed under the Treaty of Dancing Rabbit Creek. Families and clans disintegrated as spouses and clan members moved west. People were often driven off their lands by white men. But language, stickball games, cries for the dead, and traditional medicines kept them together. Fear of whites and the racism of the South isolated them, but cultural difference sustained them. Their difference was recognized by Christian missionaries, and by the 1870s and 1880s, missionary churches and schools became the new structures around which communities could gather. The missionaries brought hymns and gospels in the Choctaw language and ownership of land on which to settle landless families, making it easier to convert them and reinforce Christian virtues. Choctaws attended services, but as often as not they also played stickball and gambled on the church lawn afterward.

Churches gave Choctaws a place to meet and fostered a group of spokesmen who could present the Choctaw cause to the outside world. If Choctaw men could not be chiefs, they could be ministers and preachers. Traditional towns had disappeared, but churches and schools served as community centers, and preaching and singing were in Choctaw. In the end, the Mississippi Choctaws gained from the missionary efforts, not by adopting Christian beliefs and becoming civilized but by finding Christian churches as agents for their own survival.

Christianity is very much a part of contemporary Choctaw identity in Mississippi. The Choctaws are a vital people who have survived both despite and because of attempts to civilize them. They still say with pride, *Chahta Hapia Hoke* (We are Choctaw).

Notes

PREFACE

1. Swanton, *Source Material*, p. 2.

INTRODUCTION

1. Halbert, "Nanih Waiya," p. 230.

2. The total reservation population was 4,552. Fortune, *Mississippi Band*, pp. 3, 27.

3. See the works of McLoughlin, particularly *Cherokees and Missionaries* and *Champions of the Cherokees;* see also Milner, *With Good Intentions.*

4. Prucha, *Federal Indian Policy,* p. 21; Sheehan, *Seeds of Extinction,* pp. 262–69; Pearce, *Savagism and Civilization,* pp. 19–28; Jennings, *Invasion of America.*

5. Beaver, *Church, State, and the American Indian,* pp. 66–67.

6. Swanton, *Source Material,* p. 2; Debo, *Rise and Fall of the Choctaw Republic,* p. xii.

7. Bell, "Ethnicity and Social Change," p. 169. Cohen defines ethnicity in social terms as "a *series* of nesting dichotomizations of inclusiveness and exclusiveness" and points out that it is both subjective and objective (Cohen, "Ethnicity," p. 387). See Thompson, *Theories of Ethnicity,* for an overview of contemporary social sciences theories. See Tonkin, McDonald, Chapman, *History and Ethnicity,* for discussions of the problems of melding history and social sciences.

8. Linton, *Acculturation,* p. 463; Redfield, Linton, and Herskovits, "A Memorandum for the Study of Acculturation"; Berkhofer, *Salvation and the Savage.* White introduced the economic dependency model of culture change in *Roots of Dependency.* Cohen, "Ethnicity," p. 381.

9. See Galloway, "Confederacy." See also Peebles, "Paradise"; Smith, *Archaeology of Aboriginal Culture,* pp. 143–45.

CHAPTER 1

1. Lincecum, "Choctaw Traditions"; Cushman, *History of the Choctaw,* pp. 62–65.

2. Nanih Waiyah has never been excavated. Much of the mound and its outlying structure has been lost over time. When Gideon Lincecum saw it in 1843, the mound itself was two hundred yards in circumference at its base, eighty feet in height, with a flat surface fifty-two yards long by twenty-five yards wide on its top. It was surrounded by an embankment like a wall, in some places as high as eight feet, and from one and one-half to two miles in circumference. In 1899, H. S. Halbert described it in much its present form, "oblong in shape, . . . and about forty feet in height. Its base covers about an acre." Halbert

also described a "circular rampart, which is about a mile and a half in circumference." See Lincecum, "Choctaw Traditions"; Halbert, "Nanih Waiya." Virtually nothing remains today of the earthen rampart and the smaller mound that was assumed to be a burial mound. The original manuscript history written by Lincecum, "History of the Choctaws," from which the above is taken, is in the possession of the University of Texas Library. The manuscript, dictated to Lincecum by a Choctaw man in Texas in the 1830s, is a rich source of ethnographic information. See Campbell, "Choctaw Subsistence"; Campbell, "Medicinal Plants"; Campbell, "The Choctaw Afterworld."

3. Moundville was probably already in the first stage of collapse before European contact because its subsistence base could not sustain its large population. Its people dispersed into river valleys, absorbing other smaller groups along the way. They became part of the archaeologically identified Burial Urn Culture (so named from burials in pottery vessels), and the division of that culture on the Tombigbee watershed became the core group of the historic Choctaw tribe. Evidence from the McRae Mound in Clarke County places the protohistoric Choctaws in the Middle Woodland period. Galloway, "Confederacy;" Peebles, "Paradise," pp. 31–32; Blitz, *An Archaeological Study*, p. 22; Ford, "Analysis of Indian Village Site," pp. 44–45; Voss and Blitz, "Archaeological Investigations"; Watkins, "A Contribution"; Kinnaird and Kinnaird, "Choctaws West," p. 359.

4. Bartram, *Travels*, p. 329; Swanton, *Source Material*, p. 257; Adair, *History*, pp. 192, 305; Egmont journal in Candler, *Colonial Records* 5:57.

5. Lusser, "Journal"; "Journal of Regis du Roullet" in Rowland and Sanders, *Mississippi Provincial Archives* 1:84, 95, 151–53, 155–56; Swanton, *Source Material*, pp. 55–56; Swanton, "Early Account," p. 53. Swanton's Frenchman referred to the *ougoula tanama* in the west and the *taboka* in the south. Swanton argues that *tanama* comes from the Choctaw *tannap* ("people of the opposite side") and was used by each division to refer to the other.

6. Wright, "Choctaws," p. 215; Halbert, "Nanih Waiya," p. 230; Swanton, *Source Material*, p. 78; Romans, *Natural History*, p. 72; Edwards, "Choctaw Indians," p. 393.

7. Galloway, "Confederacy"; Halbert, "Nanih Waiya," p. 230; Cushman, *History of the Choctaw*, p. 150; Swanton, *Source Material*, pp. 76–77; Byington, *Dictionary*, p. 180.

8. Vega, *Florida*, p. 298; Smith, *Archaeology of Aboriginal Culture*, p. 143; Peebles, "Paradise," 30–34. For general discussions of the impact of disease on native communities, see Dobyns, *Their Number*; Ramenofsky, *Vectors of Death*, pp. 42–71; Thornton, *American Indian Holocaust*.

9. Where the Spanish were exactly is still a matter of conjecture. DePratter, Hudson, and Smith, "Hernando de Soto Expedition," pp. 108–26; Swanton, *Final Report*, pp. 216–17; Hudson, DePratter, and Smith, "Hernando de Soto's Expedition"; Hudson, Worth, and DePratter, "Refinements"; Bourne, 1:99

10. Reuben Gold Thwaites, *France in America*, p. 74; Galloway, "Henri de Tonti," pp. 149–50. See Woods, *French-Indian Relations*, for details of French diplomacy. See Crane, *Southern Frontier*, for an analysis of intercolonial politics and the role of Indians therein.

11. Hamilton, *Colonial Mobile*, pp. 188–204.

12. O'Neill, *Church and State*, pp. 5, 231.

13. Letter from Fr. De Poisson to Fr. ***, Oct. 3, 1727, in Thwaites, *Jesuit Relations*, 67:279.

14. Bordenave was the priest at Biloxi. Bekkers, "Catholic Church in Mississippi," p. 351. Shea, *Catholic Missions*, pp. 441–51; Rowland and Sanders, *Mississippi Provincial Archives* 2:571, 3:31; Delanglez, *French Jesuits*, pp. 76–91, 254; Thwaites, *Jesuit Relations* 69:75, 67:293; Beaudouin to Salmon, in Rowland and Sanders, *Mississippi Provincial Archives* 1:157. Beaudouin was ultimately relieved of his post because of his political activities during the events leading to the Choctaw Civil War. The mission church at Chickasawhay fell into ruin after the French Jesuits were expelled in 1764. Thwaites, *Jesuit Relations* 68:217, 70:219, 241; Axtell, *The European*, pp. 69–73; O'Neill, *Church and State*, p. 232.

15. Ru, *Journal*, p. 89. Ru accompanied Pierre Le Moyne, Sieur d'Iberville, in early explorations of the area around New Orleans. Beaudouin to Salmon, Chickasawhay, November 23, 1732, in Rowland and Sanders, *Mississippi Provincial Archives* 1:155. Using a formula of one adult male warrior to five household members, the Choctaws would have numbered anywhere from 7,330 to 25,000 people. See Wood, "Changing Population," pp. 69–93, for an assessment of colonial Choctaw demography. He cites a relatively stable population that fluctuated around the figure 15,000.

16. Beaudouin to Salmon, Chickasawhay, November 23, 1732, in Rowland and Sanders, *Mississippi Provincial Archives* 1:156.

17. *Ishtahullo* means "anything that excited surprise or suggested a hidden power," and *chito* means "large or great." Cushman, *History of the Choctaw*, p. 252; Wright, "Choctaws," pp. 180–81; Swanton, *Source Material*, p. 179.

18. Wright, "Choctaws," p. 196. Although Wright uses the term "he" in referring to the sun, the Choctaws did not specify gender in pronouns. See Byington, "Grammar," p. 355; Swanton, "An Early Account," p. 65; Cushman, *History of the Choctaw*, p. 225; Bossu, *Travels in the Interior*, pp. 166–67 (quotation); Bartram, *Travels*, pp. 328–29; Halbert, "Funeral Customs"; Romans, *Natural History*, pp. 71–72, 82; Halbert, "Nanih Waiya," p. 230; Swanton, *Source Material*, pp. 76–77.

19. Wright, "Choctaws," p. 182.

20. Journal of Elliot Mission, American Board of Commissioners for Foreign Missions, Papers, Series 18.3.4. (hereafter cited as ABCFM), vol. 1, folder 1, pp. 7–8; Cushman, *History of the Choctaw*, p. 93.

21. Romans, *Natural History*, pp. 75–78.

22. Journal of Elliot Mission, ABCFM, vol. 1, folder 1, p. 8; Cushman, *History of the Choctaw*, p. 362; Swanton, *Source Material*, p. 198; Romans, *Natural History*, pp. 75–78; Father le Petite to D'Avaugour, July 12, 1730, in Thwaites, *Jesuit Relations* 68:151.

23. See Hudson, *The Southeastern Indians*, pp. 365–75, for a discussion of the significance of the Green Corn Ceremony. Choctaws whom Wright questioned about their religion maintained that although they had heard of the dance among the Creeks, it was not one of their customs. According to the Lincecum manuscript, it was held on a yearly basis. Wright, "Choctaws"; Lincecum,

"History of the Choctaws"; Bartram, *Travels*, p. 321 (quotation). The Creek term for the dance was *bosquito*, Anglicized to "busk." The contemporary Choctaw Fair, an important annual event in Choctaw communities, is considered by tribal members to be a modern form of the Green Corn Dance. It is possible that Wright's informants were responding to his status as a Christian missionary and were aware of the bias of the missionaries against traditional Indian religious practices.

24. Cushman, *History of the Choctaw*, p. 185; Swanton, *Source Material*, pp. 141–43, 224–25; Catlin, *Letters and Notes* 1:123; Bartram, *Travels*, pp. 323–24; Cushman, *History of the Choctaw*, pp. 184–85; Edwards, "Choctaw Indians," pp. 412–13; Swanton, "An Early Account," p. 68.

25. Cushman, *History of the Choctaw*, p. 250.

26. Galloway, "Choctaw Factionalism and Civil War," pp. 292–94; Swanton, *Source Material*, p. 78.

27. Swanton, "An Early Account," p. 22.

28. Bartram, *Travels*, p. 329; Swanton, "An Early Account," pp. 65–66.

29. Swanton, "An Early Account," p. 54.

30. Galloway, "Choctaw Factionalism and Civil War, 1746–1750," pp. 126–27; Galloway, "The Chief," pp. 254–78.

31. Cushman, *History of the Choctaw*, p. 75; Cotterill, *Southern Indians*, pp. 18, 23–24; Rowland and Sanders, *Mississippi Provincial Archives* 2:39, 410–11, 3:355. Usner surveys the complex interactions of trade and culture in the colonial Southeast in *Indians, Settlers, and Slaves*.

32. Halbert, "Nanih Waiya," p. 230; Claiborne, *Mississippi*, pp. 483–84.

33. Bienville to Maurepas, New Orleans, June 26, 1736; Beaudouin to Salmon; Perier to Regis du Roullet, New Orleans, August 21, 1729, all in Rowland and Sanders, *Mississippi Provincial Archives* 1:296–97, 160–63, 17–19; Adair, *History*, pp. 306–7.

34. Adair, *History*, p. 355: Galloway, "Choctaw Factionalism and Civil War, 1746–1750," pp. 289–327; Vaudreuil to Rouille, March 3, 1749, in Rowland and Sanders, *Mississippi Provincial Archives*, ed. Galloway, 2:15–25; Paape, "Choctaw Revolt"; White, "Red Shoes"; Mooney, "Choctaw Indians"; Shea, *Catholic Missions*, p. 450; Bekkers, "The Catholic Church," p. 354. One casualty (although not by death) was the Jesuit Beaudouin, who became so active as a translator and intermediary that he was recalled to New Orleans and replaced by Father Nicholas Lefevre. Delanglez, *French Jesuits*, pp. 475–76.

35. Cotterill, *Southern Indians*, p. 31.

36. *Journal of the Congress*, pp. 24, 35, 38–39; Hamilton, *Colonial Mobile*, pp. 241–43; Cotterill, *Southern Indians*, p. 70; "Peter Chester"; White, *Roots of Dependency*, pp. 76–77.

37. Bartram, *Travels*, p. 248; Cushman, *History of the Choctaw*, p. 87; Cotterill, *Southern Indians*, p. 33; Debo, *Rise and Fall*, p. 31; Romans, *Natural History*, p. 67.

38. Cushman, *History of the Choctaw*, p. 238; O'Donnel, *Southern Indians*, p. 72.

39. Caughey, *Bernardo de Galvez*, pp. 149–211.

40. Kinnaird and Kinnaird, "Choctaws West."
41. Serrano y Sanz, *Espana y Los Indios*, pp. 82–85; Holmes, "Spanish Treaties," pp. 142–44.
42. See Coker and Watson, *Indian Traders*, for a history of these traders.
43. Holmes, *Gayoso*, pp. 152–53, 161; Holmes, "Spanish Treaties," p. 151.
44. Cotterill, *Southern Indians*, pp. 60–61; Green, *Indian Removal*, p. 76.
45. Kappler, *Indian Affairs* 2:12.
46. A Spanish census of two districts of the Choctaws, the Six Towns (Southern) and the Okla Falaya (Western), showed a total of 11,447 people and 53 villages. Holmes, "The Choctaws," pp. 33–49.

CHAPTER 2

1. Cyrus Byington to Jeremiah Evarts, Yaknokchaya, July 20, 1829, ABCFM, vol. 3, folder 93; Cushman, *History of the Choctaw*, p. 331; Morrison, *Seven Constitutions*, p. 2; White, *Roots of Dependency*, pp. 96–110; Coker and Watson, *Indian Traders*.
2. White, *Roots of Dependency*, pp. 102–3, 104–7.
3. John Sibley to General Henry Dearborn, Natchitoches, April 5, 1805, in *American State Papers* 1:725.
4. Byington to Evarts, ABCFM, vol. 3, no. 93; Stearn and Stearn, *Smallpox*, p. 84.
5. Cushman *History of the Choctaw*, pp. 167–69.
6. Halbert, "District Divisions," p. 375.
7. Draper Papers, p. 54.
8. Draper Papers, pp. 47–55; Lewis, *Chief Pushmataha*.
9. Byington to Evarts, Yaknokchaya, July 20, 1829, ABCFM, vol. 3, no. 93 (Nathaniel Folsom memoir). See McBride and McBride, "Choctaw Folsoms," for a more complete genealogy of the family.
10. McBride and McBride, "Choctaw Folsoms," p. 5.
11. Lanman, "Peter Pitchlynn"; Baird, *Peter Pitchlynn*, p. 6.
12. Ray, *Greenwood Leflore*, p. 33.
13. McBride and McBride, "A Family Makes Its Mark," pp. 1–18; Dupree, "Greenwood LeFlore."
14. Prucha, *Federal Indian Policy*, pp. 20–25. See Henri, *Southern Indians*, for a discussion of an early agent of the civilization policy.
15. Pearce, *Savagism and Civilization*, pp. 3–34; Sheehan, *Seeds of Extinction*, pp. 116–20; Horsman, *Expansion*, pp. 170–73.
16. Sheehan describes Jeffersonian Indian policy as misguided philanthropy, but Jefferson's statements about driving Indians into debt sound less benign. See Jefferson's letter to Wm. Henry Harrison in Prucha, *Documents*, p. 22. Abel, *Events*; Prucha, *The Great Father* 1:142–44.
17. James Wilkinson, Benjamin Hawkins, and Andrew Pickens to Henry Dearborn, Secretary of War, Loftus Heights, Fort Adams, December 18, 1801, in *American State Papers* 1:659.
18. Kappler, *Indian Affairs* 2:57–58; Phelps, "Stands and Travel Accommodations," p. 5; Moore, *Cotton Kingdom*, pp. 9–11.

19. Kappler, *Indian Affairs* 2:63; Coker, *Historical Sketches*, p. 22; Kappler, *Indian Affairs* 2:69–70, 87; DeRosier, *Removal*, p. 29; Coker and Watson, *Indian Traders*, p. 256.

20. Richardson, *Papers of the Presidents* 1:422–23.

21. Pickett, *History of Alabama* 2:234; Plaisance, "Choctaw Trading."

22. The Treaty of Dancing Rabbit Creek in 1830 made specific provisions of land for a group of "Wayne Warriors." Kappler, *Indian Affairs* 2:315. Sword, *Washington's Indian War:* p. 269; Wayne, *A Name in Arms*, p. 347.

23. Halbert and Ball, *The Creek War*, pp. 40–57. See Edmunds, *Shawnee Prophet*, for an account of Tecumseh, his brother Tenskwatawa, and their leadership of resistance to the American government.

24. Rogin, *Fathers and Children*, p. 161; Cushman, *History of the Choctaw*, pp. 260–62.

25. Halbert and Ball, *Creek War*, pp. 120, 215–17, 213–16. A small party of Choctaws actually joined the Red Stick Creeks in their war but were placed under sentence of death by Pushmataha for doing so. Pickett, *Alabama* 2:290–91, 322; Dowd, *A Spirited Resistance*, pp. 171–72. Martin, *Sacred Revolt*, gives a full account of the Creek War and interprets its cause as a cultural conflict between traditional religious leaders and militant war leaders. The Creek War mirrored (with a more spiritual orientation) the Choctaw Civil War of 1748–50 in revealing the basic divisions within tribes.

26. Carter, *Territorial Papers* 6:686–87; DeRosier, *Removal*, p. 37; Kappler, *Indian Affairs* 2:137.

27. Dangerfield, *Awakening*, p. 1; McLoughlin, *Cherokees and Missionaries*, p. 101; Horsman, *Race*, pp. 189–207; Rohrbough, *The Trans-Appalachian Frontier*, pp. 192–217.

28. Nye, *Cultural Life*, pp. 216–19. See Sweet, *American Culture*, for a general overview of frontier missionary efforts.

29. Sweet, *American Frontier* 2:60, 64.

30. Sweet, *American Frontier* 1:48–49, 2:60.

31. Barclay, *Methodist Missions* 1:165.

32. Tracy, "American Board," p. 78.

33. American Board, *First Ten Annual Reports*, p. 18, See also the manuscript copies of reports filed in the National Anthropological Archives, MS #3153; Hiemstra, "Presbyterian Missions"; Faust, "Growth of Presbyterian Missions," 82–123.

34. Schermerhorn, "Report," pp. 20–21.

35. Cyrus Kingsbury to William H. Crawford, Washington, D.C., May 2, 1816, in *American State Papers* 2:477.

36. Rohrbough, *Trans-Appalachian Frontier*, p. 196; Haynes, "Road to Statehood," p. 237.

37. American Board, *First Ten Annual Reports*, p. 157; Report of Samuel Worcester, National Anthropological Archives, MS #3153, p. 130.

38. Crawford to Cyrus Kingsbury, May 14, 1816, Letters of the Secretary of War Sent, Microfilm Series M15, Record Group 75, National Archives (hereafter cited as NA-LSW-S), p. 349.

39. American Board, *First Ten Annual Reports*, pp. 199–200.

40. McLoughlin, *Cherokees and Missionaries*, p. 102.

41. Brethren at Brainard to Elias Cornelius, March 18, 1818, the Brethren, cited in Ninth Annual Report of the American Board of Commissioners for Foreign Missions, National Anthropological Archives, MS #3153, p. 4.

42. Kingsbury to Samuel Worcester, Yellobusha, June 23, 1818, ABCFM, vol. 2, folder 3; Kingsbury to Worcester, Elliot, Feb. 2, 1819, ABCFM, vol. 2, folder 5; Cushman, *History of the Choctaw*, p. 135.

43. Swanton, *Source Material*, p. 2. Swanton declared that there was an "absence of pronounced native institutions" and called Choctaw beliefs and customs "simple."

44. Sweet, *Colonial America*, pp. 99–101, 245.

45. Pushmataha and Mushulatubbee to the president, Choctaw Trading House, Oct. 20, 1818, Letters to the Secretary of War—Received, Microfilm Series 271, Record Group 75, National Archives (hereafter cited as NA-LSW-R), roll 2.

CHAPTER 3

1. Kingsbury and Williams to Worcester, Yellobusha, June 29, 1818, ABCFM, vol. 1, folder 4; Loring S. Williams to Samuel Worcester, Yallobusha, June 29, 1818, ABCFM, vol. 2, folder 4.

2. American Board, *Report of the Committee on Anti-Slavery Memorials*, p. 6. Although the quotation comes from a later period, in the hindsight of experience, the missionaries still stated a deeply held principle.

3. Kingsbury and Williams to Worcester, Yellobusha, June 29, 1818, ABCFM, vol. 1, folder 4.

4. Kingsbury to Worcester, Choctaw Agency, July 21, 1818, ABCFM, vol. 2, folder 5.

5. Kingsbury to McKee, March 18, 1818, ABCFM, vol. 2, folder 1. The American Board subsequently moved to strengthen its ties with the U.S. government by appointing McKee and Col. R. J. Meigs, agent to the Cherokee, as corresponding members. American Board, *First Ten Annual Reports*, p. 199; White, *Roots of Dependency*, p. 104; John McKee to Cyrus Kingsbury, Natchez, Feb. 21, 1818, ABCFM, vol. 2, folder 1; Cyrus Kingsbury to Samuel Worcester, Choctaw Agency, July 20, 1818, ABCFM, vol. 2, folder 5.

6. American Board, *First Ten Annual Reports*, pp. 199–200.

7. Ibid,; Kingsbury to Evarts, Yallobusha, Oct. 21, 1818, ABCFM, vol. 2, folder 11; Kingsbury to Samuel Worcester, Yello Busha, Oct. 3, 1818, ABCFM, vol. 2, folder 11.

8. Kingsbury to Worcester, Choctaw Agency, July 21, 1818, ABCFM, vol. 2, folder 5; Kingsbury to Worcester, Choctaw Agency, July 30, 1818, ABCFM, vol. 2, folder 5.

9. Kingsbury to Evarts, Yellobusha, Nov. 10, 1818, ABCFM, vol. 2, folder 13.

10. Morse, *Report to the Secretary of War*, p. 183.

11. Journal of Elliot Mission, ABCFM, vol. 1, folder 1,; Kingsbury to Jeremiah Evarts, Dec. 21, 1818, ABCFM, vol. 2, folder 18; Judith Chase to Samuel Worcester, New Orleans, Dec. 28, 1818, ABCFM, vol. 2, folder 19; A. V.

Williams to Evarts, Elliott, Feb. 19, 1819, ABCFM, vol. 2, folder 179; Tracy, "American Board," p. 358.

12. Kingsbury to Cornelius, Yello Busha, Nov. 28, 1818, ABCFM, vol. 2, folder 15.

13. Kingsbury to Jeremiah Evarts, Elliot, April 1, 1819, ABCFM, vol. 2, folder 15; Journal of Elliot Mission, ABCFM, vol. 1, folder 1; American Board, *First Ten Annual Reports*, p. 243; Tracy, "American Board," pp. 78–79.

14. Journal of Elliot Mission, March 26, 1819, ABCFM, vol. 1, folder 1, pp. 1, 6; Kingsbury to Worcester, Choctaw Agency, July 30, 1818, ABCFM, vol. 2, folder 5.

15. Kingsbury to Evarts, Mrs. Claiborns, near Natchez, Jan. 12, 1819, ABCFM, vol. 2, folder 21.

16. American Board, *First Ten Annual Reports*, p. 243.

17. Ibid., p. 242; Journal of Elliot Mission, ABCFM, vol. 1, folder 1, p. 6.

18. Rohrbough, *Land Office Business*, pp. 120–21.

19. Pushmataha and Mushulatubbee to the President, Choctaw Trading House, Oct. 20, 1818, NA-LSW-R, roll 2.

20. 15th Cong., 2d sess., H. Doc. 156.

21. Watkins, "Contribution"; White, *Roots of Dependency*, pp. 113–14; Grant Foreman, *Indians and Pioneers*, pp. 137–44. Thomas Nuttall mentioned a Choctaw settlement near the town of Arkansas in 1819. See Nuttall, *Journal of Travels*, p. 363.

22. John C. Calhoun to Henry Clay, Department of War, December 5, 1818, in Calhoun, *Papers* 3:350; Moore, *Cotton Kingdom*, pp. 15–16; Dippie, *The Vanishing American*, pp. 3–11; Sheehan, *Seeds of Extinction*, pp. 167–72; Horsman, *Race*, pp. 80–93; Feller, *Public Lands*, pp. 18–22.

23. John C. Calhoun to Henry Clay, Department of War, December 5, 1818, in Calhoun, *Papers* 3:350.

24. 3 *U.S. Stat. L.*, 85, Act of March 3, 1819.

25. Prucha, *Great Father* 1:151–52.

26. James Pitchlynn to John C. Calhoun, Choctaw Nation, March 18, 1819, in *American State Papers* 2:229.

27. Andrew Jackson to John McKee, the Hermitage, near Nashville, April 22, 1819, in ibid.; Rogin, *Fathers and Children*, pp. 165–67.

28. James Pitchlynn to Major Gen. A. Jackson, Oaktibbeha, June 22, 1819, in *American State Papers* 2:231.

29. Moshatubby and Pooshmataha to Calhoun, In a Great Council, Aug. 12, 1819, NA-LSW-R, roll 2, frames 1270–71. The letter is published as Mushulatubbee and Pooshamataha, in General Council of the Choctaw Nation, Aug. 12, 1819, in *American State Papers* 2:230.

30. James Pitchlynn to John C. Calhoun, Choctaw Nation, March 18, 1819, in *American State Papers* 2:229; James Pitchlynn to Andrew Jackson, Oaktibha, Sept. 13, 1819, in Calhoun, *Papers* 4:322–23.

31. John McKee to Andrew Jackson, French Camp, Aug. 13, 1819, NA-LSW-R, roll 2, frames 1188–89.

32. Ibid.

33. Andrew Jackson to John C. Calhoun, Nashville, Aug. 24, 1819, in Calhoun, *Papers* 4:270.

34. John McKee to John C. Calhoun, Choctaw Agency, June 10, 1819, NA-LSW-R, roll 2, frame 1263.

35. Kingsbury to Samuel Worcester, French Camps, August 9, 1819, ABCFM, vol. 2, folder 31; Kingsbury to Choctaw chiefs, August 11, 1819, ABCFM, vol. 2, folder 33.

36. Journal of Elliot Mission, August 9, 1819, ABCFM, vol. 1, folder 1, p. 8; Cyrus Kingsbury to Samuel King and Robert Bell, Elliot, December 18, 1819, ABCFM, vol. 2, folder 46.

37. Moshatubby and Pooshmataha to Calhoun, In a Great Council, Aug. 12, 1819, NA-LSW-R, roll 2, frames 1270–71.

38. McKenney to Calhoun, Office of Indian Trade, Aug. 14, 1819, NA-LSW-R, roll 2, frame 1282.

39. Kingsbury to Calhoun, First Annual Report of the Mission School at Elliot, Choctaw Nation, to the autumn of 1819, Nov. 18, 1819, ABCFM, vol. 1, folder 108; American Board, *First Ten Annual Reports,* pp. 244–45.

40. Kingsbury to Jeremiah Evarts, Elliot, April 1, 1819, ABCFM, vol. 2, folder 25.

41. Journal of Elliot, April 20, 1819, ABCFM, vol. 1, folder 1, pp. 6–7, Oct. 14, 1819, p. 22, Jan. 29, 1820, folder 2, p. 5, July 27, 1823, folder 6, p. 14, Oct. 13, 1821, folder 4. Kingsbury to Worcester, Oct. 9, 1820, ABCFM, vol. 2, folder 69; Journal of Elliot, Jan. 29, 1820, ABCFM vol. 1, folder 2; Kingsbury to Samuel Worcester, Elliot, Choctaw Nation, Sept. 7, 1819, ABCFM, vol. 1, p. 63; Loring Williams to Samuel Worcester, Elliot, Oct. 4, 1819, ABCFM, vol. 2, p. 162; Kingsbury to Jeremiah Evarts, Elliot, Feb. 8, 1820, ABCFM, vol. 2, folder 49; Cyrus Byington to Jeremiah Evarts, Elliot, Choctaw Nation, Oct. 29, 1821, ABCFM, vol. 2, p. 142.

42. Journal of Elliot, April 20, 1819, ABCFM, vol. 1, folder 2, Feb. 4, 1820, pp. 6–7, Oct. 14, 1820, p. 22, July 27, 1823, folder 6, p. 14, October 13, 1821, folder 4. Kingsbury to Worcester, Elliot, October 9, 1820, ABCFM, vol. 2, folder 69; Journal of Elliot, January 29, 1820, ABCFM, vol. 1, folder 2.

43. Kingsbury to James Finley, Aug. 12, 1819, ABCFM, vol. 2, p. 32; American Board, *First Ten Annual Reports,* p. 242; Kingsbury to Calhoun, First Annual Report of the Mission School at Elliot, Choctaw Nation, to the autumn of 1819, Nov. 18, 1819, ABCFM, vol. 1, folder 108.

44. Journal of Elliot Mission, ABCFM, vol. 1, folder 2, p. 4; Hodgson, *Remarks,* p. 61.

45. Ibid., pp. 273–74.

46. Journal of Elliot Mission, June 2, 1820, ABCFM, vol. 1; Kingsbury to Evarts, Elliot, May 29, 1820, ABCFM, vol. 2, folder 61; *Missionary Herald* 16, no. 8 (August 1820): 187.

47. Journal of Elliot Mission, June 2, 1820, ABCFM, vol. 1.

48. Journal of Elliot Mission, ABCFM, vol. 1, folder 1, p. 8.

49. Journal of Elliot Mission, Oct. 5, 1819, ABCFM, vol. 1, folder 1, p. 10.

50. Samuel King to D. Folsom, Maj. John Pitchlynn's, Dec. 7, 1819, AFCFM, vol. 2, folder 45; Kingsbury to Evarts, Nov. 12, 1819, ABCFM, vol. 2, folder 39; Kingsbury to Samuel Worcester, Pigeon Roost, Dec. 4, 1819, ABCFM, vol. 2, folder 43.

51. Samuel King and Robert Bell to Cyrus Kingsbury. Maj. J. Pitchlynn's, Dec. 6, 1819, ABCFM, vol. 2, folder 44; Kingsbury to King and Bell, Elliot, Choctaw Nation, Dec. 18, 1819, ABCFM, vol. 2, folder 44; Kingsbury to Jeremiah Evarts, Elliot, February 26, 1820, ABCFM, Vol. 2, folder 52; Posey, *Presbyterian Church*, pp. 36, 40, 68.

52. Cyrus Kingsbury to Jeremiah Evarts, Elliot, Jan. 4, 1820, ABCFM, vol. 2, folder 47.

53. Kingsbury to Evarts, Elliot, May 12, 1819, ABCFM, vol. 2, folder 21; Kingsbury to Jeremiah Evarts, Elliot, Choctaw Nation, July 21, 1819, ABCFM, vol. 2, folder 30.

54. Kingsbury, Jewell, Fisk, Pride, Williams to Sam. Worcester, Sept. 7, 1819, ABCFM, vol. 1, folder 8.

55. Kingsbury to Jeremiah Evarts, Pigeon Roost, Feb. 14, 1820, ABCFM, vol. 2, folder 57; Kingsbury to Jeremiah Evarts, Oak-tib-be-ha, Feb. 26, 1820, ABCFM, vol. 2, folder 52; Kingsbury to Samuel Worcester, Oak-tib-be-ha, March 11, 1820, ABCFM, vol. 2, folder 56; *Missionary Herald* 17, no. 2 (February 1821): 48, 49; Journal of Elliot Mission, ABCFM, vol. 1, folder 2; Tracy, "American Board," p. 86.

56. Kingsbury to Evarts, Pigeon Roost, Feb. 14, 1820, ABCFM, vol. 2, folder 53.

57. Debo, *Rise and Fall*, pp. 43–44; Cushman, *History of the Choctaw*, pp. 135, 161-64; *Missionary Herald* 17, no. 5 (May 1821): 152.

58. Kingsbury to Samuel Worcester, Elliot, May 5, 1820, ABCFM, vol 2, folder 58.

59. Kingsbury to Samuel Worcester, Elliot, May 5, 1820, ABCFM, vol. 2, folder 58.

60. Jedidiah Morse to John C. Calhoun, Washington, Feb. 4, 1820, and John C. Calhoun to Jedidiah Morse, Dept. of War, Feb. 7, 1820, in Calhoun, *Papers* 4:634–35, 648–49.

61. Morse, *Report*, pp. 11, 182–83.

62. J. C. Calhoun to General A. Jackson, Dept. of War, May 23, 1820, and Jackson to Calhoun, Head-Quarters, Division of the South, Nashville, June 19, 1820, in *American State Papers* 2:229, 230.

63. Edmund Folsom to General Commissioners of the United States, who are appointed to treat with the Choctaw Indians, Sept. 13, 1820, in *American State Papers* 2:232.

64. Andrew Jackson to Hon. J. C. Calhoun, Nashville, June 19, 1820, and C. Vandeventer to Major General Andrew Jackson, Dept. of War, Aug. 21, 1820, in *American State Papers* 2:231, 232.

65. Andrew Jackson, Thomas Hinds, to the Chiefs and Warriors of the Choctaw Nation, Oct. 10, 1820, in *American State Papers* 2:236–37; Cushman, *History of the Choctaw*, pp. 121–22.

66. Andrew Jackson and Thomas Hinds to the Chiefs and Warriors of the Choctaw Nation, Oct. 13, 1820, in *American State Papers* 2:233.

67. Andrew Jackson and Thomas Hinds to the Chiefs and Warriors of the Choctaw Nation, Oct. 17, 1820, in *American State Papers* 2:239–40.

68. *American State Papers* 2:240; Kappler, *Indian Affairs* 2:193.

69. Cyrus Kingsbury to Andrew Jackson and Thomas Hinds, Treaty Ground,

Choctaw Nation, Oct. 18, 1820, NA-LSW-R, Roll 3; Kingsbury to Worcester, Choctaw Nation, Oct. 9, 1820, ABCFM, vol. 2, folder 69. A rough calculation of the proceeds of the sale of fifty-four sections at the prevailing rate of $1.25 an acre for public lands yields a figure of $43,200 for proceeds from a land cession. Kingsbury's grand plan to Calhoun would have cost over $300,000 for a period of ten years.

70. Kingsbury to Samuel Worcester, Treaty Ground, C. N., Oct. 18, 1820, ABCFM, vol. 2, folder 70.

71. Jackson and Hinds to [Monroe], Choctaw Treaty Ground, Oct. 19–21, 1820, in *American State Papers* 2:241–42.

72. Kingsbury to Samuel Worcester, Treaty Ground, C. N., Oct. 18, 1820, ABCFM, vol. 2, folder 70.

73. Cotterill, *Southern Indians*, pp. 208–9; Kappler, *Indian Affaris* 2:191–93.

CHAPTER 4

1. Miles, *Jacksonian Democracy*, pp. 19–20; Young, *Redskins*, p. 177.

2. Kingsbury to Jeremiah Evarts, Elliot, Aug. 3, 1820, ABCFM, vol. 2, folder 66; Kingsbury to James Finley, Aug. 12, 1819, ABCFM, vol. 2, folder 32; Kingsbury to Jeremiah Evarts, Elliot, Feb. 26, 1820, ABCFM, vol. 2, folder 52.

3. Calhoun to Kingsbury, Department of War, Nov. 7, 1820, in Calhoun, *Papers* 5:428; Kingsbury to Worcester, Pigeon Roost, Jan. 2, 1821, ABCFM, vol. 2, folder 72.

4. Calhoun to McKee, Oct. 11, 1820, NA-LSW-S, reel 5, p. 20.

5. *Missionary Herald* 18, no. 1 (January 1822): 154.

6. Cyrus Kingsbury to Jeremiah Evarts, Mayhew, March 26, 1821, ABCFM, vol. 2, folder 76; Kingsbury to Evarts, Mayhew, April 5, 1821, ABCFM, vol. 2, folder 77.

7. Letter of Wiliam Goodell, April 30, 1822, in *Missionary Herald* 18, no. 7 (July 1822): 223–24. The scene is remarkably reminiscent of the famous *Peaceable Kingdom* paintings by Edward Hicks.

8. Kingsbury to Evarts, Mayhew, Dec. 19, 1821, ABCFM, vol. 2, folder 93.

9. Kingsbury to Worcester, Mayhew, Jan. 22, 1821, ABCFM, vol. 2, folder 73.

10. Kingsbury to Jeremiah Evarts, Mayhew, March 2, 1821, ABCFM, vol. 2, folder 75; *Missionary Herald* 17, no. 5 (May 1821): 152, vol. 17, no. 9 (September 1821): 290, vol. 17, no. 12 (December 1821): 383–89.

11. Byington was born on March 11, 1793, in Stockbridge, Massachusetts, one of nine children of poor but respected parents. His father was a farmer, and his early education was limited, but later he studied Latin and Greek and read law at the home of Joseph Woodbridge. He was admitted to the bar in 1814 and practiced for a few years in Stockbridge and Sheffield, giving it up after a call to the ministry. He studied Hebrew and theology at Andover and was licensed to preach in September 1819. He hoped to be sent to the Armenians in Turkey, but there were no openings, and he preached in various churches in Massachusetts instead. Byington, *Dictionary*, pp. vii–viii; Baird, "Cyrus Byington," pp. 5–9; *Missionary Herald* 18, no. 1 (January 1822): 5; Tracy, "American Board," p. 338.

12. Papers of Cyrus Byington, ABCFM, series 18.3.5, vol. 1.

13. Berkhofer, *Salvation*, pp. 4–5.

14. Robert Cole was the son of a Chochumma woman and a white man. The Chochummas had been wiped out by Choctaw and Chickasaw attacks, and she had evidently been adopted into the Choctaw tribe. See "Journal of Proceedings," Entry 275, Choctaw Removal Records, case no. 2; Halbert, "District Divisions," p. 377; Journal of Elliot Mission, Aug. 3, 1821, ABCFM, vol. 1, folder 2.

15. Journal of Elliot Mission, May 28, 1822, ABCFM, vol. 1, folder 5.

16. Journal of Elliot Mission, June 9, 1821, ABCFM, vol. 1.

17. Kingsbury to Evarts, Mayhew, June 8, 1822, ABCFM, vol. 2, folder 99.

18. Journal of Elliot Mission, June 21, 1822, ABCFM, vol. 1, folder 5.

19. Journal of Elliot Mission, June 16, 1822, ABCFM, vol. 1, folder 5.

20. Journal of Elliot Mission, Feb. 6, 1823, ABCFM, vol. 1, folder 5, p. 46.

21. Mayhew Journal, July 14, 1821, ABCFM, vol. 1, folder 76.

22. Kingsbury to Jeremiah Evarts, Mayhew, March 26, 1821. ABCFM, vol. 2, folder 76.

23. Cyrus Kingsbury to J. Evarts, Esq., Mayhew, July 16, 1821, ABCFM, vol. 2, folder 81.

24. Journal of Elliot Mission, Oct. 24, 1821, ABCFM, vol. 1, folder 7.

25. Kingsbury to John C. Calhoun, Mayhew, Jan. 5, 1821, NA-LSW-R, roll 3.

26. Loring S. Williams to Jeremiah Evarts, Elliot, June 24, 1821, ABCFM, vol. 2, p. 166; Byington to Evarts, Elliot, Choctaw Nation, June 27, 1821, ABCFM, vol. 2, folder 137; Journal of Elliot Mission, June 6, 1821, ABCFM, vol. 1, folder 3; Williams to Evarts, Choctaw Nation, Jan. 3, 1822, ABCFM, vol. 2, p. 168.

27. Williams to Evarts, Bethel Mission School Choctaw Nation, Feb. 8, 1823, ABCFM, vol. 2, p. 172; Journal of Elliot Mission, June 6, 1821, vol. 1, folder 4; Kingsbury to Evarts, Mayhew, Dec. 19, 1821, ABCFM, vol. 2, folder 93.

28. Williams to Evarts, French Camp, Oct. 22, 1821, ABCFM, vol. 2, p. 167; Williams to Evarts, Choctaw Nation, Jan. 2, 1822, ABCFM, vol. 2, p. 168.

29. Williams to Evarts, Choctaw Nation, Jan. 3, 1822, ABCFM, vol. 2, p. 168.

30. Williams to Evarts, Feb. 7, 1822, ABCFM, vol. 2, p. 167.

31. Ibid.; Williams to Evarts, Choctaw Nation, Jan. 3, 1822, ABCFM, vol. 2, p. 168; Williams to Evarts, Newell Choctaw Nation, June 18, 1822, ABCFM, vol. 2, p. 169.

32. Kingsbury to John Calhoun, School Report, Jan. 20, 1822, ABCFM, vol. 1, folder 108, p. 5.

33. Mayhew Journal, March 23, 1822, ABCFM, vol. 1, folder 79; Kingsbury to Evarts, at Mingo Mushulatubbee's, Choctaw Nation, Oct. 7, 1822, ABCFM, vol. 1, folder 109.

34. Mayhew Journal, March 23, 1822, ABCFM, vol. 1, folder 79.

35. Byington to Evarts, Bethel, Choctaw Nation, April 13, 1824, ABCFM, vol. 2, folder 153.

36. See the introduction in VanDerBeets, *Held Captive*.

37. William Pride to Thomas Thacher, Mayhew, Aug. 17, 1825, Pride Papers.

38. Byington to Evarts, Bethel Choctaw Nation, April 13, 1824, ABCFM, vol. 2, folder 153.

39. Journal of Mayhew, May 1, 1822, ABCFM, vol. 1, folder 82.

40. Extracts from the Journal of Mayhew Mission, Dec. 13, 1822, ABCFM, vol. 1, folder 94.

41. Mayhew Journal, Sept. 1, 1822, ABCFM, vol. 1, folder 82; Mayhew Journal, June 26, 1822, and July 30, 1822, ABCFM, vol. 1, folder 82.

42. Mayhew Journal, Sept. 1, 1822, ABCFM, vol. 1, folder 82.

43. Journal of Elliot Mission, July 1, 1821, ABCFM, vol. 1, folder 75; July 26, 1821, ABCFM, vol. 1, folder 75; Kingsbury to Evarts, Mayhew, Oct. 16, 1821, ABCFM, vol. 2, folder 90.

44. Mayhew Journal, March 29, 1822, ABCFM, vol. 1, folder 81.

45. Kingsbury to Evarts, at Mingo Mushulatubbee's, Choctaw Nation, Oct. 7, 1822, ABCFM, vol. 2, folder 108.

46. Kingsbury to Evarts, Mayhew, Sept. 27, 1822, ABCFM, vol. 2, folder 106; Kingsbury to Evarts, at Mingo Mushulatubbee's, Choctaw Nation, Oct. 7, 1822, ABCFM, vol. 2, folder 108.

47. Mayhew Journal, Oct. 23, 1822, ABCFM, vol. l, folder 89.

48. Ibid.

49. Kingsbury to Evarts, at Mingo Mushulatubbee's, Choctaw Nation, Oct. 7, 1822, ABCFM, vol. 2, folder 108; Mayhew Journal, Oct. 23, 1822, ABCFM, vol. 1, folder 89.

50. Kingsbury to Evarts, at Mingo Mushulatubbee's, Choctaw Nation, Oct. 7, 1822, ABCFM, vol. 2, folder 108.

51. Extracts from the Journal at Mayhew, Nov. 7, 1822, ABCFM, vol. 1, folder 94.

52. Kingsbury to Evarts, Mayhew, Aug. 22, 1822, ABCFM, vol. 2, folder 103; Kingsbury to Evarts, Mayhew, Sept. 27, 1822, ABCFM, vol. 2, folder 106; Kingsbury to Evarts, at Mingo Mushulatubbee's, Choctaw Nation, Oct. 7, 1822, ABCFM, vol. 2, folder 108; Kingsbury to Evarts, Mayhew, Oct. 29, 1822, ABCFM, vol. 2, folder 109; Kingsbury to Evarts, Six Towns, July 26, 1823, ABCFM, vol. 2, folder 120; Kingsbury to John Calhoun, School Report, October 1823, ABCFM, vol. 1, folder 121.

53. Kingsbury to Evarts, Pigeon Roost, C. N., June 12, 1823, ABCFM, vol. 2, folder 115; Mayhew Journal, May 28, 1823, ABCFM, vol. 1, folder 102, p. 22.

54. Kingsbury to Evarts, Pigeon Roost, Choctaw Nation, June 12, 1823, ABCFM, vol. 2, folder 115.

55. "Agreement between Mooshulatubbee & Pushamatahaw and Captains & Warriors of their respective districts," May 12, 1823, ABCFM, vol. 2, folder 100. The signatories also included Little Leader and David Folsom.

56. Kingsbury to Evarts, Pigeon Roost, C. N., June 12, 1823, ABCFM, vol. 2, folder 115; Kingsbury to Evarts, Six Towns, July 26, 1823, ABCFM, vol. 2, folder 120.

57. Mayhew Journal, May 13, 1823, ABCFM, vol. 1, folder 101, p. 17; Kingsbury to Evarts, Pigeon Roost, C.N., June 12, 1823, ABCFM, vol. 2, folder 115; Kingsbury to Evarts, Six Towns, July 26, 1823, ABCFM, vol. 2, folder 120; Mayhew Journal, May 28, 1823, ABCFM, vol. 1, folder 102, p. 22; Kingsbury to Evarts, Mayhew, July 14, 1823, ABCFM, vol. 1, folder 103.

58. Kingsbury to Evarts, Six Towns, July 26, 1823, ABCFM, vol. 2, folder 120.

59. Kingsbury to Evarts, Mayhew, Oct. 9, 1823, ABCFM, vol. 2, folder 123.

60. Journal of Elliot Mission, Feb. 6, 1823, ABCFM, vol. 1, folder 5; Kingsbury to Evarts, Mayhew, Oct. 9, 1823, ABCFM, vol. 2, folder 123.

61. Kingsbury to Evarts, Mayhew, June 7, 1824, ABCFM, vol. 2, folder 128; Extracts from Journal at Mayhew, June 5, 1824, ABCFM, vol. 1, folder 106; Extracts from Journal at Mayhew, June 22, 1824, ABCFM, vol. 1, folder 107.

62. Kingsbury to Evarts, Mayhew, July 19, 1824, ABCFM, vol. 2, folder 134.

63. Journal of Elliot Mission, June 21, 1822, ABCFM, vol. 1, folder 5; Kingsbury to Evarts, Pigeon Roost, C. N., June 12, 1823, ABCFM, vol. 2, folder 115.

64. Journal of Elliot Mission, July 4, 1823, ABCFM, vol. 1, folder 6, p. 50.

65. Kingsbury to John Calhoun, School Report, Oct. 1823, ABCFM, vol. 1, folder 122. Mission personnel included Cyrus Byington, Dr. William Pride, Joel Wood (schoolmaster), John Smith, and Zechariah Howes at Elliot; Cyrus Kingsbury, William Hooper (schoolmaster), Calvin Cushman, Philo Stewart, and Samuel Wisner at Mayhew; Loring S. Williams and Stephen B. Macomber at Bethel; Moses Jewell and Anson Gleason at Emmaus; and Alfred Wright, Anson Dyer, and Elijah Bardwell at Yokena Chukamah. Mayhew Journal, May 6, 1821, ABCFM, vol. 1, folder 74; Morse, *Report*, p. 165; *Missionary Herald* 17, no. 9 (September 1821): 292, vol. 18, no. 1 (January 1822): 8.

CHAPTER 5

1. Extracts from Journal at Mayhew, Nov. 21, 1822, ABCFM, vol. 1, folder 94.

2. Mayhew Journal, Nov. 21, 1822, ABCFM, vol. 1, folder 94.

3. Journal of Elliot Mission, July 2, 1821, ABCFM, vol. 1, folder 2.

4. Mayhew Journal, July 6, 1821, ABCFM, vol. 1, folder 75.

5. Mayhew Journal, June 11, 1821, ABCFM, vol. 1, folder 74.

6. Journal of Elliot Mission, June 19, 1821, ABCFM, vol. 1, folder 5.

7. Kingsbury to Evarts, Elliot, May 12, 1819, ABCFM, vol. 2, folder 26.

8. *Missionary Herald* 17, no. 11 (November 1821): 349–51.

9. William Ward to Thomas McKenney, October 27, 1824, Office of Indian Affairs, Letters Received, Microfilm Series 234, Record Group 75, National Archives (hereinafter cited as NA-OIA), roll 169.

10. Mayhew Journal, April 29, 1821, ABCFM, vol. 1, folder 74.

11. Mayhew Journal, Jan. 17, 1822, ABCFM, vol. 1, folder 79.

12. Mayhew Journal, Jan. 13, 1822, ABCFM, vol. 1, folder 79.

13. Mayhew Journal, May 28, 1822, ABCFM, vol. 1, folder 82.

14. Loring Williams to Evarts, Newell Choctaw Nation, June 18, 1822, ABCFM, vol. 2, folder 169.

15. Journal of Elliot Mission, Feb. 18, 1821, and Sept. 2, 1821, ABCFM, vol. 1, folder 1.

16. Journal of Elliot Mission, April 18, 1821, ABCFM, vol. 1, folder 3.

17. Williams to Evarts, Newell Choctaw Nation, June 18, 1822, ABCFM, vol. 2, folder 169.

18. Journal of Elliot Mission, Oct. 19, 1821, vol. 1, folder 4.

19. Journal of Elliot Mission, Feb. 23, 1822, ABCFM, vol. 1, folder 5; *Missionary Herald* 19, no. 7 (July 1823): 203–204.

20. Journal of Elliot Mission, Feb. 22, 1822, ABCFM, vol. 1, folder 5; *Missionary Herald* 18, no. 6 (June 1822): 181.

21. *Missionary Herald* 18, no. 6 (June 1822): 181.

22. Extracts from the Journal of Elliot Mission, May 25, 1823, ABCFM, vol. 1, folder 51.

23. Williams to Evarts, Choctaw Nation, Sept. 19, 1822, ABCFM, vol. 2, folder 171.

24. Kingsbury to Evarts, Mayhew, Jan. 6, 1824, ABCFM, vol. 2, folder 125.

25. Kingsbury to Evarts, Mayhew, June 16, 1824, ABCFM, vol. 2, folder 130.

26. The Missionary Society of the Methodist Episcopal Church was founded on April 5, 1819, soon after the passage of the Civilization Act on March 3 of that year. Barclay, *Methodist Missions* 2:114; Kingsbury to Jeremiah Evarts, Elliot, June 26, 1820, ABCFM, vol. 2, folder 64; Mayhew Journal, Aug. 5, 1821, vol. 1, folder 76; Mayhew Journal, Jan. 4, 1821, vol. 1, folder 74; Jones, *History of Methodism* 2:34; *Minutes of the Annual Conferences of the Methodist Episcopal Church* 1:429; Bangs, *History of the Missions*, p. 152.

27. Kingsbury to Evarts, Mayhew, June 16, 1824, ABCFM, vol. 2, folder 130.

28. William Winans to Rev. Zechariah Williams, Wilkinson, Mississippi, July 2, 1824, Winans Papers.

29. Berkhofer, *Salvation*, p. 92.

30. William Winans to Bishop R. R. Roberts, Aug. 6, 1824, Winans Papers.

31. Jones, *History of Methodism* 2:34.

32. Mayhew Journal, Aug. 8, 1822, ABCFM, vol. 1, folder 86.

33. *Missionary Herald* 29, no. 1 (January 1823): 6.

34. Mayhew Journal, Aug. 8, 1822, ABCFM, vol. 1, folder 86.

35. Mayhew Journal, Aug. 26, 28, 1822, ABCFM, vol. 1, folder 86.

36. Morse, *Report*, pp. 37–38.

37. Byington to Evarts, Elliot, Choctaw Nation, June 27, 1821, ABCFM, vol. 2, folder 137.

38. Kingsbury to Evarts, Mayhew, Sept. 14, 1821, ABCFM, vol. 2, folder 86; Kingsbury to Evarts, Mayhew, Aug. 19, 1822, ABCFM, vol. 2, folder 103.

39. The food prepared and consumed at the mission in an average week included five hundred pounds of beef, fourteen bushels of potatoes, forty large loaves of bread, two hundred gallons of *tomfullah* (corn soup), sixty gallons of coffee, and three pecks of beans and peas. See Extracts from the Journal of Elliot Mission, Oct. 31, 1819, ABCFM, vol. 1, folder 2.

40. 23d Cong., 1st sess., S. Doc. 1230, pp. 65, 86. This document is the Armstrong census taken in 1831 in preparation for removal under the Treaty of Dancing Rabbit Creek. It showed 62 slaves in the Southern District, with the greatest number (20) owned by Charles Juzan, 190 slaves in the Northeastern District, and 247 slaves in the Western District, that closest to the cotton-growing region of the Mississippi Delta. The mission journals at Elliot and Mayhew record the presence of slaves at public worship services and in the fields and kitchens of the missions.

41. See DeRosier, "Pioneers," for a discussion of Choctaw attitudes toward slavery. See McLoughlin, "Red Indians," for a general overview of the topic.

For a comparative view of a different tribe, see Perdue, *Slavery and the Evolution of Cherokee Society.*

42. Byington to Evarts, Elliot, July 24, 1821, ABCFM, vol. 2, folder 141; Byington to Evarts, Elliot, Choctaw Nation, Dec. 27, 1821, ABCFM, vol. 2, folder 144.

43. Byington to Warren Fay, April 5, 1822, ABCFM, vol. 2, folder 145.

44. Ibid.

45. Sweet, *American Culture*, p. 208.

46. Byington to Evarts, Mayhew, May 12, 1824, ABCFM, vol. 2, folder 154.

47. Williams to Evarts, Bethel, April 1824, ABCFM, vol. 2, folder 177.

48. Byington to Evarts, Mayhew, May 12, 1824, ABCFM, vol. 2, folder 154.

49. Kingsbury to Evarts, Mayhew, Oct. 6, 1825, ABCFM, vol. 3, folder 14.

50. Ibid,; Moses Jewell to Evarts, Emmaus, June 17, 1824, ABCFM, vol. 2, folder 214; Philena Thacher to Thomas Thacher, Columbus, Aug. 5, 1821, Pride Papers.

51. Resolution, Mayhew, Oct. 15, 1824, ABCFM, vol. 3, folder 4.

52. Kingsbury to Evarts, Mayhew, Oct. 4, 1826, ABCFM, vol. 3, folder 20.

53. Byington to Evarts, Bethel, Choctaw Nation, April 13, 1824, ABCFM, vol. 2, folder 153.

54. Ong discusses the profound intellectual and philosophical implications of the introduction of writing in cultures that previously depended on the spoken word. See his works *The Presence of the Word* and *Orality and Literacy.*

55. Journal of Elliot Mission, March 3, 1822, ABCFM, vol. 1, folder 5.

56. Byington to Evarts, Elliot, Dec. 17, 1821, ABCFM, vol. 2, folder 143; Journal of Elliot Mission, Feb. 23, 1822, ABCFM, vol. 1, folder 36; Journal of Elliot Mission, Dec. 30, 1821, and March 3, 1822, ABCFM, Vol. 1, folders 5, 6.

57. American Board, *First Ten Annual Reports*, pp. 44, 198.

58. Byington to Evarts, Elliot, Choctaw Nation, June 27, 1821, ABCFM, vol. 2, folder 137.

59. Journal of Elliot Mission, Jan. 12, 31, 1823, ABCFM, vol. 1, folders 45, 46.

60. Journal of Mayhew Mission, Sept. 13, 1821, ABCFM, vol. 1, folder 77; Kingsbury to Evarts, Mayhew, Sept. 14, 1821, ABCFM, vol. 2, folder 86; Byington to Evarts, Mayhew Choctaw Nation, April 1, 1823, ABCFM, vol. 2, folder 151.

61. Journal of Elliot Mission, Dec. 6, 23, 1822, ABCFM, vol. 1, folder 5; Journal of Elliot Mission, April 12, 1823, ABCFM, vol. 1, folder 7.

62. Kingsbury to Evarts, Mayhew, March 17, 1825, ABCFM, vol. 3, folder 7.

63. Byington to Evarts, Mayhew, Choctaw Nation, April 1, 1823, ABCFM, vol. 2, folder 151.

64. Williams to Evarts, Bethel, Feb. 14, 1824, ABCFM, vol. 2, folder 174; Byington to Evarts, Aikhunnah, Dec. 22, 1824, ABCFM, vol. 3, folder 67.

65. Byington to Evarts, Aikhunnah, Dec. 22, 1824, ABCFM, vol. 3, folder 67.

66. Mayhew Journal, Sept. 13, 1821, ABCFM, vol. 1, folder 77; Mayhew Journal, Jan. 17, 1822, ABCFM, vol. 1, folder 79; Kingsbury to John Calhoun, School Report, Oct. 1823, ABCFM, vol. 1, folder 122.

67. He had preached in Choctaw 120 times and in English only 45 times. Byington to Evarts, Aikhunnah, Dec. 22, 1824, ABCFM, vol. 3, folder 67.

68. Byington to Evarts, Aikhunna, May 16, 1825, ABCFM, vol. 3, folder 68.
69. Extracts from the Journal at Mayhew, June 25, 1824, ABCFM, vol. 1, folder 107, p. 9.
70. Prudential Committee Report, 1825, National Anthropological Archives, MS #3153, p. 66; Kingsbury to Evarts, Mayhew, Aug. 8, 1825, ABCFM, vol. 3, folder 12; Byington to Evarts, Aikhunna, May 16, 1825, ABCFM, vol. 3, folder 68; Evarts to Byington, Boston, Sept. 9, 1825, ABCFM, vol. 5, pp. 376–77; Byington to Evarts, Aikhunna, Nov. 28, 1825, folder 73.
71. Wright and Byington, A spelling Book. See Pilling, Bibliography, for a list of extant early Choctaw texts.
72. Byington to Evarts, Gibeon, Sept. 2, 1826, ABCFM, vol. 3, folder 78; Byington to Evarts, Aikhuna, July 7, 1826, ABCFM, vol. 3, folder 77; Byington to Evarts (extract), Aikhunna, July 1, 1826, ABCFM, vol. 3, folder 76.
73. Byington to Evarts, Aikhunna, May 18, 1825, ABCFM, vol. 3, folder 69; Moseley, Missionary Meetings, p. 1. Participants at the meeting were Kingsbury, Byington, Dyer, Cushman, Pride, and William Chamberlin from the Cherokee mission. Byington was also directed to visit the Presbytery in Mississippi or in Alabama to be ordained. The organization affiliated with both the American Board and the Presbyterian Synod of South Carolina and Georgia. "Meeting of Missionaries in the Chikasha Chahta & Cherokee Nations, was held at Monroe this day agreeably to a note passed at the Meeting at Mayhew May 6, 1825, Monroe Chickasha Nation, May 21, 1826" ABCFM, vol. 3, folder 75; Moseley, Missionary Meetings, p. 3.
74. Moseley, Missionary Meetings, p. 2.
75. "At a meeting of the missionary Brethren of the Choctaw Mission, holden at Eliot, Nov. 3, 1825," ABCFM, vol. 3, folder 72.
76. McKenney to Kingsbury, Dept. of War, April 10, 1826. ABCFM, vol. 4, 258.
77. Kingsbury to McKenney, Mayhew, May 5, 1826, ABCFM, vol. 4, folder 278.
78. Ibid.
79. Cyrus Kingsbury, "Ninth annual report of schools in the Chahta Nation for the year ending Sept. 30th, 1827," Mayhew, C. N., Nov. 1827, ABCFM, vol. 3, folder 25, no. 2.
80. Moseley, Missionary Meetings, p. 4.
81. Ibid., pp. 7, 9.
82. Wright to Evarts, Goshen, Dec. 23d, 1826, ABCFM, vol. 3, folder 105.
83. Wright and Byington, Second Chahta Book; Wright and Byington, Choctaw Hymnbook. See Pilling, Bibliography, for a listing of works in the Choctaw language.
84. Missionary Herald 25, no. 6 (June 1829): 186; American Board, Report . . . Twentieth Annual Meeting, p. 72.
85. Williams to Evarts, Choctaw Nation, Dec. 28, 1825, ABCFM, vol. 3, folder 57.
86. Kingsbury to Calhoun, Mayhew, C. N., Nov. 1827, ABCFM, vol. 3, folder 25, no. 2, pp. 9, 14, 18, 20.
87. Byington to Evarts, Yaknokchaya, July 21, 1929, ABCFM, vol. 3, folder 93

(Nathaniel Folsom memoir); Cushman, *History of the Choctaw,* pp. 166–67; Swanton, *Source Material,* pp. 177–79.

88. Journal of Elliot Mission, Sept. 22, 1821, ABCFM, vol. 1, folder 1.

89. Kingsbury noted that Christmas was a great day among the Choctaws. They visited each other, had "folies," and "got drunk"—behavior that he attributed to "their intercourse with the *civilized* part of the world." See Journal of Elliot Mission, Dec. 25, 1819, ABCFM, vol. 1, folder 1.

CHAPTER 6

1. Prucha, *Great Father* 1:154.

2. *Arkansas Gazette* 2, no. 8 (January 6, 1821).

3. *Arkansas Gazette* 2, no. 42 (September 1, 1821); William Woodward, Commissioner for Ark. Territory, to John C. Calhoun, Dec. 15, 1821, in Calhoun, *Papers* 6:570–71; DeRosier, *Removal,* pp. 54–55.

4. Calhoun to Thomas H. Williams and Christopher Rankin, Department of War, Nov. 15, 1824, in Calhoun, *Papers* 9:383–84. Williams was a senator and Rankin a representative to Congress from Mississippi.

5. John Calhoun to Thos. Hinds & Wm. Woodward esqrs., May 5, 1823, John Calhoun to Wm. Woodward, Dec. 31, 1823, and John Calhoun to William Ward, Jan. 29, 1824, NA-LSW-S, reel 5, frame 436, reel 6, frames 26, 36.

6. Ward to Calhoun, Choctaw Agency, May 28, 1824, NA-OIA, roll 169, frame 122.

7. Ibid.; D. W. Wright to James Monroe, Oct. 8, 1824, NA-LSW-R, roll 169, frame 146.

8. William Ward to John Calhoun, Choctaw Agency, Sept. 23, 1824, NA-LSW-R, roll 169, frame 128.

9. McKenney to Kingsbury, Nov. 5, 1824, in Calhoun, *Papers* 9:371.

10. Calhoun to Choctaw Delegation, Washington, Nov. 9, 1824, Choctaw Delegation to Calhoun, Washington, Nov. 12, 1824, Calhoun to Choctaw Delegation, Washington, Nov. 15, 1824, Calhoun to Thomas H. Williams and Christopher Rankin, Nov. 15, 1824, J. L. McDonald to Calhoun, Washington, Nov. 16, 1824, Calhoun to Choctaw Delegation, Nov. 19, 1824, David Folsom and J. L. McDonald to Calhoun, Washington, Nov. 20, 1824, Choctaw Delegation to Calhoun, Washington, Nov. 22, 1824, Calhoun to Choctaw Delegation, Nov. 27, 1824, and David Folsom and J. L. McDonald to Calhoun, Nov. 30, 1824, in Calhoun, *Papers* 9:374–75, 379–80, 383–84, 384–85, 388, 390–91, 397–99, 407, 411–12. See also *American State Papers* 2:554–55. An account of the negotiations is also given in Viola, *Thomas L. McKenney,* pp. 124–34.

11. Calhoun, *Papers* 11:xxix. As befitted a military hero, Pushmataha was buried in the congressional cemetery in Washington, D.C., where his tombstone may still be seen.

12. Bill for Choctaw Delegation, Jan. 1825, NA-LSW-R, reel 3; Debo, *Rise and Fall,* p. 50.

13. David Folsom and J. L. McDonald to Calhoun, Dec. 1, 1824, Calhoun to Choctaw Delegation, Dec. 28, 1824, Calhoun to Choctaw Delegation, Dec. 31, 1824, Choctaw Delegation to Calhoun, Jan. 3, 1825, Calhoun to Choctaw

Delegation, Jan. 5, 1825, and Calhoun to Choctaw Delegation, Jan. 15, 1825, in Calhoun, *Papers* 9:414, 465–66, 469, 472–73, 475, 498; Kappler, *Indian Affairs* 2:213–14. The signatories of the treaty were J. C. Calhoun, Mooshulatubbee, Robert Cole, Daniel McCurtain, Talking Warrior, Red Fort, Nittuckachee, David Folsom, and J. L. McDonald.

14. Kappler, *Indian Affairs* 2:212.

15. Folsom to Evarts, Washington, Jan. 19, 1825, ABCFM, vol. 4, folder 214.

16. Kingsbury to Evarts, Mayhew, March 17, 1825, ABCFM, vol. 3, folder 7.

17. Loring Williams to Jeremiah Evarts, Bethel, Feb. 14, 1824, ABCFM, vol. 2, folder 174; John Calhoun to William Ward, Dec. 31, 1822, NA-LSW-S, reel 5, frame 375.

18. Loring Williams to Jeremiah Evarts, Bethel, April 1824, ABCFM, vol. 2, folder 177.

19. Kingsbury to Evarts, Choctaw Agency, Oct. 18, 1824, ABCFM, vol. 3, folder 1.

20. Kingsbury to Evarts, Jan. 13, 1824, ABCFM, vol. 2, folder 126; Kingsbury to Evarts, Oct. 8, 1824, ABCFM, vol. 3, folder 1; Tracy, "American Board," p. 147.

21. Kingsbury to Evarts, Oct. 8, 1824, ABCFM, vol. 3, folder 1; Kingsbury to William Winans, Mayhew, Jan. 28, 1825, ABCFM, vol. 3, folder 5.

22. Kingsbury to William Winans, Mayhew, Jan. 28, 1825, ABCFM, vol. 3, folder 5; John C. Calhoun to Choctaw Delegation, Dec. 3, 1824, ABCFM, vol. 4, folder 252.

23. Barclay, *Methodist Missions* 2:135; Miller, *North Mississippi Methodism*, p. 29.

24. Mission personnel included the following: (Elliot) Joel Wood, Anson Dyer, and Lucy Hutchinson, teachers, John Smith, farmer, and Zechariah Howes, mechanic; (Bethel) Stephen Macomber, teacher; (Captain Harrison's, near Puckshanubbee's residence on the Pearl River) Anson Gleason, teacher; (Mayhew) Kingsbury, William Pride, physician, Calvin Cushman, farmer, Samuel Wisner and Philo Stewart, mechanics, William Hooper, Anna Burnham, and Philena Thatcher, teachers; (Aikhunna) Cyrus Byington and David Wright, teacher; (Emmaus) Mr. and Mrs. Moses Jewell and David Gage, teacher, and his wife; (Mr. Juzan's) James T. Hadden, teacher, assisted by Arfasus Nash, a Methodist; (Goshen) Alfred Wright, missionary, Elijah Bardwell, teacher, and Ebenezer Bliss, farmer and mechanic.

25. Prudential Committee Report, 1825, National Anthropological Archives, MS #3153, p. 66; ABCFM, vol. 3, folder 12.

26. Kingsbury to Evarts, Mayhew, Jan. 13, 1824, ABCFM, vol. 2, folder 126; Kingsbury to Henry Hill, June 21, 1824, ABCFM, vol. 1, folder 34.

27. Kingsbury to War Department, Mayhew, July 6, 1825, ABCFM, vol. 3, folder 12.

28. Gibbs to Evarts, Hohtak, June 1825, ABCFM, vol. 4, folder 221.

29. Kingsbury to Thomas L. McKenney, Mayhew, Sept. 28, 1825, in 26th Cong., 2d sess., H. Doc. 109 (cited hereafter as H. Doc. 109).

30. Jno. Coleman, Sampson Muncrief, John Jones, Joseph Riddle, Isaac

Gaunee, Samuel Jones, Jeremiah Gardner, John Walker to Rev Cyrus Kingsbury, Choctaw Trading House, June 27, 1825, H. Doc. 109, p. 7.

31. Thomas McKenney to Chiefs of the Choctaw Nation, Oct. 21, 1825, ABCFM, vol. 4, folder 259.

32. Kingsbury to Thomas McKenney, Mayhew, September 28, 1825, H. Doc. 109, pp. 12–13.

33. Hudson, *Southeastern Indians*, p. 377; Council at Trading House, Choctaw Nation, June 12, 1825, NA-OIA, reel 169, frame 160.

34. J. L. McDonald to Tho. L. McKenney, Jackson, Mississippi, April 25, 1826, NA-OIA, reel 169, frames 326–29.

35. Kingsbury to War Department, Mayhew, July 6, 1825, ABCFM, vol. 3, folder 12.

36. Posey, *Baptist Church*, pp. 84–85.

37. Elias Cornelius to Cyrus Kingsbury, March 8, 1820, quoted in ibid., p. 84.

38. W. Ward to James Barbour, Choctaw Agency, June 26, 1825, H. Doc. 109, p. 4; Kingsbury to Evarts, Mayhew, Aug. 8, 1825, ABCFM, vol. 3, folder 12; Posey, *Baptist Church*, pp. 83–84.

39. Meyer, *Richard M. Johnson*, pp. 336–37; Resolution of Board of Managers of the Baptist General Convention, Dec. 25, 1825, Miscellaneous Choctaw Removal Records, Entry 267, Choctaw Removal Records, box 8; Foreman, "Choctaw Academy," p. 454.

40. William Staughton to the Secretary of War, submitting the plan and regulations of the Choctaw Academy, Dec. 8, 1825, H. Doc. 109, p. 21–22.

41. Tho. McKenney to Tho. Henderson, Feb. 28, 1826, Miscellaneous Choctaw Removal Records, Entry 267, Choctaw Removal Records, box 8.

42. Rouse, "Johnson's Choctaw Academy," p. 97; Foreman, "Choctaw Academy," p. 460.

43. Kingsbury to Evarts, Mayhew, July 24, 1826, ABCFM, vol. 3, folder 16.

44. Kingsbury to Evarts, Mayhew, July 24, 1826, ABCFM, vol. 3, folder 16; Thomas McKenney, Plan and Regulations of the Choctaw Academy, Office of Indian Affairs, Department of War, December 9, 1825, and William Staughton, Corresponding Secretary, Board of Managers of the Baptist General Convention, to Rev. Thomas Henderson, Missionary of the Choctaw Academy in Scott County, Kentucky, both in H. Doc. 109, p. 22.

45. Miscellaneous Choctaw Removal Records, Entry 267, Choctaw Removal Records, box. 8.

46. Thomas L. McKenney to Thomas Henderson, Office of Indian Affairs, Feb. 7, 1828, H. Doc. 109, p. 35.

47. Kingsbury to McKenney, Mayhew, May 5, 1826, ABCFM, vol. 4, folder 278; *Missionary Herald* 24, no. 1 (January 1828): p. 9.

48. Kingsbury to Evarts, Mayhew, Sept. 14, 1825, ABCFM, vol. 3, folder 13.

49. Kingsbury to Evarts, Mayhew, Aug. 8, 1825, ABCFM, vol. 3, folder 12, no. 4.

50. Kingsbury to Evarts, Mayhew, June 21, 1827, ABCFM, vol. 3, folder 24.

51. American Board, *Report . . . Seventeenth Annual Meeting*, p. 105; Foreman, "Foreign Mission School at Cornwall," pp. 242–44. The school at Cornwall closed in 1827 for lack of support.

52. *Missionary Herald* 22, no. 1 (January 1826): 3, no. 8 (August 1826), 234–35.

53. Tuttle, *Conversations* 2:36.

54. Greenwood LeFlore to James Barbour, Choctaw Academy, June 17, 1827, and Charles Juzan to James Barbour, Choctaw Academy, Oct. 17, 1827, H. Doc. 109, pp. 38–39; David Folsom to Richard M. Johnson, Dec. 10, 1829, ABCFM, vol. 4, folder 216.

55. Foreman, "Choctaw Academy," p. 461.

56. Ibid.

57. Christopher Rankin to Monroe, March 14, 1825, NA-OIA, roll 169, frames 202–3.

58. James Monroe to the Senate and House of Representatives of the United States, Washington, Jan. 27, 1825, in Richardson, *Papers of the Presidents* 2:280–82.

59. McCoy, *Baptist Indian Missions,* pp. 217–18.

60. Ibid., pp. 265, 274.

61. L. R. Bakewell to J. P. Barbour, Sept. 2, 1825, NA-OIA, reel 169, frame 153.

62. William Ward to Tho. L. McKenney, Choctaw Agency, March 16, 1826, NA-OIA, reel 169, frames 336–37.

63. Mingo Mushulatubbee, Mingo Robert Cole, Mingo Tappenahhomah, Astonocohajo, Hosheshahomah, Ahacatubbee, Coleman Cole to James Barbour, Sec. of War, March 18, 1826, NA-OIA, reel 169, frames 341–42.

64. David Folsom to Thomas L. McKenney, Gibeon, Chachta Nation, June 27, 1826, NA-OIA, reel 169, frames 277–79.

65. J. Pitchlynn to James Barbour, Choctaw Nation, Feb. 2, 1826, and John McKee to James Barbour, Talapoosa, Sept. 13, 1826, NA-OIA, reel 185.

66. Kingsbury to Evarts, Mayhew, Aug. 8, 1825, ABCFM, folder 11, no. 4.

67. David Folsom to Tho. L. McKenney, Gibeon, Chachta Nation, May 29, 1826, NA-OIA, reel 169, frames 272–75.

68. David Folsom to Thomas L. McKenney, Gibeon, Chachta Nation, June 27, 1826, NA-OIA, reel 169, frames 277–79.

69. David Folsom to Tho. L. McKenney, Gibeon, June 27, 1826, NA-OIA, reel 169, frames 272–75, 277–79; Ray, *Greenwood Leflore,* pp. 47–49.

70. Ray, *Greenwood Leflore,* p. 47; Swanton, *Source Material,* p. 104. See also Morgan, *Ancient Society,* p. 167. The book, first published in 1877, was based on information furnished largely by Indian agents and missionaries, and Morgan mentions how a man asked Kingsbury, by that time with the tribe in Indian Territory, how he could become a citizen of the United States so that he could leave his property to his children rather than having it go to his brothers and sisters as it would under the old Choctaw system.

71. American Board, *Report . . . Eighteenth Annual Meeting,* pp. xxvi–xxvii; Kingsbury to ABCFM, vol. 3, folder 35; William Ward to Thomas McKenney, Aug. 9, 1826, NA-OIA, roll 169. The document was signed by "Tapanahuma, David Folsom and Greenwood Lefleur."

72. American Board, *Report . . . Eighteenth Annual Meeting,* pp. xxvi–xxvii; Kingsbury to ABCFM, vol. 3, folder 35; William Ward to Thomas McKenney, Aug. 9, 1826, NA-OIA, roll 169.

73. David Folsom to Tho. L. McKenney, Gibeon, Chachta Nation, June 27, 1826, NA-OIA, roll 169, frames 277–79; J. L. McDonald to Tho. L. McKenney, Jackson, Miss., April 25, 1826, NA-OIA, roll 169, frames 277–79.

74. L. R. Bakewell to J. P. Barbour, Sept. 2, 1825, NA-OIA, roll 169, frame 153.

75. *Missionary Herald* 18, no. 9 (September 1827): 281.

76. Ibid.

77. L. R. Bakewell to J. P. Barbour, Sept. 2, 1825, NA-OIA, roll 169, frame 153.

78. Kingsbury to Evarts, Mayhew, July 24, 1826, ABCFM, vol. 3, folder 16.

79. Kingsbury to Evarts, Mayhew, Aug. 15, 1826, ABCFM, vol. 3, folder 19.

80. Kingsbury to Evarts, Mayhew, Nov. 10, 1824, ABCFM, vol. 3, folder 4.

81. Kingsbury to Folsom, Mayhew, Aug. 2, 1826, ABCFM, vol. 4, folder 263: Kingsbury, Cushman, Cooper, and Gleason to Evarts, Mayhew, April 24, 1827, ABCFM, vol. 4, folder 265; Kingsbury to Evarts, Mayhew, Aug. 15, 1826, ABCFM, vol. 3, folder 19.

82. *Missionary Herald* 23 (September 1827): 277–78.

CHAPTER 7

1. Thomas McKenney to Eli Baldwin, Oct. 28, 1829, quoted in Prucha, *Federal Indian Policy*, pp. 22–23; Kingsbury to Evarts, Mayhew, Aug. 8, 1825, ABCFM, vol. 1, folder 11, no. 4; Schultz, *Indian Canaan*, pp. 59–81; Prucha, *Great Father* 1:191–93; Rogin, *Fathers and Children*, 206–17; Remini, *Andrew Jackson*, p. 60.

2. Kingsbury to Evarts, Mayhew, June 23, 1830, ABCFM, vol. 3, folder 48; Mushulatubbee, Netuchache, et al., to J. H. Eaton, Secretary of War, Choctaw Nation, June 2, 1830, in *Indian Removals* 2:58–59.

3. Kingsbury to Evarts, Mayhew, June 23, 1830, ABCFM, vol. 3, folder 48.

4. McKenney, *Reports*, p. 4.

5. Ibid., p. 26.

6. Ibid., p. 27.

7. Ibid.

8. In deference to the sensitivity of Leflore's position as a chief, McKenney deleted his name from the published record of his mission, but he included it in his written report to Secretary of War Barbour. McKenney to Barbour, Choctaw Agency, Oct. 17, 1827, NA-OIA, roll 169.

9. "Greenwood Leflore," 2:72.

10. Kingsbury to Evarts, Mayhew, June 21, 1827, ABCFM, vol. 3, folder 24.

11. Kingsbury to Evarts, Elliot, Jan. 15, 1827, ABCFM, vol. 3, folder 22; Kingsbury to Evarts, Mayhew, Aug. 13, 1827, ABCFM, vol. 3, folder 25.

12. Barclay, *Methodist Missions* 2:135–36; Talley to Winans, Opelousa, Sept. 12, 1827, Talley Papers, box 1, folder 9; Holder, *Mississippi Methodists*, p. 33.

13. Sweet, *American Frontier* 2:60; Elsbree, *Missionary Spirit*, p. 30.

14. Talley to Winans, Choctaw Nation, Leflores, June 3, 1828, and Talley to Winans, Doaks Stand, Aug. 27, 1828, Talley Papers, box 1, folder 10.

15. Talley to Winans, Leflore's, June 3, 1828, Talley to Winans, Dokes Stand,

Aug. 27, 1828, and Talley to Winans, Choctaw Nation, Big Land, Oct. 28, 1829, Talley Papers, box 1, folder 10.

16. Zeddock Brashears to Kingsbury, June 21, 1828, ABCFM, vol. 3, folder 26; Kingsbury to Leflore, Mayhew, July 30, 1828, Leflore to Kingsbury, N.W. District, Aug. 8, 1828, and Deposition by Susannah Lyles, ABCFM, vol. 3, folder 26; Kingsbury to Evarts, Mayhew, Oct. 6, 1828, ABCFM, vol. 3, folder 32.

17. Talley to Winans, Choctaw Nation, Leflore's, June 3, 1828, Talley Papers, box l, folder 10; Talley to Winans, Choctaw Nation, Big Land, Oct. 28, 1829, Talley Papers, box 2, folder 12.

18. Talley to Winans, Choctaw Nation, Leflore's, Talley Papers, box 1, folder 10.

19. Talley to Winans, Choctaw Nation, Leflores, June 3, 1828, and Talley to Winans, Doaks Stand, August 27, 1828, Talley Papers, box 1, folder 10.

20. Williams to Evarts, Aiikhunnah, Chahta Nation, Feb. 2, 1829, ABCFM, vol. 3, folder 60.

21. Kingsbury to the Office of the Board, Mayhew, Jan. 28, 1829, ABCFM, vol. 3, folder 35.

22. Williams to Evarts, Aiikhunnah, Chahta Nation, Feb. 2, 1829, ABCFM, vol. 3, folder 60.

23. Wright to Evarts, Goshen, June 26, 1829, ABCFM, vol. 3, folder 107.

24. Talley to Winans, Benton, Yazoo, Sept. 21, 1829, Talley Papers; Smith to Winans, at Captain Cobb's, Chakta Nation, November 3, 1828, Winans Papers, box 1, folder 10.

25. Kingsbury to Evarts, Mayhew, July 23, 1829, ABCFM, vol. 3, folder 39.

26. "T" is probably a man named Tunupinchuffa, who is mentioned several times in Williams's journal. Williams to Evarts, Aiikhunnah, May 4, 1829, ABCFM, vol. 3, folder 61.

27. Talley to Winans, Dokes Stand, Aug. 27, 1828, Talley to Winans, Choctaw Nation, June 1, 1829, and Talley to Winans, Choctaw Nation, Big Land, Oct. 28, 1829, Talley Papers, box 2, folder 12; *Tenth Annual Report of the Missionary Society*, p. 7.

28. Kingsbury to Evarts, Mayhew, May 13, 1829, ABCFM, vol. 3, folder 38.

29. *Niles' Weekly Register* 35, no. 905 (January 17, 1829): 330.

30. David Folsom to Thos. L. McKenney, Chahta Nation, Gibeon, Oct. 14, 1828, NA-OIA, roll 169, frames 500–502.

31. Kingsbury to Evarts, Mayhew, Jan. 29, 1829, ABCFM, vol. 3, no. 35.

32. Byington to Evarts, Yoknokchaya, Sept. 23, 1829, ABCFM, vol. 2, no. 97.

33. Ibid.

34. See Prucha, *Cherokee Removal*. Prucha's introductory essay summarizes Evarts's activities.

35. *Missionary Herald* 25, no. 12 (December 1829): 382.

36. Thomas L. McKenney to P. B. Porter, Dept. of War, Nov. 1, 1828, in *New American State Papers* 1:73.

37. J. L. McDonald to Tho. L. McKenney, Jackson, Miss., April 25, 1826, NA-OIA, M234, roll 169, frames 326–29; Viola, *Thomas L. McKenney*, p. 193.

38. *Laws of the State of Mississippi*, p. 141.

39. Ibid.

40. May, *John A. Quitman*, p. 40; Miles, *Jacksonian Democracy*, p. 24.

41. Andrew Jackson, First Annual Message to Congress, in Richardson, *Papers of the Presidents* 3:1021.

42. Ibid.

43. Kappler, *Indian Affairs* 2:193; Byington to Evarts, Yoknokchaya, Sept. 23, 1829, ABCFM, vol. 3, no. 97.

44. Byington to Evarts, Yoknokchaya, Sept. 23, 1829, ABCFM, vol. 3,no. 97. Choctaw Chiefs to William Ward, Nov. 7, 1829, NA-OIA, roll 169 (quotation).

45. Message from Andrew Jackson to the Choctaws, Washington, Oct. 15, 1829, ABCFM, vol. 4, folder 272.

46. T. Child to ?, Port Gibson, July 11, 1829, NA-OIA, roll 185.

47. William Juzan, Anderson Perry, William Riddle, Samuel Worcester, Basil Leflore, Noel Gardner, Lyman Collins, Levi Franklin, Zadoc Harrison, James Brewer, John Adams, Robert B. Nail, Samuel McCurtin, Robert M. Jones, To Friends and Countrymen, Choctaw Academy, Kentucky, Oct. 10, 1829, ABCFM, vol. 4, folder 313.

48. Mushulatubbee to John Eaton, Choctaw Academy, Kentucky, Sept. 28, 1829, NA-OIA, roll 185.

49. William Juzan, Anderson Perry, William Riddle, Samuel Worcester, Basil Leflore, Noel Gardner, Lyman Collins, Levi Franklin, Zadoc Harrison, James Brewer, John Adams, Robert B. Nail, Samuel McCurtin, Robert M. Jones, To Friends and Countrymen, Choctaw Academy, Kentucky, Oct. 10, 1829, ABCFM, vol. 4, folder 313.

50. David Folsom to Richard M. Johnson, Chahta Nation, Dec. 10, 1829, ABCFM, vol. 4, folder 216; letter from Folsom appended to letter from boys at Choctaw Academy, ABCFM, vol. 4, folder 313.

51. Kingsbury to Evarts, Mayhew, May 6, 1830, ABCFM, vol. 3, folder 45.

52. David Folsom to William Ward, Chakta Nation, Nov. 22, 1829, and Mackey to John Eaton, Choctaw Nation, Nov. 27, 1829, NA-OIA, roll 185; Talley to Winans, Dokes Stand, July 5, 1830, Talley Papers, box 10, folder 10.

53. William Ward to the secretary of war, Oct. 11, 1830, and Nov. 14, 1830, NA-OIA, roll 169.

54. Amendments to the latter act were proposed that would have deprived the Choctaws of the right to vote and to serve as jurors, but these failed. See *Journal of the House of Representatives of the State of Mississippi*, p. 36; *Laws of the State of Mississippi*, p. 141; *Code of Mississippi*, p. 136.

55. "Patriot Letter," *Natchez* 1, no. 7 (February 13, 1830): 53.

56. *Niles' Weekly Register* 37, no. 947 (November 7, 1829): 172.

57. William Winans to E. Smith, Esq., Centreville, Amite, March 10, 1830, Winans Papers, microfilm copy.

58. Talley to William Winans, Queens School, July 19, 1830, Winans Papers, box 2, folder 12.

59. Kingsbury to Evarts, Mayhew, Feb. 15, 1830, ABCFM, vol. 3, folder 43.

60. Kingsbury to Evarts, May 28, 1830, Statement of Captain Johnson of Kentucky, May 3, 1830, and Ward to Kingsbury, Choctaw Agency, May 7, 1830, ABCFM, vol. 3, folder 46.

61. J. R. Nicholson to Winans, Nicholson, Miss., Sept. 10, 1830, Winans Papers.

62. Kingsbury to Evarts, Mayhew, May 6, 1830, ABCFM, vol. 3, folder 45; Byington to Evarts, Yoknachaya, March 18, 1830, ABCFM, vol. 3, folder 100; Talley to Winans, Choctaw Nation, March 20, 1830, Winans Papers, box 2, folder 12; Debo, *Rise and Fall*, p. 52.

63. Byington to Evarts, Yoknachaya, March 18, 1830, ABCFM, vol. 3, folder 100.

64. Kingsbury to Evarts, Mayhew, May 6, 1830, ABCFM, vol. 3, folder 45; Talley to Winans, Dokes Stand, July 5, 1830, Talley Papers; DeRosier, *Removal*, pp. 113–14; Kingsbury to Thomas L. McKenney, Mayhew, C. N., March 22, 1830, ABCFM, vol. 3, folder 43.

65. Talley to William Winans, Queens School, July 19, 1830, Winans Papers, box 2, folder 12.

66. Byington to Evarts, Yoknachaya, March 18, 1830, ABCFM, vol. 3, folder 100.

67. Talley to Winans, Dokes Stand, July 5, 1830, Talley Papers; Richardson, *Papers of the Presidents* 10:478–79.

68. 4 *U.S. Stat. L.*, 411–12. 4 (1830): 411–12. See Satz, *American Indian Policy*, for a complete discussion of congressional actions and debates concerning the passage of the removal bill.

69. McCoy, *Baptist Indian Missions*, p. 400.

70. Wright to Evarts, Goshen, June 26, 1829, ABCFM, vol. 3, folder 107; Byington to Evarts, Yaknokchaya, May 19, 1830, ABCFM, vol. 3, no. 101.

71. Greenwood Leflore to Mushulatubbee, Big Sand, April 1830, copy in Leflore Papers.

72. Mushulatubbee, Netuchache, et al. to John Eaton, Choctaw Nation, June 2, 1830, in *Indian Removals* 2:58–59. A statement at the end of the letter, signed by John Pitchlyn, M. Mackey, and P. P. Pitchlynn, certifies that the statement "is the talk of the principal chiefs and headmen of the northeast and southern districts."

73. Kingsbury to Evarts, Mayhew, May 6, 1830, ABCFM, vol. 3, folder 45; Talley to Winans, Dokes Stand, July 5, 1830, Talley Papers, box 1, folder 7.

74. Wright to Evarts, Goshen, June 26, 1829, ABCFM, vol. 3, folder 107.

75. Kingsbury to Evarts, Mayhew, July 23, 1830, ABCFM, vol. 3, folder 39.

76. Talley to Winans, Dokes Stand, July 5, 1830, Talley Papers, box 1, folder 10.

77. Mushulatubbee and Nittukaichee to William Ward, April 17, 1830, NA-OIA, roll 169.

78. Kingsbury to Evarts, Mayhew, June 23, 1830, ABCFM, vol. 3, folder 48; Debo, *Rise and Fall*, p. 54.

79. Claiborne, *Mississippi*, p. 509.

80. William Ward to Col. Richard Johnson, Choctaw Agency, Aug. 7, 1830, NA-OIA, roll 185. The text of Ward's letter appears in Foreman, *Indian Removal*, pp. 25–26.

81. Debo, *Rise and Fall*, p. 54, citing *Niles' Register* 38 (1830): 457–58.

82. Kingsbury to Henry Hill, Mayhew, July 26, 1830, ABCFM, vol. 3, folder 50.

83. Mushulatubbee and Nitakeche to Eaton, Aug. 16, 1830, NA-OIA, roll 169; R. D. Smith to Winans, Queen's School, Oct. 1, 1830, Winans Papers, box 2, folder 12.

84. Andrew Jackson to the Choctaws, Franklin, Tennessee, Aug. 23, 1830, Documents Concerning the Negotiation of Ratified Indian Treaties, 1801–1869, Microfilm Series T494, roll 2.

85. Cyrus Kingsbury, Cyrus Byington, Loring S. Williams, and Calvin Cushman to Eaton and Coffee, Sept. 17, 1829, Journal of Proceedings, pp. 39–40, in Documents Concerning the Negotiation of Ratified Indian Treaties, 1801–1869, Microfilm Series T494, roll 2; Kingsbury to Evarts, Mayhew, received Oct. 11, 1820, ABCFM, vol. 5, folder 2; Kingsbury to Evarts, Mayhew, Nov. 24, 1830, ABCFM, vol. 5, folder 6.

86. Halbert, "Story of the Treaty," p. 375; Talley to Drake, Treaty Ground, Sept. 19, 1830, cited by C. M. Thayer to Winans, Sept. 25, 1830, Talley Papers, box 2, folder 12.

87. Journal of Proceedings, Treaty of Dancing Rabbit Creek, Documents Concerning the Negotiation of Ratified Indian Treaties, 1801–1869, Microfilm Series T494, roll 2.

88. Kingsbury to Evarts, Mayhew, Sept. 29, 1830, ABCFM, vol. 5, folder 3.

89. Kappler, *Indian Affairs* 2:310–11.

90. Halbert, "Story of the Treaty"; Kappler, *Indian Affairs* 2:313.

91. Kappler, *Indian Affairs* 2:311.

92. Ibid., pp. 313–14.

93. Byington to David Greene, Yoknokhaya, Dec. 1, 1830, ABCFM, vol. 5, folder 156.

94. Choctaw Captains of 6 Towns, Cafowanee and Chickasawhey, to Eaton, in Council at Yakniachukma, Oct. 16, 1830, and Iyachuhopia to Eaton, n.d., NA-OIA, roll 185.

95. Kingsbury to Evarts, Mayhew, Sept. 29, 1830, ABCFM, vol. 5, folder 3.

96. Kingsbury to Evarts, Mayhew, Nov. 24, 1830, ABCFM, vol. 5, folder 6.

97. 22d Cong., 1st sess., H. Doc. 194, pp. 1–5.

98. Ibid., p. 3.

99. *Missionary Herald* 20, no. 1 (January 1824): 3; Gaines, "Reminiscences," p. 158; American Board, *Monthly Paper*.

100. 22d Cong., 1st sess., H. Doc. 194, p. 14.

101. American Board, *Monthly Paper*, pp. 11–12; American Board, *Report . . . Twenty-Second Annual Meeting*, p. 104.

102. Kingsbury noted in 1825, "The greatest part of the scholars, at those schools where they are boarded in the mission families, are the children of half-breeds" (Kingsbury to Rufus Anderson, Mayhew, June 24, 1825, ABCFM, vol. 3, folder 11).

103. By 1830 there were fourteen schools among the white population of the state of Mississippi, although statistics are not readily available on the number who attended. See Lucas, "Education in Mississippi," 1:356.

104. American Board, *Monthly Paper*, p. 12.

105. Ibid., pp. 11–12; American Board, *Report . . . Twenty-Third Annual Meeting*, p. 104; Kingsbury to Calhoun, Mayhew, Choctaw Nation, Oct. 1829, ABCFM, vol. 3, folder 41.

106. American Board, *Memorial Volume*, p. 321.

CHAPTER 8

1. Tocqueville, *Democracy in America,* pp. 298–99

2. Foreman's account of the removal documents the conditions of the removal and the suffering of many Choctaws. Parties of Choctaws continued to move from Mississippi to Indian Territory through 1849. See Foreman, *Indian Removal,* pp. 56–104.

3. Mushaletubee, Oklabbee, Ispiahhomah, Charles King, James M. King, Hiram King, and Peter King to Andrew Jackson, Dec. 23, 1830, cited in Foreman, "Choctaw Academy," p. 475.

4. Kingsbury to Evarts, Mayhew, May 6, 1830, ABCFM, vol. 3, folder 45.

5. Isaac Folsom, Robert Folsom, John Folsom, et al., Choctaw Nation, March 19, 1831, ABCFM, vol. 5, folder 9.

6. Moseley, *Missionary Meetings,* p. 107; McCoy, *Baptist Indian Missions,* p. 401.

7. American Board, *Memorial Volume,* p. 302; Debo, *Rise and Fall,* pp. 60–61, 65. See Coleman, *Presbyterian Missionary Attitudes,* for a discussion of American Board activities in Indian Territory.

8. Wood, *Report,* p. 20; *Constitution and Laws of the Choctaw Nation,* pp. 70–71; Littlefield, *Okah Tubbee,* p. 10; 28th Cong., 2d sess., H. Rep. 193.

9. Lewit, "Indian Missions."

10. American Anti-Slavery Society, *Slavery and the American Board,* pp. 1–20. See correspondence between Kingsbury and Byington and officers of the Presbyterian Church, in Presbyterian Historical Society, *American Indian Correspondence,* box 2, vol. 2; Lewit, "Indian Missions," pp. 50–54.

11. Benson, *Life among the Choctaw,* p. 28; American Board, *Memorial Volume,* p. 259.

12. Debo, *Rise and Fall,* p. 75.

13. Benson, *Life among the Choctaw,* p. 29. For an example of laws, see *Chahta oklahi nanulhpisa.* This text was also published in English. For an example of the gospel, see American Bible Society, *The Books of Genesis.*

14. Debo, *Rise and Fall,* pp. 65, 76–77, 109; Stuart, *Sketch of the Cherokee,* pp. 31–32.

15. Benson, *Life among the Choctaw,* pp. 50–51.

16. Spicer, "European Expansion"; Blu, *The Lumbee Problem;* Finger, *The Eastern Band;* Rountree, *Pocahontas's People;* Merrell, *The Indians' New World;* Paredes, *Indians.*

17. See Claiborne, *Mississippi,* p. 519, for funeral and mourning customs; Brown, *Newton County,* pp. 14–15, for ball games; Kenaston, "Sharecropping," p. 131, for persistence of beliefs in witchcraft and traditional curing in the Tennessee Choctaw community that split off from the Mississippi group; Bremer, *Chata Indians,* for persistence of community organization in Louisiana; Sawyer, "Choctaw Indians," pp. 209–10.

18. Peterson, "The Mississippi Band," p. 40; T. C. Stuart to I. L. Cochran, Philadelphia, Oct. 31, 1848, NA-OIA, roll 186. See also Usner, "American Indians"; Phillips to Harris, Natchez, Dec. 8, 1836, Miscellaneous Choctaw Removal Records, Entry 267, Choctaw Removal Records; Testimony of Tanampishubbee, Case 261, "Journal of Proceedings."

19. Eggan, "Historical Changes," p. 39. The terminology recorded by By-ington in about 1860 in Indian Territory showed a pattern grouping the father's sister's son and his descendents through the male line under the term "fa-ther"—a male-oriented system. See Swanton, *Source Material*, p. 86. Eggan found this same terminology among the Mississippi Choctaws in the 1930s, but Edwards, who had collaborated with Byington in collecting data in Indian Territory, recalled an earlier, and definitely matrilineal, system that classified the father's sisters and their female offspring as aunts, a matrilineal system that Edwards summarized as "aunts in a row." (Edwards, "Choctaw Indians," p. 400.) See also Eggan, *American Indian*, and Spoehr, *Changing Kinship*, for discussions of changing kinship patterns as evidence of historial change.

20. Testimony of Nokaanchatubbee, Case 320, "Journal of Proceedings."

21. Gaines to Crawford, Yazoo Old Village, Sept. 22, 1844, NA-OIA, roll 185; Deposition of Toba-Chubba, Oct. 21, 1833, NA-OIA, roll 188; Testimony of Toblachubbee, Case 347, "Journal of Proceedings."

22. See the tabular lists of claims presented by Commissioners Murray and Vroom in 1838 and printed in U.S. Court of Claims, "The Choctaw Nation of Indians v. the United States" (hereafter cited as "Choctaw Nation v. U.S."), 1:218–81.

23. "General Roll of Choctaw Families," Census Roll, Entry 260, Choctaw Removal Records.

24. Kappler, *Indian Affairs* 2:313.

25. Moore, *Cotton Kingdom*, p. 19; Rohrbough, *Trans-Appalachian Frontier*, p. 298.

26. "Choctaw Nation v. U.S.," 1:18.

27. George W. Martin to Lewis Cass, Chocchuma, Sept. 15, 1833, "Choctaw Nation v. U.S.," 1:38–39; Letter from John M. Moore, Acting Commissioner of the General Land Office, to Elbert Herring, Commissioner of Indian Affairs, June 17, 1833, in 24th Cong., 1st sess., S. Doc. 69, p. 3.

28. T. S. Sumrall, Registrar, Mt. Salus Land Office, to Ethan A. Brown, Commissioner of the General Land Office, Dec. 11, 1835, in 24th Cong., 1st sess., S. Doc. 69, p. 20; Young, *Redskins*, pp. 52–53; Rohrbough, *Land Office Business*, pp. 222–23.

29. Case no. 2, "Journal of Proceedings."

30. Testimony of G. W. Martin, April 18, 1836, 24th Cong., 1st sess., H. Doc. 1523, p. 677. See Young, *Redskins*, for a complete account of the role of land speculators in the disposition of land in Indian cessions in the Southeast.

31. 24th Cong., 1st sess., H. Doc. 89; 24th Cong., 2d sess., *Petition*; 24th Cong., 1st sess., H. Doc. 119.

32. Miles, *Jacksonian Democracy*, pp. 133–34.

33. 5 *U.S. Stat. L.*, 2, chapter 39.

34. P. D. Vroom, J. Murray, Roger Barton, Leflore's place, Mississippi, to C. A. Harris, Commissioner of Indian Affairs, March 1, 1838, "Choctaw Nation v. U.S.," 1:126.

35. Journal of Hearings Held by Murray and Vroom, Entry 271, Choctaw Removal Records; 24th Cong., 1st sess., H. Rep. 663, pp. 32–33; William Ward to Samuel S. Hamilton, Choctaw Agency, June 21, 1831, NA-OIA, roll 185;

George W. Martin to Lewis Cass, Secretary of War, Sept. 11, 1833, "Choctaw Nation v. U.S.," 1:37.

36. S. A. Phillips, Natchez, Dec. 9, 1836, NA-OIA, roll 185.

37. Rister, *Baptist Missions*, p. 94.

38. John McRae to H. Crawford, Hopakha, Feb. 6, 1843, NA-OIA, roll 185.

39. Murray and P. D. Vroom to the President, "Choctaw Nation v. U.S.," 1:131–36.

40. 28th Cong., 1st sess., S. Doc. 168, pp. 53–55.

41. Claiborne, *Proceedings*.

42. "Choctaw Nation v. U.S.," 1:494–95; 29th Cong., 1st sess., H. Doc. 189, pp. 2–3; Choctaw Patents, Bureau of Land Management.

43. 28th Cong., 2d sess., S. Doc. 86.

44. Crawford to John McRae, at Paulding, Mississippi, Dec. 2, 1842, N.A. Microfilm 234, roll 185; McRae to Crawford, Hopahka, Sept. 22, 1843, Miscellaneous Choctaw Removal Records, Entry 267, Choctaw Removal Records.

45. "General Roll of Choctaw Families," Entry 260, Census Roll, Choctaw Removal Records.

46. Cornelius Janssens, to Director of Board of Catholic Indian Missions, Feb. 16, 1888, Board of Catholic Indian Missions, Papers (hereafter cited as BCIM), series I, box 21, folder 17.

47. LeBreton, *Chata-Ima*, pp. 168, 201–208, 222–24, 238.

48. Peterson, "Louisiana Choctaw Life," pp. 106–7. Bushnell, *Bayou Lacomb*, reveals the persistence of this way of life into the early twentieth century. Kenaston, "Sharecropping," describes the existence of some elements of this life-style in Tennessee in the 1950s.

49. Rowland, *Military History*, p. 787.

50. Compiled Service Records of Confederate Soldiers.

51. Mississippi State Archives, Record Group 69, vol. 24, folder 17.

52. Peterson, "The Mississippi Band," p. 50.

53. Kappler, *Indian Affairs* 2:313; Report of the Secretary of the Interior, 1871, I, 755, cited in Davis, "Mississippi Choctaws," p. 260.

54. 28th Cong., 1st sess., S. Doc. 168; 5 *U.S. Stat. L.*, 513–16; "Choctaw Nation v. U.S.," Argument of Thomas Simons for the Defendants, 1:179.

55. "Choctaw Nation v. U.S.," Evidence, 1:494–95.

56. *U.S. Stat. L.*, 777.

57. Proclamation from Council, September 21, 1843, Report on Removal, William Wilkins, Secretary of War, February 6, 1845, A. Harris to W. Medill, Washington, June 30, 1846, Armstrong to Medill, Washington, July 1, 1846, and Medill to Marcy, February 11, 1848, NA-OIA, roll 186.

58. U.S. Department of the Interior, *Report of the Commissioner of Indian Affairs*, p. 214.

59. Debo, *Rise and Fall*, pp. 180–81.

60. "Choctaw Nation v. U.S.,"1:22.

61. Baird, *Peter Pitchlynn*, p. 97.

62. G. W. Manypenny to D. H. Cooper, April 4, 1855, Miscellaneous Choctaw Removal Records, Entry 267, Choctaw Removal Records.

63. Gibson, *The Chickasaws*; Debo, *Rise and Fall*, p. 171.

64. Kappler, *Indian Affairs* 2:706; Debo, *Rise and Fall*, p. 71; Gibson, *The Chickawaws*, pp. 219–23.

65. Baird, *Peter Pitchlynn*, pp. 97–107.

66. Ibid., pp. 98–99; Kappler, *Indian Affairs* 2:706.

67. "Choctaw Nation v. U.S.," 1:36.

68. Kappler, *Indian Affairs* 2:918–31.

69. *The Choctaw Nation.*

CHAPTER 9

1. Prentiss, *Memoir* 1:130–31.

2. The Baptist Church numbered 400 churches and 21,485 members in 1845. Pillar, "Religious and Cultural Life," p. 382; Rister, *Baptist Missions*, p. 94; Farr, "Religious Assimilation," pp. 26–27.

3. McLemore, *Mississippi Baptists*, p. 3; *Minutes of the Forty-Second Annual Session*, p. 6.

4. *Christian Advocate* 36, no. 15 (April 11, 1889): 2.

5. Archives of the Diocese of Jackson, File: Janssens, C.; Halbert to Draper, Crawford, Lowndes Co., May 11, 1886, Draper Papers, pp. 172, 354.

6. T. L. Mellen, Missionary Secretary, Mission Conference, Canton, Mississippi, to the editor of the *Christian Advocate,* January 29, 1897, see *Christian Advocate* 44, no. 6 (February 11, 1897): 1, vol. 48, no. 41 (October 10, 1901): 2, vol. 36, no. 31 (August 1, 1889): 2.

7. *Christian Advocate* 39, no. 19 (May 12, 1892): 1.

8. Ibid. Halbert, "Indians in Mississippi," p. 536.

9. Gerow, *Catholicity*, pp. 259–62.

10. *Christian Advocate* 43, no. 46 (November 12, 1896): 3.

11. McLemore, *Mississippi Baptists*, p. 149. The Baptist missionary was Rev. N. L. Clarke of Decatur. Halbert to Draper, House P.O., Neshoba Co., Mississippi, June 24, 1887, Draper Papers.

12. Farr, "Religious Assimilation," p. 28.

13. *Minutes of the Eighth Annual Meeting*, pp. 8–9; *Proceedings of the General Association . . . Held with Bethel Church*, p. 4; *History of the Harmony Baptist Association*, p. 26; *Minutes of the General Association . . . Held with Zion Hill Church*, p. 3; *Minutes of the General Association . . . Held with Poplarville Church*, pp. 5–6; Farr, "Religious Assimilation," p. 28; *History of the Harmony Baptist Association*, p. 30; *Minutes of the General Association . . . Held with Fellowship Church*, p. 3; *Minutes of the General Association . . . Held with Decatur Church*, p. 3.

14. Tolbert, "Study of the Choctaw Indians," p. 220; Farr, "Religious Assimilation," pp. 32, 75; *Christian Advocate* 36, no. 31 (August 1, 1889): 2; *Proceedings of the General Association . . . Held with Shady Grove Church*, p. 5; *Minutes of the General Association . . . Held with Oakland Church*, pp. 7–8; *History of the Harmony Baptist Association*, pp. 15–16; *Minutes of the Fifty-fourth Annual Session*, p. 7; Brown, *Newton County*, pp. 20–27, 273.

15. *Minutes of the Seventy-Eighth Annual Session*; *Christian Advocate* 38, no. 53 (December 31, 1891): 2, vol. 39, no. 18 (May 5, 1892): 1, no. 24 (June 16, 1982), no. 35 (September 1, 1892): 2.

16. Brown, *Newton County*, p. 22; Jones, *Methodism*, p. 62; "Proceedings of the Eightieth Session," p. 39; "Proceedings of the Eighty-Third Session," p. 36; *Christian Advocate* 39, no. 41 (October 13, 1892): 2, vol. 40, no. 10 (March 9, 1893): 1, vol. 42, no. 11 (April 25, 1895): 5, vol. 43, no. 10 (March 5, 1896): 3, vol. 45, no. 7 (February 17, 1898): 5; "Proceedings of the Eighty-Fifth Session," p. 35; Farr, "Religious Assimilation," p. 33; "Proceedings of the Eighty-Seventh Session"; *Christian Advocate* 42, no. 26 (June 27, 1895): 3, vol. 47, no. 39 (September 27, 1900): 1, vol. 46, no. 3 (January 19, 1899): 3; *Journal of the 89th Session*, p. 49; *Journal of the 90th Session*.

17. Halbert, "Indians in Mississippi," p. 536; Brown, *Newton County*, pp. 20–27; *Christian Advocate* 39, no. 18 (May 5, 1892): 1, no. 35 (September 1, 1892): 2, vol. 39, no. 35 (September 1, 1892): 2, vol. 40, no. 10 (March 9, 1893): 1, vol. 40, no. 11 (March 16, 1893): 2.

18. Brown, *Newton County*, pp. 26–27. See Draper, "Abba Isht tuluwa," for a discussion of the significant hymns in the Choctaw language in contemporary Mississippi Choctaw communities.

19. Brown, *Newton County*, pp. 20–21; Claiborne, *Mississippi*, pp. 504–5; Beckett, "Choctaw Indians," pp. 63–64; Blanchard, *Mississippi Choctaws*, pp. 40–43.

20. Lickteig, "Indian Apostolate," p. 69.

21. *Minutes of the Fifty-First Annual Session*, p. 7; Halbert, "Indian Schools," p. 24. A major part of ball games was gambling on the outcome, and the Mississippi legislature passed a law in 1898 prohibiting gambling at Indian ball games. Blanchard, *Mississippi Choctaws*, pp. 41–42.

22. Brown, *Newton County*, pp. 20–27, 273; *Minutes of the General Association of Regular Baptists*, p. 12; Jones, *Methodism*, p. 62; "Proceedings of the Eightieth Session," p. 39; *Christian Advocate* 38, no. 53 (December 31, 1891): 2; *Minutes of the Seventy-Eighth Annual Session; Christian Advocate* 39, no. 41 (October 13, 1892): 2, vol. 40, no. 10 (March 9, 1893): 1, vol. 48, no. 41 (October 10, 1901): 2, vol. 45, no. 5 (February 3, 1898): 2, Report of Catholic Indian Missions for 1907, BCIM, series 2, box 4, folder 17.

23. *Christian Advocate* 46, no. 3 (January 19, 1899): 3, vol. 46, no. 36 (September 7, 1899): 3.

24. Ibid. 48, no. 41 (October 10, 1901): 1.

25. Bernard, *Sisters of Mercy*, p. 132.

26. Bekkers, "Indian Mission of Tucker," p. 3; Janssens to Director Board of Catholic Indian Missions, Dec. 20, 1889, and Sister Mary Bernard, St. Aloysius Academy, Meridian, to W. H. Ketcham, Washington, D.C., April 5, [1917], BCIM, series I, box 24, folder 2, and series 1, box 107, folder 1; Halbert to Draper, House P.O., Neshoba Co., Mississippi, June 24, 1887, Draper Papers.

27. Mississippi Laws, 1882, chapter 41, in *Annotated Code*, p. 77; Janssens to Director of Board of Catholic Indian Missions, Feb. 16, 1888, BCIM, series I, box 21, folder 17; Prucha, *Churches*, p. 2; Halbert, "Indians in Mississippi," pp. 534–45; Halbert, "Indian Schools in Mississippi," pp. 574–76; Halbert, "Indian Schools," pp. 23–30; Halbert, "Mississippi Choctaws."

28. Halbert, "Indian Schools in Mississippi," p. 574; Halbert, "Mississippi Choctaws," p. 35.

29. "Proceedings of the Eighty-Third Session," p. 36; *Christian Advocate* 42 (April 25, 1895): 5, vol. 43, no. 10 (March 5, 1896): 3, vol. 45, no. 7 (February 17, 1898): 5.

30. Halbert, "Indian Schools in Mississippi," p. 574.

31. Sawyer, "Choctaw Indians," p. 209.

CHAPTER 10

1. Washburn, *Indian Tribalism*, pp. 68–73; Roosevelt, *Presidential Addresses* 1:549; Hoxie, *Final Promise*. Hofstadter's presentation of the American agrarian ideal in *The Age of Reform* is still classic. See Otis, *The Dawes Act*, for a succinct summary of the legislative history of the Dawes Act and its impact on Indian tribes.

2. 30 *U.S. Stat. L.*, 495, Act of June 28, 1898; Debo, *Rise and Fall*, pp. 246–62.

3. Debo, *Rise and Fall*, 181–84.

4. Indian Affairs Kappler, 2:313.

5. For acts conferring citizenship, see *Laws of the Choctaw Nation*, pp. 26, 45; *Constitution and Laws of the Choctaw Nation, Together with the Treaties*, p. 53; Debo, *Still the Waters*, p. 181.

6. 30 *U.S. Stat. L.*, 83; U.S. Commission, *Annual Report [Fifth] of the Commission to the Five Civilized Tribes*, p. 24.

7. 57th Cong., 2d sess., S. Doc. 319; Debo, *Still the Waters*, pp. 43–44.

8. Breek to Bishop Meerschaert, Feb. 2, 1903, BCIM, series 1, box 45, folder 5.

9. Breek to Eugene Easton, Antlers, I.T., Jan. 23, 1903, Eugene Easton to Ketcham, Jan. 26, 1903, and Eugene Easton to Rev. Bishop Meerschaert, Guthrie, I.T., BCIM, series 1, box 45, folder 5.

10. K. S. Murchison, Philadelphia, Miss., to Charles Lusk, Feb. 5, 1901, Aug. Breek, Tucker, to Right Rev. Mgr. J. A. Stephan, Feb. 15, 1901, and W. H. Ketcham to Aug. Breek, Feb. 19, 1901, BCIM, series 1, box 42, folder 9.

11. W. H. Ketcham to Aug. Breek, Feb. 19, 1901, BCIM, series 1, box 42, folder 9.

12. Aug. Breek, Tucker, to W. H. Ketcham, March 6, 1901, BCIM, series 1, box 42, folder 9.

13. Lusk to Murchison, March 25, 1901, and Ketcham to Breek, March 25, 1901, BCIM, series 1, box 42, folder 9.

14. Breek to Ketcham, [March 1901], BCIM, series 1, box 42, folder 9.

15. Halbert, "Mississippi Choctaws," pp. 36–37; U.S. Commission, *Annual Report [Sixth] of the Commission to the Five Civilized Tribes*, p. 92; U.S. Commission, *Annual Report [Seventh] of the Commission to the Five Civilized Tribes*, p. 16; Sawyer, "Choctaw Indians," p. 164.

16. Roberts, "Second Choctaw Removal," p. 103; U.S. Commission, *Annual Report [Eleventh] of the Commission to the Five Civilized Tribes*, p. 19; Report of H. Van Smith to Commissioner of Indian Affairs, Muskogee, Aug. 16, 1903, Entry 168, Federal Record Center, Fort Worth, Texas; Breek to Ketcham, Aug. 11, 1903, BCIM, series 1, box 45, folder 5.

17. Kappler, *Indian Affairs* 3:17; Debo, *Still the Waters*, pp. 97–98.

18. U.S. Commission, *Final Rolls.*

19. Swanton, *Source Material*, p. 5; Peterson, "The Mississippi Band," p. 109; Mississippi Band, *Overall Economic Development Plan*, p. 17.

20. *Journal of the 92nd Session; Journal of the 95th Session; Journal of the 98th Session; Journal of the 101st Session*, p. 90; *Christian Advocate* 52, no. 6 (February 9, 1905): 3 (quotation); Breek to Ketcham, Aug. 11, 1903, Tams Bixby, chairman, Dawes Commission, Muskogee, to William Ketcham, Sept. 17, 1903, Ketcham to Rt. Rev. T. Heslin, Natchez, Feb. 9, 1903, Breek to Ketcham, Sept. 10, 1903, Breek to Ketcham, Oct. 30, 1903, Ketcham to Most Rev. Diomede Falconio, Apostolic Delegate, Washington, Nov. 13, 1903, Ketcham to Breek, Dec. 21, 1903, and Ketcham to Falconio, Dec. 21, 1903, BCIM, series 1, box 45, folder 5.

21. Beckett, "Choctaw Indians," pp. 36–37; Farr, "Religious Assimilation," pp. 32–33; Peterson, "The Mississippi Band," pp. 89, 97; *Minutes of the General Association of Regular Baptists*, p. 6.

22. Halbert, "Mississippi Choctaws," p. 37; Farr, "Religious Assimilation," p. 19; Tolbert, "Study of the Choctaw," pp. 125–26; Osoinach, 'Choctaw Society." p. 31.

23. 64th Cong., 2d sess., H. Doc. 1464, p. 25.

24. Breek to Ketcham, Aug. 11, 1903, Breek to Ketcham, [1903], Breek to Ketcham, May 22, 1903, Breek to Ketcham, Sept. 10, 1903, Ketcham to Most Rev. Diomede Falconio, Apostolic Delegate, Washington, Nov. 13, 1903, Ketcham to Breek, Dec. 21, 1903, and Ketcham to Falconio, Dec. 21, 1903, BCIM, series 1, box 45, folder 5; Report of Catholic Indian Missions for 1908, BCIM, series 2/2, box 4, folder 17; School Report, 1910, BCIM, series 2/1, box 13, folder 3; Report of Catholic Indian Missions for 1910, BCIM series 2/2, box 4, folder 17.

25. Report of Catholic Indian Missions for 1907, BCIM, series 2k/2, box 4, folder 17.

26. Enis to Ketcham, March 26, 1917, BCIM, series 1, box 107, folder 1; Ketcham to Ahern, June 9, 1916, P. J. Wendel, S.V.D, Meridian, Miss., to Ketcham, July 31, 1916, Wendel to Ketcham, Aug. 5, 1916, Ahern to Ketcham, Dec. 15, 1916, Ahern to Ketcham, Dec. 16, 1916, Ketcham to Ahern, Dec. 20, 1916, and Ketcham to Ahern, Dec. 26, 1916, BCIM, series 1, box 102, folder 6; Ahern to Ketcham, June 16, 1917, and Ketcham to Ahern, Nov. 10, 1917, BCIM, series 1, box 107, folder 1.

27. Minutes of the General Association, p. 6, 14; Minutes of the General Association, p. 11.

28. Secretary of Board of Catholic Indian Missions to Enis, St. Mary's Institute, Chatowa, Miss, Dec. 31, 1913, BCIM, series 1, box 86, folder 10; *Indian Sentinal* 1, (1916): 26–27, vol. 1, no. 3 (January 1917): 20.; Ketcham to Wendel, Dec. 23, 1916, BCIM, series 1, box 102, folder 6; Ahern to Ketcham, Jan. 8, 1917, and Ahern to Ketcham, [April 24, 1917], BCIM, series 1, box 107, folder 1. Ahern himself learned to say the Rosary in Choctaw. (Ahern to Ketcham, Dec. 16, 1916, BCIM, series 1, box 102, folder 6.)

29. Ahern to Ketcham, Jan. 1, 1917, BCIM, series 1, box 107, folder 1.

30. Proceedings of the Sixty-Second Annual Session of the Harmony Baptist Association, p. 32; *Minutes of the Third Annual Session of the New Choctaw Baptist Association*, p. 8; *Minutes of the Fourth Annual Session of the New Choctaw Baptist Association*, p. 3; Minutes of the Seventh Annual Session of the New Choctaw Baptist Association; Farr, "Religious Assimilation," pp. 70–71.

31. U.S. Commission, *Annual Report [Eighth] of the Commission to the Five Civilized Tribes*, pp. 18–19.

32. U.S. Commission, pp. 161–70; Coker, "Pat Harrison's Efforts," pp. 38–39.

33. Debo, *Still the Waters*, pp. 267–68; Coker, "Pat Harrison's Efforts," p. 40.

34. Coker, "Pat Harrison's Efforts," pp. 46–47.

35. Ibid., pp. 41–42.

36. U.S. Department of the Interior, *Report of Inspector James McLaughlin*, pp. 3–31.

37. *Proposed Legislation for the Full-Blood*, p. 19.

38. J. E. Arnold, Washington, D.C., to Rev. Father Enis, Philadelphia, Miss., March 27, 1913, BCIM, series 1, box 86, folder 10.

39. Ketcham to Enis, June 17, 1913, BCIM, series 1, Box 86, folder 10.

40. *Proposed Legislation for the Full-Blood*, pp. 8–9, 19; Enis to Ketcham, June 12, 1913, BCIM, series 1, box 86, folder 10.

41. Coker, "Pat Harrison's Efforts," pp. 52–53.

42. 39 *U.S. Stat. L.*, 123, 128.

43. 64th Cong., 2d sess., H. Doc. 1464, pp. 2, 6, 11, 14, 24, 25, 28.

44. *Condition of the Mississippi Choctaws*, pp. 117, 131, 160, 134, 150.

45. Prucha, *Churches*, p. 205. In the records of the Board of Catholic Indian Missions, letters in Choctaw addressed to Ketcham begin to appear in January 1917, and they continue through 1921. See the correspondence files of BCIM. *Indian Sentinel* 1, no. 7 (January 1918): 24.

46. Ketcham to Gunn, October 17, 1917, BCIM, series 1, box 107, folder 1.

47. Minutes of the Seventh Annual Session of the New Choctaw Baptist Association; Lindquist, *The Red Man*, p. 115; Jim Davis, Union, to Ketcham, Jan. 3, 1918, BCIM, series 1, box 11, folder 17; Mrs. J. E. Arnold to Culberson Davis, Jan. 3, 1918, BCIM, series 1, box 111, folder 17; Ahern to Ketcham, Feb. 19, 1918, John William, Union, to Ketcham, Feb. 18, 1918, and Ketcham to John William, Union, [March 1918], BCIM, series 1, box 111, folder 17.

48. Ketcham to Ahern, November 21, 1917, BCIM, series 1, box 107, folder 1; Ketcham to Ahern, February 27, 1918, BCIM, series 1, box 111, folder 17.

49. The decrease in funding was primarily because of the war effort. J. E. Arnold to R. J. Ahern, Oct. 25, 1917, BCIM, series 1, box 107, folder 1; Ketcham to Ahern, Feb. 27, 1918, BCIM, series 1, box 111, folder 17.

50. Secretary of the Board of Catholic Indian Missions to Ahern, May 1, 1918, and [Ketcham to S. W. Stoliby, April 1918], BCIM, series 1, box 111, folder 17.

51. Ketcham to Ahern, July 29, 1918, and Aug. 12, 1918, BCIM, series 1, box 111, folder 17.

52. Ketcham to Ahern, Oct. 31, 1917, BCIM, series 1, box 107, folder 1; *Condition of the Mississippi Choctaws*, p. 21.

53. J. A. Charley, Philadelphia, to Ketcham, April 17, 1918, Culberson Davis

to Ketcham, Aug. 5, 1918, Willie Solomon, Decatur, to Ketcham, Sept. 25, 1918, John Williams, Union, to Ketcham, Sept. 28, 1918, and Ketcham to Ahern, Aug. 12, 1918, BCIM, series 1, box 111, folder 17; Blanchard, *Mississippi Choctaws*, pp. 43–44.

54. George Polk to Ketcham, Oct. 27, 1918, and Ahern to Ketcham, Feb. 19, 1919, BCIM, series 1, box 111, folder 17; Jimmie Davis, Union, to Ketcham, March 31, 1919, BCIM, series 1, box 116, folder 19.

55. Swanton, *Source Material*, p. 5; Peterson, "The Mississippi Band," p. 109; Mississippi Band, *Overall Economic Development Plan*, p. 17.

56. Peterson, "The Mississippi Band," p. 111.

57. Ahern to Ketcham, [Nov. 11, 1918], Ketcham to Ahern, Nov. 11, 1918, Ketcham to Gunn, Nov. 29, 1918, and Ahern to Ketcham, Nov. 30, 1918, BCIM, series 1, box 111, folder 17.

Bibliography

MANUSCRIPTS

American Board of Commissioners for Foreign Missions. Papers, Series 18.3.4. Houghton Library, Harvard University.

Archives of the Baptist Church, State of Mississippi. Clinton College, Clinton, Mississippi.

Archives of the Diocese of Jackson. Jackson, Mississippi. File: Janssens, C.

Archives of the Methodist Episcopal Church South. Millsaps College, Jackson, Mississippi.

Beckett, Charles Mitchell. "Choctaw Indians in Mississippi since 1830." Oklahoma State University, Stillwater, 1949.

Bekkers, B. J. "History of the Indian Mission of Tucker, Neshoba County, Mississippi." Typescript copy of the journal of Fr. Bekkers. Holy Rosary Mission, Tucker, Mississippi.

Board of Catholic Indian Missions. Papers. Special Collections, Marquette University Library, Milwaukee, Wisconsin.

Choctaw Patents. Bureau of Land Management, Vol. 324. Arlington, Virginia.

Compiled Service Records of Confederate Soldiers Who Served in Organizations from the State of Mississippi. Microfilm Publications, Microcopy No. 269, Roll 7. Record Group 109, National Archives, Washington, D.C.

Documents Concerning the Negotiation of Ratified Indian Treaties, 1801–1869. Microfilm Series T494. Record Group 75, National Archives, Washington, D.C.

Draper, Lyman. Papers. Wisconsin Historical Society, Series 10yy. Madison, Wisconsin.

Entry 168. Federal Record Center, Fort Worth, Texas. Record Group 75, National Archives, Washington, D.C.

"General Roll of Choctaw Families, Residing East of the Mississippi River and in the States of Mississippi, Louisiana and Alabama . . . dated May the 23rd, 1855." Census Roll, Entry 260, Choctaw Removal Records. Record Group 75, National Archives, Washington, D.C.

Hotchkin, Ebenezer. "History of the Presbyterian Church in Oklahoma." Manuscript on microfilm at the Foundation of the Presbyterian and Reformed Churches, Montreat, North Carolina.

Journal of Hearings Held by Murray and Vroom. Entry 270, Choctaw Removal Records. Record Group 75, National Archives, Washington, D.C.

"Journal of Proceedings." Entry 275, Choctaw Removal Records. Record Group 75, National Archives, Washington, D.C.

Leflore, Greenwood. Papers. Greenwood Public Library, Greenwood, Mississippi.

Letters of the Secretary of War—Sent. Microfilm Series M15. Record Group 75, National Archives, Washington, D.C.

Letters to the Secretary of War—Received. Microfilm Series 271. Record Group 75, National Archives, Washington, D.C.

Lincecum, Gideon. "History of the Choctaws." Manuscript in the Rare Book Collection of the library at the University of Texas at Austin. Typescript copy, Neshoba County Library, Philadelphia, Mississippi.

Miscellaneous Choctaw Removal Records. Entry 267, Choctaw Removal Records. Record Group 75, National Archives, Washington, D.C.

Mississippi State Department of Archives and History. Record Group 69, Vol. 24, Folder 17. Jackson.

National Anthropological Archives, MS #3153. Smithsonian Institution, Washington, D.C.

Office of Indian Affairs, Letters Received. Microfilm Series 234. Record Group 75, National Archives, Washington, D.C.

Osoinach, H. Kirkland. "The dynamics of Mississippi Choctaw Society: An Exploratory Formulation." [Chicago: University of Chicago, Department of Anthropology, 1960.] Manuscript, Choctaw Collection, Mississippi State University Library, Mississippi State, Mississippi.

Pride, William. Papers. Mississippi State Department of Archives and History. Jackson.

Talley, Alexander. Papers. Archives of the Methodist Episcopal Church South. Millsaps College, Jackson, Mississippi.

U.S. Court of Claims. "The Choctaw Nation of Indians v. the United States." No. 12742, December Term, 1885–86. Printed Records, vol. 112 (in 2 vols.), Pleadings, Petition, and Evidence.

Winans, William. Papers. Archives of the Methodist Episcopal Church South. Millsaps College, Jackson, Mississippi.

JOURNAL, MINUTES, AND PROCEEDINGS

Journal of the 89th Session of the Mississippi Annual Conference of the Methodist Episcopal Church South, Held at Natchez, Mississippi, December 11–15, 1902. N.p, n.d.

Journal of the 90th Session of the Mississippi Annual Conference of the Methodist Episcopal Church South, Held at Jackson, Mississippi, December 9–14, 1903. N.p, n.d.

Journal of the 92nd Session of the Mississippi Annual Conference of the Methodist Episcopal Church South, Held at Gloster, Mississippi, December 13–18, 1905. N.p, n.d.

Journal of the 95th Session of the Mississippi Annual Conference of the Methodist Episcopal Church South, Held at Yazoo City, Mississippi, December 9–14, 1908. N.p, n.d.

Journal of the 98th Session of the Mississippi Annual Conference of the Methodist Episcopal Church South, Held at Meridian, Mississippi, December 6–11, 1911. N.p, n.d.

Journal of the 101st Session of the Mississippi Annual Conference of the Methodist Episcopal Church South, Held at Columbia, Mississippi, December 9–14, 1914. N.p, n.d.

Minutes of the Annual Conferences of the Methodist Episcopal Church, 1773–1845. 3 vols. New York: Published by T. Mason and G. Lane, 1840–45.

Minutes of the General Association of Regular Baptists of the State of Mississippi for 1903, 1904, 1906. Archives of the Baptist Church, State of Mississippi, Clinton College, Clinton, Mississippi.

Minutes of the Eighth Annual Meeting of the Choctaw and Chickasaw Baptist Association, Hebron, September 19, 1879. Dennison, Tex.: M. F. Dearing, Lessee Herald Job Office, 1879.

Minutes of the Forty-Second Annual Session of the Mt. Pisgah Baptist Association, Held with Bethel Church, Newton Co., Miss., September 20, 1879. Meridian, Miss.: Southern Baptist, 1879.

Minutes of the Fifty-First Annual Session of the Mt. Pisgah Baptist Association Held with Rock Branch Church, Newton County, Miss., September 15, 16, and 17th, 1888. Meridian, Miss.: Union Baptist Publishing Company, 1888.

Minutes of the Fifty-fourth Annual Session of the Mt. Pisgah Baptist Association, Held with New Prospect Church, Newton Co., Miss., September 19, 20, and 21, 1891. Meridian, Miss.: John J. Dement, Printer, 1891.

Minutes of the General Association of Regular Baptists of the State of Mississippi Held with Zion Hill Church, Smith County, Miss., October 26 to 29th, 1883. Meridian, Miss.: Southern Baptist Print, 1883.

Minutes of the General Association of Regular Baptists of the State of Mississippi Held with Poplarville Church, Marion County, Miss., October 25 to 28, 1884. Meridian, Miss.: Southern Baptist Print, 1884.

Minutes of the General Association of Regular Baptists of the State of Mississippi Held with Fellowship Church, Jasper County, Miss., October 4 to 6, 1885. Meridian, Miss.: Southern Baptist Print, 1885.

Minutes of the General Association of Regular Baptists of the State of Mississippi Held with Decatur Church, Newton County, Miss., October 28th to November 1st, 1886. Meridian, Miss.: Southern Baptist Print, 1886.

Minutes of the General Association of Regular Baptists of the State of Mississippi Held with Enon Church, Jasper County, Miss., October 29th to 31st, 1887. Meridian, Miss.: Baptist Union Publishing Company, 1887.

Minutes of the General Association of Regular Baptists of the State of Mississippi held with Oakland Church, Newton County, Miss., October 26 to 29th 1889. Meridian, Miss.: Press of Democrat Publishing Company, 1889.

Minutes of the General Association of Regular Baptists of the State of Mississippi. Meridian, Miss.: Press of Democrat Publishing Co., 1896.

Minutes of the Third Annual Session of the New Choctaw Baptist Association (Chowtaws), Held with the Hopewell Baptist Church, Leake County, Mississippi, October 17 and 18, 1913. Newton, Miss.: Price Printing Company, Printers, 1914.

Minutes of the Fourth Annual Session of the New Choctaw Baptist Association (Choctaws) Held with the Mt. Zion Baptist Church Leake County, Mississippi, October 17, 18, 19, 1914. Newton, Miss.: Price Printing Company, Printers, 1914.

Minutes of the Seventh Annual Session of the New Choctaw Baptist Association (Choctaw) Held with the Hope Baptist Church, Neshoba County, Mississippi, November 15, 16, 17, 1918. Baptist Archives, Clinton College, Clinton, Mississippi.

Proceedings of the General Association of Regular Baptists of the State of Mississippi Held with Bethel Church, Newton Co., Miss., Commencing Saturday, October 28, 1882. Enterprise, Miss.: Printed at the Courier Book and Job Office, 1882.

Proceedings of the General Association of Regular Baptists of the State of

Mississippi Held with Shady Grove Church, Jasper County, Miss., October 27th, 28th, and 29th, 1888. Meridian, Miss.: Union Baptist Publishing Company, 1888.

Proceedings of the Sixty-Second Annual Session of the Harmony Baptist Association, October 20, 21, 22, 1911. Archives of the Baptist Church, State of Mississippi, Clinton College, Clinton, Mississippi.

Proceedings of the 80th Session of the Missionary Society of the Methodist Episcopal Church, Hazelhurst, December 7–11, 1893. Methodist Episcopal Church South, Millsaps College, Jackson, Mississippi.

Proceedings of the 83rd Session of the Methodist Missionary Society, Port Gibson, December 2–6, 1896. Methodist Episcopal Church South, Millsaps College, Jackson, Mississippi.

Proceedings, 85th Session, [Methodist Missionary Society], Hattiesburg, December 29, 1898–January 2, 1899. Methodist Episcopal Church South, Millsaps College, Jackson, Mississippi.

Proceedings of 87th Session, [Methodist Missionary Society], Brookhaven, December 13–17, 1900. Methodist Episcopal Church South, Millsaps College, Jackson, Mississippi.

GOVERNMENT DOCUMENTS

Condition of the Mississippi Choctaws: Hearing before the Committee on Investigation of the Indian Service. House of Representatives, Union, Mississippi, March 16, 1917. Vol. 2. Washington: Government Printing Office, 1917.

U.S. Commission to the Five Civilized Tribes. *Annual Report [5th] of the Commission to the Five Civilized Tribes in the Indian Territory to the Secretary of the Interior, 1898.* Washington: Government Printing Office, 1898.

————. *Annual Report [6th] of the Commission to the Five Civilized Tribes in the Indian Territory to the Secretary of the Interior, 1899.* Washington: Government Printing Office, 1899.

————. *Annual Report [7th] of the Commission to the Five Civilized Tribes in the Indian Territory to the Secretary of the Interior, 1900.* Washington: Government Printing Office, 1900.

————. *Annual Report [8th] of the Commission to the Five Civilized Tribes in the Indian Territory to the Secretary of the Interior, 1901.* Washington: Government Printing Office, 1901.

————. *Annual Report [11th] of the Commission to the Five Civilized*

Tribes in the Indian Territory to the Secretary of the Interior, 1903.
Washington: Government Printing Office, 1903.

_____. *The Final Rolls of Citizens and Freedmen of the Five Civilized Tribes in Indian Territory, Prepared by the Commission and Commissioner to the Five Civilized Tribes, and Approved by the Secretary of the Interior on or Prior to March 4, 1907.* [Washington: Government Printing Office, 1907.]

U.S. Department of the Interior. *Report of Inspector James McLaughlin on Bills for Enrollment with the Five Civilized Tribes, July 2, 1914.* Washington: Government Printing Office, 1916.

_____. *Report of the Commissioner of Indian Affairs, November 30, 1846.* Washington: Government Printing Office, 1846.

15th Cong. 2d sess. H. Doc. 156. "Emigration of the Choctaws," December 1, 1818. *American State Papers* 1:180.

22d Cong., 1st sess. H. Doc. 194. Board of Commissioners—Foreign Missions, *Memorial of the Prudential Committee of the American Board of Commissioners for Foreign Missions, Respecting the Property of the Board in the Choctaw Nation,* April 2, 1832.

23d Cong., 1st sess., S. Doc. 1230, "In Relation to the Location of Reservations under the Choctaw Treaty of the 27th of September, 1830," April 11, 1834. *American State Papers* 2:1–139.

23d Cong., 2d sess., H. Rep. 1315. "Claims to Choctaw Reservations," February 9, 1835. *American State Papers* 7:627–52.

24th Cong., 1st sess., S. Doc. 69. *Report of the Secretary of the Treasury, in Compliance with a Resolution of the Senate Concerning the Location of the Choctaw Claims and Reservations,* January 20, 1836.

24th Cong., 1st sess., H. Doc. 89. *Indian Claims in Mississippi, Petition of the Citizens of the State of Mississippi, Remonstrating against Indian Claims,* February 1, 1836.

24th Cong., 1st sess., H. Doc. 119. *Choctaw Indians, by Andrew Hays, Agent,* February 1, 1836.

24th Cong., 1st sess., H. Doc. 1523. *On Claims to Reservations under the Fourteenth Article of the Treaty of Dancing Rabbit Creek, with the Choctaw Indians, Communicated to the House of Representatives,* May 11, 1836.

24th Cong., 1st sess., H. Rep. 663. *Land Claims, &c. under 14th Article Choctaw Treaty,* May 11, 1836.

24th Cong., 2d sess., S. Doc. 91. *Petition of a Number of Citizens of Mississippi Praying Congress to Institute an Inquiry into the Claims of*

Choctaw Indians to Reservations under the Treaty of Dancing Rabbit Creek, January 21, 1837.

26th Cong., 2d sess., H. Doc. 109. *Choctaw Treaty—Dancing Rabbit Creek*, March 2, 1841.

27th Cong., 2d sess., H. Doc. 231. *Choctaw Academy*, May 20, 1842.

28th Cong., 1st sess., S. Doc. 168. *Message from the President of the United States, Transmitting the Correspondence in Relation to the Proceedings and Conduct of the Choctaw Commission, under the Treaty of Dancing Rabbit Creek*, January 30, 1844.

28th Cong., 2d sess., S. Doc. 86. *Report of the Secretary of War—Information in Relation to the Contracts Made for the Removal and Subsistence of the Choctaw Indians*, February 7, 1845.

28th Cong., 2d sess., H. Rep. 193. *Choctaw Academy in Kentucky*, March 3, 1845.

29th Cong., 1st sess., H. Doc. 189. *Choctaw Treaty, Message from the President of the United States Transmitting a Report of the Secretary of War Relative to the Claims Arising under the Choctaw Treaty, in Compliance with a Resolution of the House of Representatives of the 31st of December Last*, April 27, 1846.

57th Cong., 2d sess., S. Doc. 319. *Rights of Mississippi Choctaws in the Choctaw Nation*, April 24, 1902.

64th Cong., 2d sess., H. Doc. 1464. John T. Reeves, *Additional Land and Indian Schools in Mississippi*, December 7, 1916.

DISSERTATIONS, THESES, AND PAPERS

Coe, Pamela. "Lost in the Hills of Home: Outline of Mississippi Choctaw Social Organization." Master's thesis, Columbia University, 1960.

Farr, Eugene Ijams. "Religious Assimilation: A Case Study of the Adoption of Christianity by the Choctaw Indians of Mississippi." Ph.D. diss., New Orleans Baptist Theological Seminary, 1948.

Galloway, Patricia. "Confederacy as a Solution to Chiefdom Dissolution: Historical Evidence in the Choctaw Case." Paper presented at the 1985 meeting of the American Society for Ethnohistory, Chicago, Illinois.

Kenaston, Monte Ray. "Sharecropping, Solidarity, and Social Cleavage: The Genesis of a Choctaw Subcommunity in Tennessee." Ph.D. diss., Southern Illinois University, 1972.

McBride, Ralph Folsom, and Alberta Patrick McBride. "Choctaw Folsoms." Paper delivered at Hibernian Hall, Charleston, South Carolina, on August 11, 1979, at the 64th Annual Reunion and 70th Anniversary of the Folsom Family Association of America, Inc.

Paape, Charles William. "The Choctaw Revolt: A Chapter in the Intercolonial Rivalry in the Old Southwest." Ph.D. diss., University of Illinois, 1946.

Peterson, John H., Jr. "The Mississippi Band of Choctaw Indians: Their Recent History and Current Social Relations." Ph.D. diss., University of Georgia, 1970.

Tolbert, Charles Madden. "A Sociological Study of the Choctaw Indians in Mississippi." Ph.D. diss., Louisiana State University, 1958.

PERIODICALS AND NEWSPAPERS

Arkansas Gazette.

Christian Advocate. Published by the Methodist Episcopal Church South, New Orleans, Louisiana.

Indian Sentinal. Published by the Bureau of Catholic Indian Missions, Washington, D.C.

Missionary Herald. Published by the American Board of Commissioners for Foreign Missions, Boston, Massachusetts.

Natchez.

Niles' Weekly Register.

BOOKS AND ARTICLES

Abel, Annie Heloise. *Events Leading to the Consolidation of American Indian Tribes West of the Mississippi River.* Washington, D.C.: American Historical Association. 1906.

Adair, James. *Adair's History of the American Indians,* edited by Samuel Cole Williams. New York: Promontory Press, 1930.

American Anti-Slavery Society. *Slavery and the American Board of Commissioners for Foreign Missions.* New York: American Anti-Slavery Society, 1859.

American Bible Society. *The Books of Genesis, Exodux, Leviticus, Numbers, and Deuteronomy Translated into the Choctaw Language— Chenesis, Eksotus, Lefitikus, Numbas, Mihce tutelonomi Holisso Aiena Kut Toshowut Chahta Anumpa toba Hoke.* New York: American Bible Society, 1867.

American Board of Commissioners for Foreign Missions. *First Ten Annual Reports of the American Board of Commissioners for Foreign Missions, with Other Documents of the Board.* Boston: Printed by Crocker and Brewster, 1834.

―――――. *Memorial Volume of the First Fifty Years of the American Board of Commissioners for Foreign Missions.* Boston: Published by the Board, 1861.

―――――. *Monthly Paper,* no. 3 (June 1823).

―――――. *Report of the American Board of Commissioners for Foreign Missions, Compiled from Documents Laid before the Board, at the Seventeenth Annual Meeting, Which Was Held in Middletown, (Con.) Sept. 14, and 15, 1826.* Boston: Printed for the Board by Crocker and Brewster, 1826.

―――――. *Report of the American Board of Commissioners for Foreign Missions, Compiled from Documents Laid before the Board, at the Eighteenth Annual Meeting, Which Was Held in the City of New York, October 10, 11, 12, 13 & 15, 1827.* Boston: Printed for the Board by Crocker and Brewster, 1827.

―――――. *Report of the American Board of Commissioners for Foreign Missions, Compiled from Documents Laid before the Board, at the Twentieth Annual Meeting, Which Was Held in the City of Albany, Oct. 7, 8, and 9, 1829.* Boston: Printed for the Board by Crocker and Brewster, 1829.

―――――. *Report of the American Board of Commissioners for Foreign Missions, Read at the Twenty-Second Annual Meeting, Which Was Held in the City of New Haven, Conn., Oct. 5, 6, and 7, 1831.* Boston: Printed for the Board by Crocker and Brewster, 1831.

―――――. *Report of the American Board of Commissioners for Foreign Missions, Read at the Twenty-Third Annual Meeting, Which Was Held in the City of New York, Oct. 3, 4, and 5, 1832.* Boston: Printed for the Board by Crocker and Brewster, 1832.

―――――. *Report of the Committee on Anti-Slavery Memorials, September 1845, with a Historical Statement of Previous Proceedings.* Boston: Press of T. R. Marvin, 1845.

American State Papers: Documents, Legislative and Executive, of the Congress of the United States. 38 vols. Washington, D.C.: Gales and Seaton, 1832–61. Series 2, *Indian Affairs,* 2 vols.

The Annotated Code of the General Statue Laws of the State of Mississippi, Prepared by R. H. Thompson, George G. Dillard, and R. B. Campbell *and Reported to and Amended and Adopted by the Legislature at Its Regular Session in 1892.* Nashville: Marshall and Brue, Law Publishers, 1892.

Axtell, James. *The European and the Indian: Essays in the Ethnohistory of Colonial North America.* Oxford, Eng.: Oxford University Press, 1981.

————. *The Invasion Within: The Contest of Cultures in Colonial North America.* New York: Oxford University Press, 1985.

Baird, W. David. "Cyrus Byington and the Presbyterian Choctaw Mission." In *Churchmen and the Western Indians, 1820–1920,* edited by Clyde A. Milner II and Floyd A. O'Neil. Norman: University of Oklahoma Press, 1985.

————. *Peter Pitchlynn: Chief of the Choctaws.* Norman: University of Oklahoma Press, 1972.

Bangs, Nathan. *An Authentic History of the Missions under the Care of the Missionary Society of the Methodist Episcopal Church.* New York: Published by J. Emory and B. Waugh, for the Methodist Episcopal Church, 1832.

Barclay, Wade C. *History of Methodist Missions: Part One, Early American Methodism, 1769–1844; Part Two, The Methodist Episcopal Church, 1845–1939; Part Three, Twentieth Century Perspectives, Methodist Episcopal Church, 1896–1939* (by J. Tremayne Copplestone). 4 vols. New York: Board of Missions and Church Extension of the Methodist Church, 1949–73.

Bartram, William. *The Travels of William Bartram.* Edited by Francis Harper. New Haven: Yale University Press, 1958.

Beaver, R. Pierce. *Church, State, and the American Indian.* St. Louis: Concordia Publishing House, 1966.

Bekkers, B. J. "The Catholic Church in Mississippi during Colonial Times." *Publications of the Mississippi Historical Society* 6 (1902): 351–57.

Bell, Daniel. "Ethnicity and Social Change." In *Ethnicity: Theory and Experience,* edited by Nathan Glazer and Daniel P. Moynihan, pp. 141–74. Cambridge: Harvard University Press, 1975.

Benson, Henry C. *Life among the Choctaw Indians, and Sketches of the South-west.* Cincinnati: Published by L. Swormstedt and A. Poe, for the Methodist Episcopal Church, 1860. Reprint, New York: Johnson Reprint Corporation, 1970.

Berkhofer, Robert F., Jr. *Salvation and the Savage: An Analysis of Protes-*

tant Missions and American Indian Response, 1787–1862. New York: Atheneum, 1972.

Bernard, Mother Mary. The Story of the Sisters of Mercy in Mississippi. New York: Kennedy and Sons, 1931.

Blanchard, Kendall. The Mississippi Choctaws at Play: The Serious Side of Leisure. Urbana: University of Illinois Press, 1981.

Blitz, John Howard. An Archaeological Study of the Mississippi Choctaw Indians. Archaeological Report No. 16. Jackson, Miss.: Department of Archives and History, 1985.

Blu, Karen I. The Lumbee Problem: The Making of an American Indian People. Cambridge, Eng.: Cambridge University Press, 1980.

Bossu, Jean Bernard. Travels in the Interior of North America, 1751–62. Translated and edited by Seymour Feiler. Norman: University of Oklahoma Press, 1962.

Bourne, Edward Gaylord, ed. Narratives of the Career of Hernando de Soto in the Conquest of Florida as Told by a Knight of Elvas and in a Relation by Luys Hernandez de Biedma, Factor of the Expedition. Translated by Buckingham Smith. 2 vols. New York: Allerton Book Company, 1922. Reprint, New York: AMS Press, 1973.

Bremer, Cora. The Chata Indians of Pearl River. New Orleans: Picayune Job Print, [ca. 1907].

Brown, A. J. History of Newton County, Mississippi, from 1834 to 1894. Jackson, Miss.: Clarion-Ledger Company, 1894.

Bureau of Catholic Indian Missions. Kiahlik Iksa nana-Aiyimmika, I Katikisma. Washington, D.C.: Bureau of Catholic Indian Missions, 1916.

Bushnell, David I., Jr. The Choctaw of Bayou Lacomb, St. Tamany Parish, Louisiana. Smithsonian Institution, Bureau of American Ethnology, Bulletin 48. Washington: Government Printing Office, 1909.

Byington, Cyrus. A Dictionary of the Choctaw Language. Edited by J. R. Swanton and H. S. Halbert. Smithsonian Institution, Bureau of American Ethnography, Bulletin 46. Washington: Government Printing Office, 1915.

_____. "Grammar of the Choctaw Language." Proceedings of the American Philosophical Society, 11 (1870): 317–67.

Calhoun, John C. The Papers of John C. Calhoun. Edited by W. Edwin Hemphill. 19 vols. Columbia: Published by the University of South Carolina Press for the South Caroliniana Society, 1957–.

Campbell, T. N. "The Choctaw Afterworld." Journal of American Folklore 73 (1959): 146–54.

————. "Choctaw Subsistence: Ethnographic Notes from the Lincecum Manuscript." *Florida Anthropologist* 12 (1959): 9–24.

————. "Medicinal Plants Used by Choctaw, Chickasaw, and Creek Indians in the Early Nineteenth Century." *Journal of the Washington Academy of Sciences* 41, no. 9 (1951): 285–90.

Candler, Allen D., ed. *The Colonial Records of the State of Georgia.* 26 vols. Atlanta: Franklin Printing and Publishing Company, G. S. Harrison, State Printer, 1904–16.

Carter, Clarence E., ed. *Territorial Papers of the United States.* 27 vols. Washington, D.C.: Government Printing Office, 1934–69.

Catlin, George. *Letters and Notes on the Manners, Customs, and Condition of the North American Indians.* 2 vols. New York: Dover Press, 1973.

Caughey, John Walton. *Bernardo de Galvez in Louisiana, 1776–1783.* Berkeley: University of California Press, 1934.

Chahta oklahi nanulhpisa noshbobo micha nanvlhpisa: Mikmvt afamih 1837, 1855, 1865, 1866 kash nanitimapisa tok (treaties) aiena ho chata oklah nanvpisa chito vt vpisa toko anotaka hosh A. R. Durant, vt vlht uka yosh holisso achafa ilapa foki noke; Davis Homer micha Ben Watkins, apilvchi. Tvllis, Teksis: J. F. Worley, 1894.

The Choctaw Nation vs. the United States. Washington, D.C.: David M'Intosh, printer, 1872.

Claiborne, J.F.H. *Mississippi as a Province, Territory, and State.* Vol. 1. Jackson, Miss.: Power and Barksdale, 1880.

————. *Proceedings of the Board of Choctaw Commissioners, Col. Claiborne's Statement.* Natchez: N.P., 1843.

Code of Mississippi: Being an Analytical Compilation of the Public and General Statutes of the Territory and State with Tabular References to the Local and Private Acts from 1798 to 1848, with the National and State Constitutions, Assigns of the Country by the Choctaw and Chickasaw Indians, and Acts of Congress for the Survey and Sale of the Lands and Granting Domations Thereof to the State. By A. Hutchinson, Jackson, Miss.: Published for the compiler by Price and Fall, State Printing, 1848.

Cohen, Ronald. "Ethnicity: Problem and Focus in Anthropology." *Annual Review of Anthropology* 7 (1978): 379–404.

Coker, William S. *Historical Sketches of Panton, Leslie and Company.* Gainesville: University Presses of Florida, 1976.

————. "Pat Harrison's Efforts to Reopen the Choctaw Citizenship Rolls." *Southern Quarterly* 3 (October 1964): 36–60.

Coker, William S., and Thomas D. Watson. *Indian Traders of the Southeastern Spanish Borderlands: Panton Leslie & Company and John Forbes & Company, 1783–1847.* Pensacola: University of West Florida Press, 1986.

Coleman, Michael C. *Presbyterian Missionary Attitudes toward American Indians, 1837–1893.* Jackson: University Press of Mississippi, 1985.

The Constitution and Laws of the Choctaw Nation. Park Hill, Cherokee Nation: Mission Press, Edwin Archer, Printer, 1847. Reprint, Wilmington, Del.: Scholarly Resources, 1975.

Constitution and Laws of the Choctaw Nation, Together with the Treaties of 1837, 1855, 1865 and 1866, Published by Authority of the General Council by A. R. Durant and Davis Homer and Ben Watkins. Dallas, Tex.: John F. Worley, Printer and Publisher, 1894. Reprint, Wilmington, Del.: Scholarly Resources, 1973.

Cotterill, Robert. *The Southern Indians.* Norman: University of Oklahoma Press, 1954.

Crane, Verner. *The Southern Frontier, 1670–1732.* New York: W. W. Norton, 1981.

Cushman, H. B. *History of the Choctaw, Chickasaw, and Natchez Indians.* Greenville, Tex.: Headlight Printing House, 1899. Reprint, edited by Angie Debo. New York: Russell and Russell, 1962.

Dangerfield, George. *The Awakening of American Nationalism: 1815–1828.* New York: Harper and Row, 1965.

Davis, Edward. "The Mississippi Choctaws." *Chronicles of Oklahoma* 10 (June 1932): 257–66.

Debo, Angie. *And Still the Waters Run.* Princeton: Princeton University Press, 1972.

————. *The Rise and Fall of the Choctaw Republic.* Norman: University of Oklahoma Press, 1934.

Delanglez, Jean. *The French Jesuits in Lower Louisiana (1700–1763).* Washington, D.C.: Catholic University of America, 1935.

Densmore, Frances. *Choctaw Music.* Bureau of American Ethnology, Bulletin 136. Washington: Government Printing Office, 1943.

Department of Commerce, Bureau of the Census. *Thirteenth Census of the United States Taken in the Year 1910, Supplement for Mississippi.* Washington: Government Printing Office, 1913.

DePratter, Chester B., Charles Hudson, and Marvin T. Smith. "The Hernando de Soto Expedition: From Chiaha to Mabila." In *Alabama and Its Borderlands from Prehistory to Statehood,* edited by Reid

Badger and Lawrence A. Clayton. University: University of Alabama Press, 1985.

DeRosier, Arthur H., Jr. "Pioneers with Conflicting Ideals: Christianity and Slavery in the Choctaw Nation." 21 (1959): 174–89.

_____. *The Removal of the Choctaw Indians.* New York: Harper and Row Publishers, 1972.

Dippie, Brian W. *The Vanishing American: White Attitudes and U.S. Indian Policy.* Middletown, Conn.: Wesleyan University Press, 1982.

Dobyns, Henry. *Their Number Become Thinned.* Knoxville: University of Tennessee Press, 1983.

Dowd, Gregory Evans. *A Spirited Resistance: The North American Indian Struggle for Unity, 1745–1815.* Baltimore and London: Johns Hopkins University Press, 1992.

Draper, David. "Abba Isht tuluwa: The Christian Hymns of the Mississippi Choctaw." *American Indian Culture and Research Journal* 6, no. 1 (1982): 43–61.

Dupree, (Mrs.) N. D. "Greenwood LeFlore." *Publications of the Mississippi Historical Society* 12 (1903): 141–52.

Edmunds, R. David. *The Shawnee Prophet.* Lincoln: University of Nebraska Press, 1983.

Edwards, John. "The Choctaw Indians in the Middle of the Nineteenth Century." *Chronicles of Oklahoma* 10 (1932): 392–425.

Eggan, Fred. *The American Indian: Perspectives for the Study of Social Change.* Chicago: Aldine Publishing Company, 1966.

_____. "Historical Changes in the Choctaw Kinship System." *American Anthropologist* 39 (1937): 34–52.

Elsbree, Oliver Wendell. *The Rise of the Missionary Spirit in America, 1790–1815.* Williamsport, Pa.: Williamsport Printing and Binding Company, 1928.

Faust, Harold S. "The Growth of Presbyterian Missions to the American Indians during the National Period." *Journal of the Presbyterian Historical Society* 22 (1944): 82–123, 137–71.

Feller, Daniel. *The Public Lands in Jacksonian Politics.* Madison: University of Wisconsin Press, 1984.

Finger, John R. *The Eastern Band of Cherokees, 1819–1900.* Knoxville: University of Tennessee Press, 1984.

Ford, James A. *Analysis of Indian Village Site Collections from Louisiana and Mississippi.* Anthropological Study No. 2, State of Louisiana. New Orleans: Department of Conservation, Louisiana Geological Survey, 1936.

Foreman, Carolyn Thomas. "The Choctaw Academy." *Chronicles of Oklahoma* 6 (December 1928): 453–80; 9 (December 1931): 382–411; 10 (March 1932): 77–114.

———. "The Foreign Mission School at Cornwall, Connecticut." *Chronicles of Oklahoma* 7 (September 1929): 242–59.

Foreman, Grant. *The Five Civilized Tribes.* Norman: University of Oklahoma Press, 1934.

———. *Indian Removal: The Emigration of the Five Civilized Tribes of Indians.* Norman: University of Oklahoma Press, 1972.

———. *Indians and Pioneers: The Story of the American Southwest before 1830.* Rev. ed. Norman: University of Oklahoma Press, 1936.

Fortune, Jim C. *Mississippi Band of Choctaw Indians: Demographic Census, July, 1990.* [Philadelphia: Mississippi Band of Choctaw Indians, 1990.]

Gaines, George S. "Reminiscences." *Alabama Historical Quarterly* 24 (Fall and Winter 1964): 133–229.

Galloway, Patricia. "'The Chief Who Is Your Father': Choctaw and French Views of the Diplomatic Relation." In *Powhatan's Mantle: Indians in the Colonial Southeast,* edited by Peter H. Wood, Gregory A. Waselkov, and M. Thomas Hatley. Lincoln: University of Nebraska Press, 1989.

———. "Choctaw Factionalism and Civil War." *Journal of Mississippi History* 44 (November 1982): 289–327.

———. "Choctaw Factionalism and Civil War, 1746–1750." In *The Choctaw before Removal,* edited by Carolyn Keller Reeves. Jackson: University Press of Mississippi, 1985.

———. "Henri de Tonti du Village des Chacta, 1702: The Beginning of the French Alliance." In *La Salle and His Legacy: Frenchmen and Indians in the Lower Mississippi Valley,* edited by Patricia K. Galloway. Jackson: University Press of Mississippi, 1982.

Geertz, Clifford. *The Interpretation of Cultures.* New York: Basic Books, 1973.

Gentleman of Elvas. *The Discovery and Conquest of Terra Florida, by Don Ferdinando de Soto, and Six Hundred Spaniards His Followers, Written by a Gentleman of Elvas, Employed in all the Action, and translated out of Portugese by Richard Hakluyt.* 1611. Reprint, edited by Luis Hernandez de Biedma. London: Printed for the Hakluyt Society, 1851.

Gerow, Richard Oliver. *Catholicity in Mississippi.* Natchez: Hope Haven Press, 1939.

Gibson, Arrell M. *The Chickasaws.* Norman: University of Oklahoma Press, 1971.

Green, Michael D. *The Politics of Indian Removal: Creek Government and Society in Crisis.* Lincoln: University of Nebraska Press, 1983.

"Greenwood Leflore." In *Encyclopedia of Mississippi History: Comprising Sketches of Counties, Towns, Events, institutions, and Persons,* edited by Dunbar Rowland. Madison, Wis.: S. A. Brant, 1907.

Halbert, H. S. "District Divisions of the Choctaw Nation." *Publications of the Alabama Historical Society, Miscellaneous Collection* 1 (1901): 375–85.

_____. "Funeral Customs of the Mississippi Choctaws." *Publications of the Mississippi Historical Society* 3 (1900): 353–66.

_____. "Indian Schools." In *Biennial Report of the State Superintendent of Public Education to the Legislature of Mississippi for Scholastic Years 1895–96 and 1896–97,* pp. 23–30. Jackson, Miss.: Clarion Ledger Print, 1898.

_____. "Indian Schools in Mississippi." In *Biennial Report of the State Superintendent of Public Education to the State Superintendent of Public Education to the Legislature of Mississippi for Scholastic Years 1891–92 and 1892–93,* pp. 574–76. Jackson, Miss.: Clarion-Ledger Print, 1894.

_____. "The Indians in Mississippi and Their Schools." In *Biennial Report of the State Superintendent of Public Education to the Legislature of Mississippi for Scholastic Years 1893–94 and 1894–95,* pp. 534–45. Jackson, Miss.: Clarion-Ledger Printing Establishment, 1895.

_____. "The Mississippi Choctaws." In *Biennial Report of the State Superintendent of Public Instruction, to the Legislature of Mississippi, for Scholastic Years 1897–98 and 1898–99.* Jacksonville, Fla.: Lance Printing Company, 1900.

_____. "Nanih Waiya, the Sacred Mound of the Choctaws." *Publications of the Mississippi Historical Society* 2 (1899): 223–34.

_____. "The Story of the Treaty of Dancing Rabbit Creek." *Publications of the Mississippi Historical Society* 6 (1902): 373–402.

Halbert, H. S., and T. H. Ball. *The Creek War of 1813 and 1814.* Chicago: Donohue and Henneberry; Montgomery: White, Woodruff, and Fowler, 1895.

Hamilton, Peter J. *Colonial Mobile.* Rev. ed. 1910. Reprint, edited by Charles G. Summersell. Southern Historical Publications No. 20. University: University of Alabama Press, 1976.

Haynes, Robert V. "The Road to Statehood." In *A History of Missis-*

sippi, edited by Richard Aubrey McLemore. Hattiesburg: University and College Press of Mississippi, 1973.

Henri, Florette. *The Southern Indians and Benjamin Hawkins, 1796-1816.* Norman: University of Oklahoma Press, 1986.

Hiemstra, William L. "Early Presbyterian Missions among the Choctaw and Chickasaw." *Journal of Mississippi History* 10 (January 1948): 8–16.

History of the Harmony Baptist Association, 1849–1909. N.p., n.d.

Hodgson, Adam. *Remarks during a Journey through North America in the Years 1819, 1820, and 1821, in a Series of Letters: With an Appendix, Containing an Account of Several of the Indian Tribes, and the Principal Missionary Stations, &c. Also, a letter to M. Jean Baptiste Say, on the Comparative Expense of Free and Slave Labour.* Collected, Arranged, and Published by Samuel Whiting. New York: J. Seymour, 1823.

Hofstadter, Richard. *The Age of Reform.* New York: Alfred A. Knopf, 1955.

Holder, Ray. *The Mississippi Methodists, 1799–1983.* N.p.: Maverick Prints, 1984.

Holmes, Jack D. L. "The Choctaws in 1795." *Alabama Historical Quarterly* 30 (1968): 33–49.

————. "Spanish Treaties with West Florida Indians, 1784–1802." *Florida Historical Quarterly* 48 (1969): 140–45.

————. *Gayoso: The Life of a Spanish Governor in the Mississippi Valley, 1789–1799.* Baton Rouge: Louisiana State University Press for the Louisiana Historical Association, 1965.

Horsman, Reginald. *Expansion and American Indian Policy, 1783–1812.* [Lansing]: Michigan State University Press, 1967.

————. *Race and Manifest Destiny.* Cambridge: Harvard University Press, 1981.

Howard, James H., and Victoria Lindsay Levine. *Choctaw Music and Dance.* Norman: University of Oklahoma Press, 1990.

Hoxie, Fred. *A Final Promise.* Lincoln: University of Nebraska Press, 1984.

Hudson, Charles. *The Southeastern Indians.* Knoxville: University of Tennessee Press, 1976.

Hudson, Charles, Chester DePratter, and Marvin T. Smith. "Hernando de Soto's Expedition through the Southern United States." In *First Encounters: Spanish Explorations in the Caribbean and the United States, 1492–1570*, edited by Jerald T. Milanich and Susan Milbrath. Gainesville: University of Florida Press, 1989.

Hudson, Charles M., John E. Worth, and Chester B. DePratter. "Refinements in Hernando de Soto's Route through Georgia and South Carolina." In *Columbian Consequences*, vol. 2, edited by David Hurst Thomas, pp. 107–20. Washington, D.C.: Smithsonian Institution Press, 1990.

The Indian Removals: Document 512 of the U.S. Senate 23rd Congress, 1st Session. 3 vols. New York: AMS Press, 1974.

Jennings, Francis. *The Invasion of America: Indians, Colonialism, and the Cant of Conquest.* Chapel Hill: University of North Carolina Press, 1975.

Jones, John G. *A Complete History of Methodism as Connected with the Mississippi Conference of the Methodist Episcopal Church, South.* 2 vols. Nashville: Publishing House of the Methodist Episcopal Church, South, for the author, 1908.

Journal of the Congress of the Four Southern Governors, and the Superintendent of That District with the Five Nations of Indians, at Augusta, 1763. South Carolina, Charles-town: Printed by Peter Timothy, 1764.

Journal of the House of Representatives of the State of Mississippi at Their Thirteenth Session, Held in the Town of Jackson. Jackson, Miss.: Printed by Peter Isler, 1830.

Kappler, Charles J. *Indian Affairs: Laws and Treaties.* 5 vols. Washington: Government Printing Office, 1904–41.

Kinnaird, Lawrence, and Lucia B. Kinnaird. "Choctaws West of the Mississippi River, 1766–1800." *Southwestern Historical Quarterly* 63 (1979–80): 349–70.

Lanman, Charles. "Peter Pitchlynn, Chief of the Choctaws," *Atlantic Monthly*, April 1870, p. 486.

Laws of the Choctaw Nation Passed at the Regular Session of the General Council Convened at Tushka Humma, October 7, 1889, and Adjourned November 15, 1889. Atoka, I.T.: Indian Citizen Publishing Company, 1890. Reprint, Wilmington, Del.: Scholarly Resources, 1975.

Laws of the State of Mississippi, Passed at the Eleventh Session of the General Assembly Held in the town of Jackson. Jackson, Miss.: Peter Isler, State Printer, 1828.

LeBreton, Dagmar Renshaw. *Chata-Ima: The Life of Adrien-Emmanuel Roquette.* Baton Rouge: Louisiana State University Press, 1947.

Lewis, Anna. *Chief Pushmataha, American Patriot: The Story of the Choctaws' Struggle for Survival.* New York: Exposition Press, 1959.

Lewit, Robert T. "Indian Missions and Antislavery Sentiment: A Conflict of Evangelical and Humanitarian Ideals." *Mississippi Valley Historical Review* 50 (1963–64): 39–55.

Lickteig, Franz-Bernard. "The Choctaw Indian Apostolate, History, Part II." *Sword* 19, no. 2 (June 1969): 63–78.

Lincecum, Gideon. "Choctaw Traditions about their Settlement in Mississippi and the Origin of Their Mounds." *Publications of the Mississippi Historical Society* 8 (1904): 524–42.

Lindquist, G.E.E. *The Red Man in the United States: An Intimate Study of the Social, Economic, and Religious Life of the American Indian, Made under the Direction of G.E.E. Lindquist, with a Foreword by Honorable Charles H. Burke.* New York: George H. Doran Company, 1923.

Linton, Ralph, ed. *Acculturation in Seven American Indian Tribes.* Gloucester, Mass.: Peter Smith, 1963.

Littlefield, Daniel, Jr., ed. *The Life of Okah Tubbee.* Lincoln: University of Nebraska Press, 1988.

Lucas, Aubrey Keith. "Education in Mississippi from Statehood to the Civil War." In *A History of Mississippi*, edited by Richard Aubrey McLemore. 2 vols. Hattiesburg: University and College Press of Mississippi, 1973. I, 352–77.

Lusser, J. "Journal of the Journey That I Made in the Choctaw Nation by Order of Mr. Perier, Beginning on January 12th, 1730, and Lasting until March 23rd of the Same Year." In *Mississippi Provincial Archives, French Dominion*, edited by Dunbar Rowland and A. G. Sanders, 1:81–117. Jackson: Press of the Mississippi Department of Archives and History, 1927–32.

McBride, Ralph Folsom, and Alberta Patrick McBride. *A Family Makes Its Mark: The Leflores of Mississippi.* Sponsored by the Louis Leflore Family Association. Jacksonville, Fla.: McBride, 1976.

McCoy, Isaac. *History of Baptist Indian Missions: Embracing Remarks on the Former and Present Condition of the Aboriginal Tribes, Their Settlement within the Indian Territory, and Their Future Prospects.* Washington, D.C.: William M. Morrison; New York: H. & S. Raynor, and Bennett, Backus and Hawley, 1840.

McKenney, Thomas L. *Reports and Proceedings of Col. McKenney, on the Subject of His Recent Tour among the Southern Indians, as Submitted to Congress with the Message of the President.* Washington, D.C.: Printed by Gales and Seaton, 1826 [1827].

McLemore, Richard Aubrey, ed. *A History of Mississippi.* 2 vols. Hattiesburg: University and College Press of Mississippi, 1973.

————. *A History of Mississippi Baptists, 1780–1970*. [Jackson]: Mississippi Baptist Convention Board, [1971].

McLoughlin, William G. *Champions of the Cherokees: Evan and John B. Jones*. Princeton: Princeton University Press, 1990.

————. *Cherokees and Missionaries, 1789–1839*. New Haven: Yale University Press, 1984.

————. "Red Indians, Black Slavery, and White Racism: America's Slaveholding Indians." *American Quarterly* 26, no. 4 (October 1974): 367–85.

Martin, Joel. *Sacred Revolt: The Muskogees' Struggle for a New World*. Boston: Beacon Press, 1991.

May, Robert. *John A. Quitman, Old South Crusader*. Baton Rouge: Louisiana State University Press, 1985.

Merrell, James. *The Indians' New World: The Catawbas and Their Neighbors from European Contact through the Era of Removal*. Chapel Hill: Published for the Institute of Early American History and Culture, Williamsburg, Virginia, by the University of North Carolina Press, 1989.

Meyer, Leland Winfield. *The Life and Times of Colonel Richard M. Johnson of Kentucky*. New York, 1932.

Miles, Edwin A. *Jacksonian Democracy in Mississippi*. James Sprunt Studies in History and Political Science, vol. 42. Chapel Hill: University of North Carolina Press, 1960.

Miller, Gene Ramsey. *A History of North Mississippi Methodism 1820–1960*. Nashville, Tenn.: Parthenon Press, 1966.

Milner, Clyde A. *With Good Intentions: Quaker Work among the Pawnees, Otos, and Omahas in the 1870s*. Lincoln: University of Nebraska Press, 1982.

Missionary Society of the Methodist Episcopal Church. *Tenth Annual Report of the Missionary Society of the Methodist Episcopal Church*. New York: Printed at the Conference Office, Crosby Street, 1829.

Mississippi Band of Choctaw Indians. *Chahta Hapia Hoke: We Are Choctaw*. Philadelphia, Miss.: Mississippi Band of Choctaw Indians, [ca. 1981].

————. *Overall Economic Development Plan, 1978–1982*. Philadelphia: Mississippi Band of Choctaw Indians, 1977.

Mooney, James. "Choctaw Indians." In *Catholic Encyclopedia*, 7: 692–93. New York: Robert Appleton Company, 1908.

Moore, John Hebron. *The Emergence of the Cotton Kingdom in the Old*

Southwest: Mississippi, 1770–1860. Baton Rouge: Louisiana State University Press, 1988.

Morgan, Lewis Henry. *Ancient Society; or, Researches in the Lines of Human Progress from Savagery through Barbarism to Civilization.* 1877. Reprint, edited by Eleanor Burke Leacock. Cleveland: World Publishing Company, Meridian Books, 1963.

Morrison, James P. *Seven Constitutions (Anumpa Ulhpisa Untuklo): Government of the Choctaw Republic, 1826–1906.* Durant: Choctaw Bilingual Education Program, Southeastern Oklahoma State University, 1977.

Morse, Jedidiah. *A Report to the Secretary of War of the United States, on Indian Affairs, Comprising a Narrative of a Tour Performed in the Summer of 1820, under a Commission from the President of the United States, for the Purpose of Ascertaining, for the Use of the Government, the Actual State of the Indian Tribes in Our Country. . . .* New Haven: Published by Davis and Force, 1822.

Moseley, John W., ed. *A Record of Missionary Meetings Held in the Chahta and Chikesha Nations and the Records of Tombigbee Presbytery from 1825 to 1838.* West Point, Miss.: West Point Leader Printing, n.d.

New American State Papers, Indian Affairs. 13 vols. Wilmington, Del.: Scholarly Resources, 1972.

Nuttall, Thomas. *Journal of Travels into the Arkansa Territory, during the Year 1819, with Occasional Observations on the Manners of the Aborigines.* Vol. 13, *Early Western Travels,* ed. Reuben Gold Thwaites. New York: AMS Press, 1966.

Nye, Russel Blaine. *The Cultural Life of the New Nation, 1776–1830.* New York: Harper and Row, Publishers, 1960.

O'Donnel, James H., III. *Southern Indians in the American Revolution.* Knoxville: University of Tennessee Press, 1973.

O'Neill, Charles Edwards. *Church and State in French Colonial Louisiana: Policy and Politics in 1732.* New Haven: Yale University Press, 1966.

Ong, Walter. *Orality and Literacy: The Technologizing of the Word.* London: Methuen, 1982.

————. *The Presence of the Word: Some Prolegomena for Cultural and Religious History.* Minneapolis: University of Minnesota Press, 1967.

Otis, D. S. *The Dawes Act and the Allotment of Indian Land.* Norman: University of Oklahoma Press, 1973.

Paredes, J. Anthony, ed. *Indians of the Southeastern United States in the Late Twentieth Century.* Tuscaloosa: University of Alabama Press, 1992.

Pearce, Roy Harvey. *Savagism and Civilization: A Study of the Indian and the American Mind.* Baltimore: Johns Hopkins University Press, 1964.

Peebles, Christopher S. "Paradise Lost, Strayed, and Stolen: Prehistoric Social Devolution in the Southeast." In *The Burden of Being Civilized: An Anthropological Perspective on the Discontents of Civilization,* edited by Miles Richardson and Malcolm C. Webb, pp. 24–40. Southern Anthropological Proceedings, No. 18. Athens: University of Georgia Press, 1986.

Perdue, Theda. *Slavery and the Evolution of Cherokee Society.* Knoxville: University of Tennessee Press, 1979.

"Peter Chester, Third Governor of the Province of West Florida under British Dominion, 1770–1781." *Publications of the Mississippi Historical Society* 5 (1925).

Peterson, John H., Jr. "Louisiana Choctaw Life at the End of the Eighteenth Century." In *Four Centuries of Southern Indians,* edited by Charles Hudson. Athens: University of Georgia Press, 1975.

Phelps, Dawson A. "Stands and Travel Accommodations on the Natchez Trace." *Journal of Mississippi History* 11, no. 1 (January 1949).

Pickett, A. J. *History of Alabama and Incidentally of Georgia and Mississippi, from the Earliest Period.* 3d ed., 2 vols. Charleston: Walker and James, 1851. Reprint, New York: Arno Press and the New York Times, 1971.

Pillar, James C. "Religious and Cultural Life, 1817–1860." In *A History of Mississippi,* edited by Richard Aubrey McLemore. Hattiesburg: University and College Press of Mississippi, 1973. Pp. 378–419.

Pilling, James Constantine. *Bibliography of the Muskhogean Languages.* Washington: Government Printing Office, 1889.

Plaisance, A. "The Choctaw Trading House, 1803–1822." *Alabama Historical Quarterly* 16 (1954): 393–423.

Posey, Walter Brownlow. *The Baptist Church in the Lower Mississippi Valley, 1776–1845.* Lexington: University of Kentucky Press, 1957.

————. *The Presbyterian Church in the Old Southwest, 1778–1838.* Richmond, Va.: John Knox Press, 1952.

Prentiss, S. S. *A Memoir of S. S. Prentiss,* edited by [George Prentiss]. 2 vols. New York: Charles Scribner, 1855.

Presbyterian Historical Society. *American Indian Correspondence: The Presbyterian Historical Society Collection of Missionaries Letters, 1833–1893.* Westport, Conn.: Greenwood Press, 1978.

Proposed Legislation for the Full-Blood and Identified Choctaws of Mississippi, Louisiana, and Alabama, with Memorial, Evidence, and Brief. Washington, D.C.: Judd and Detweiler, [1913].

Prucha, Francis Paul. *Cherokee Removal: The "William Penn" Essays and Other Writings.* Knoxville: University of Tennessee Press, 1981.

————. *Churches and the Indian Schools, 1888–1912.* Lincoln: University of Nebraska Press, 1979.

————. *Federal Indian Policy in United States History.* Lincoln: University of Nebraska Press, 1981.

————. *The Great Father: The United States Government and the American Indians.* 2 vols. Lincoln: University of Nebraska Press, 1984.

————, ed. *Documents of U.S. Indian Policy.* Lincoln: University of Nebraska Press, 1975.

Ramenofsky, Ann. *Vectors of Death.* Albuquerque: University of New Mexico Press, 1987.

Ray, Florence Rebecca. *Chieftain Greenwood Leflore and the Choctaw Indians of the Mississippi Valley: Last Chief of Choctaws East of Mississippi River.* 2d ed. Memphis, Tenn.: C. A. Davis Printing Company, 1936.

Redfield, Robert, Ralph Linton, and Melville J. Herskovits. "A Memorandum for the Study of Acculturation." *American Anthropologist* 38 (1936): 149–52.

Reeves, Carolyn Keller, ed. *The Choctaw before Removal.* Jackson: University Press of Mississippi, 1985.

Remini, Robert V. *The Legacy of Andrew Jackson: Essays on Democracy, Indian Removal, and Slavery.* Baton Rouge: Louisiana State University Press, 1988.

Richardson, James D. *A Compilation of the Messages and Papers of the Presidents, 1789–1897.* 10 vols. Washington: Government Printing Office, 1899.

Rister, Carl C. *Baptist Missions among the American Indians.* Atlanta: Home Mission Board, Southern Baptist Convention, 1944.

Roberts, Charles. "The Second Choctaw Removal, 1903." In *After Removal: The Choctaw in Mississippi,* edited by Samuel J. Wells and Roseanna Tubby. Jackson: University Press of Mississippi, 1986.

Rogin, Michael Paul. *Fathers and Children: Andrew Jackson and the Subjugation of the American Indian.* New York: Alfred A. Knopf, 1973.

Rohrbough, Malcolm. *The Land Office Business: The Settlement and Administration of American Public Lands, 1789–1837.* New York: Oxford University Press, 1968.

————. *The Trans-Appalachian Frontier: People, Societies, and Institutions, 1775–1850.* New York: Oxford University Press, 1978.

Romans, Bernard. *A Concise Natural History of East and West Florida: Containing an Account of the Natural Produce of All the Southern Part of British America in the Three Kingdoms of Nature Particularly the Animal and Vegetable, Illustrated with Twelve Copper Plates and Two Whole Sheet Maps.* Vol. 1. New York: Printed for the Author, 1775.

Roosevelt, Theodore. *Presidential Addresses and State Papers of Theodore Roosevelt.* 2 vols. New York: P. F. Collier and Son; New York: Krause Reprint Company, 1970.

Rountree, Helen C. *Pocahontas's People: The Powhatan Indians of Virginia through Four Centuries.* Norman: University of Oklahoma Press, 1990.

Rouse, Shelley D. "Colonel Dick Johnson's Choctaw Academy: A Forgotten Educational Experiment." *Ohio Archaeological and Historical Quarterly* 25, no. 1 (January 1916): 88–117.

Rowland, Dunbar. *Military History of Mississippi, 1803–1898, Taken from the Official and Statistical Register of the State of Mississippi, 1908.* Spartanburg, S.C.: Reprint Company, Publishers, 1978.

Rowland, Dunbar, and A. G. Sanders, eds. *Mississippi Provincial Archives, French Dominion.* 3 vols. Jackson: Press of the Mississippi Department of Archives and History, 1927–32.

————. *Mississippi Provincial Archives, French Dominion, 1729–1748.* Revised and edited by Patricia Kay Galloway. 2 vols. Baton Rouge: Louisiana State University Press, 1984.

Ru, Paul du. *Journal of Paul du Ru.* Translated and edited by Ruth Lapham Butler. Chicago: Caxton Club, 1934.

Satz, Ronald N. *American Indian Policy in the Jacksonian Era.* Lincoln: University of Nebraska Press, 1975.

Sawyer, Charles H., "The Choctaw Indians of Mississippi. Parts 1 and 2. *Twin Territories* 4, no. 6 (June 1902): 160–64; no. 7 (July 1902): 205–11.

Schermerhorn, John F. "Report Respecting the Indians Inhabiting the Western Parts of the United States." *Collections of the Massachusetts*

Historical Society, 2d ser., 2 (1814). Reprint, Boston: Charles C. Little and James Brown, 1846.

Schultz, George A. *An Indian Canaan: Isaac McCoy and the Vision of an Indian State*. Norman: University of Oklahoma Press, 1972.

Serrano y Sanz, Manuel. *España y Los Indios Cherokis y Chactas en la Segunda Mitad del Siglo XVIII*. Seville: Tip. de la "Guia Oficial," 1916.

Shea, John D. G. *History of the Catholic Missions among the Indian Tribes of the United States, 1529–1854*. New York: E. Dunigan, 1855.

Sheehan, Bernard W. *Seeds of Extinction: Jeffersonian Philanthropy and the American Indian*. Chapel Hill: Published for the Institute of Early American History and Culture at Williamsburg, Virginia, by the University of North Carolina Press, 1973.

Silverberg, Robert. *The Mound Builders*. Greenwich, Conn.: New York Graphic Society, 1970.

Smith, Marvin T. *Archaeology of Aboriginal Culture Change in the Interior Southeast: Depopulation during the Early Historic Period*. Gainesville: University of Florida Press/Florida State Museum, 1987.

Spicer, Edward. "European Expansion and the Enclavement of Southwestern Indians." *Arizona and the West* 1 (Summer 1959): 132.

Spoehr, Alexander. *Changing Kinship Systems: A Study in the Acculturation of the Creeks, Cherokee, and Choctaw*. Anthropological Series, no. 33 Chicago: Field Museum, 1947.

Stearn, E. Wagner, and Allen E. Stearn. *The Effect of Smallpox on the Destiny of the Amerindian*. Boston: Bruce Humphries, 1945.

Stuart, John. *A Sketch of the Cherokee and Choctaw Indians*. Little Rock: Printed by Woodruff and Pew, 1837.

Swanton, John. "An Early Account of the Choctaw Indians." *Memoirs of the American Anthropological Association* 5 (1918): 1–118.

————. *Final Report of the United States De Soto Expedition Commission*. Washington: Government Printing Office, 1939. Reprint, Washington, D.C.: Smithsonian Institution Press, 1985.

————. *The Indians of the Southeastern United States*. Smithsonian Institution Bureau of American Ethnology, Bulletin 137. Washington: Government Printing Office, 1946.

————. *Source Material for the Social and Ceremonial Life of the Choctaw Indians*. Bureau of American Ethnology Bulletin 103. Washington: Government Printing Office, 1931.

Sweet, William Warren. *Religion in Colonial America*. New York: Cooper Square Publishers, 1965.

_____. *Religion in the Development of American Culture, 1765–1840*. Gloucester, Mass.: Peter Smith, 1963.

_____. *Religion on the American Frontier*. 4 vols. New York: Henry Holt and Company, 1931–46.

Sword, Wiley. *President Washington's Indian War: The Struggle for the Old Northwest, 1790–1795*. Norman: University of Oklahoma Press, 1985.

Thompson, Richard H. *Theories of Ethnicity: A Critical Appraisal*. Westport, Conn.: Greenwood Press, 1989.

Thornton, Russell. *American Indian Holocaust and Survival*. Norman: University of Oklahoma Press, 1988.

Thwaites, Reuben Gold. *France in America, 1497–1763*. New York: Harper and Brothers Publishers, 1905. Reprint, Westport, Conn.: Greenwood Press, Publishers, 1970.

_____, ed. *The Jesuit Relations and Allied Documents: Travels and Explorations of the Jesuit Missionaries in New France, 1610–1791*. 73 vols. Cleveland: Burrows Brothers Company, 1896–1901.

Tocqueville, Alexis de. *Democracy in America*. Translated by George Lawrence. Edited by J. P. Mayer and Max Lerner. New York: Harper and Row, Publishers, 1966.

Tonkin, Elizabeth, Maryon McDonald, and Malcolm Chapman, eds. *History and Ethnicity*. Association of Social Anthropologists Monograph 27. London: Routledge, 1989.

Tracy, Joseph. "History of the American Board of Commissioners for Foreign Missions, Compiled Chiefly from the Published and Unpublished Documents of the Board." In *History of American Missions to the Heathen from Their Commencement to the Present Time*. Worcester, Mass.: Spooner and Howland, 1840.

Tuttle, Sarah. *Conversations on the Choctaw Mission*. 2 vols. Boston: Printed by T. R. Marvin, for the Massachusetts Sabbath School Union, 1830.

Usner, Daniel B., Jr. "American Indians in Colonial New Orleans." In *Powhatan's Mantle: Indians in the Colonial Southeast*, edited by Peter H. Wood, Gregory A. Waselkov, and M. Thomas Hatley, pp. 104–27. Lincoln: University of Nebraska Press, 1989.

_____. *Indians, Settlers, and Slaves in a Frontier Exchange Economy: The Lower Mississippi Valley Before 1783*. Chapel Hill: Published for the Institute of Early American History and Culture, Williamsburg, Virginia, by the University of North Carolina Press, 1992.

VanDerBeets, Richard. *Held Captive by Indians: Selected Narratives, 1642–1836.* Knoxville: University of Tennessee Press, 1973.

Vega, Garcilaso de la. *The Florida of the Inca.* Translated and edited by John Grief Varner and Jeannette Johnson Varner. Austin: University of Texas Press, 1988.

Viola, Herman J. *Thomas L. McKenney, Architect of America's Early Indian Policy: 1816–1830.* Chicago: Sage Books, Swallow Press, 1974.

Voss, Jerome A., and John H. Blitz. "Archaeological Investigations in the Choctaw Homeland." *American Antiquity* 53, no. 1 (1988): 125–45.

Washburn, Wilcomb E. *The Assault on Indian Tribalism: The General Allotment Law (Dawes Act) of 1887.* Philadelphia: J. B. Lippincott Company, 1975.

Watkins, John A. "A Contribution to Chacta History," *American Antiquarian (and Oriental Journal)* 16 (1894): 257–65.

Wayne, Anthony. *Anthony Wayne, A Name in Arms: Soldier, Diplomat, Defender of Expansion Westward of a Nation. The Wayne-Knox-Pickering-McHenry Correspondence.* Edited by Richard C. Knopf. Pittsburgh: University of Pittsburgh Press, 1960.

Wells, Samuel J., and Roseanna Tubby, eds. *After Removal: The Choctaw in Mississippi.* Jackson: University Press of Mississippi, 1986.

White, Richard. "Red Shoes: Warrior and Diplomat." In *Struggle and Survival in Colonial America,* edited by David G. Sweet and Gary B. Nash, pp. 49–68. Berkeley: University of California Press, 1981.

————. *Roots of Dependency: Subsistence, Environment, and Social Change among the Choctaws, Pawnees, and Navajos.* Lincoln: University of Nebraska Press, 1983.

Wood, George W. *Report of Mr. Wood's Visit to the Choctaw and Cherokee Missions, 1855.* Boston: Press of T. R. Marvin, 1855.

Wood, Peter. "Changing Population of the Colonial South." In *Powhatan's Mantle: Indians in the Colonial Southeast,* edited by Peter H. Wood, Gregory A. Waselkov, and M. Thomas Hatley. Lincoln: University of Nebraska Press, 1989.

Woods, Patricia Dillon. *French-Indian Relations on the Southern Frontier, 1699–1762.* Ann Arbor, Mich.: UMI Research Press, 1980.

Wright, Alfred. "Choctaws, Religious Opinions, Traditions, etc." *Missionary Herald* 24 (June 1828): 178–83, 214–16.

Wright, Alfred, and Cyrus Byington. *Chahta Holisso a tukla, or the Second Chahta Book: Containing Translations of Portions of the Scriptures, Biographical Notices of Henry Obokiah and Catharine Brown, a*

Catechism, and Dissertations on Religious Subjects. Cincinnati: Printed by Morgan, Lodge and Fisher, 1827.

————. *Chahta uba isht taloa holisso, or Choctaw Hymnbook*. Boston: Crocker and Brewster, 1829.

————. *A Spelling Book, Written in the Chahta Language, with an English Translation, Prepared and Published under the Direction of the Missionaries in the Chahta Nation, with the Aid of Captain David Folsom, Interpreter*. Cincinnati: Published by Morgan, Lodge and Fisher for the Missionary Society, 1825.

Young, Mary Elizabeth. *Redskins, Ruffleshirts, and Rednecks: Indian Allotments in Alabama and Mississippi, 1830–1860*. Norman: University of Oklahoma Press, 1961.

Index